Latin America in the Twentieth Century

Peter Calvert
Professor of Comparative and International Politics
Department of Politics, University of Southampton

and

Susan Calvert
Visiting Fellow
Department of Politics, University of Southampton

Second Edition

St. Martin's Press   New York

First edition published in the United States of America in 1990
Second edition 1993

Printed in Hong Kong

ISBN 0-312-09103-6

Library of Congress Cataloging-in-Publication Data
Calvert, Peter.
Latin America in the twentieth century / Peter Calvert and Susan
Calvert. —2nd ed.
p. cm.
Includes bibliographical references and index.
ISBN 0-312-09103-6
1. Latin America—Politics and government—20th century. 2. Latin
America—Economic conditions—1918– 3. Latin America—Social
conditions. I. Calvert, Susan. II. Title.
F1414.2.C23 1993
980.03'3—dc20   90–31061
                                                      CIP

Contents

List of Maps

List of Plates

List of Tables

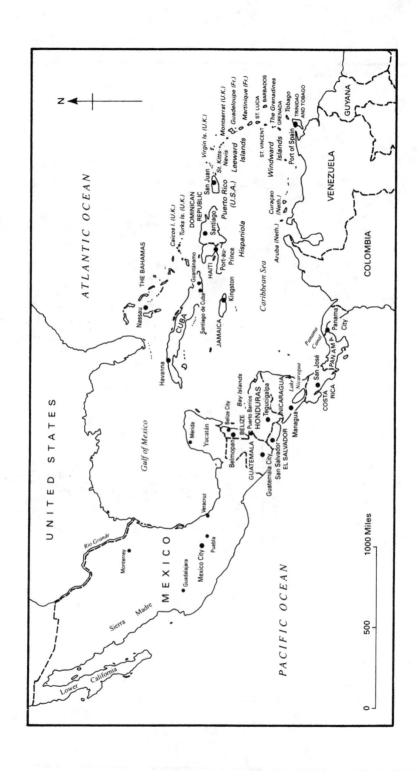

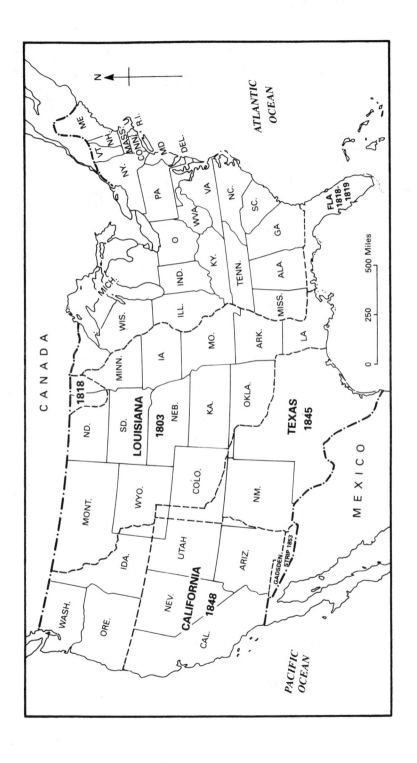

Preface to the Second Edition

Earthquakes, hurricanes and military coups are the events that hit the headlines. Hence Latin America has long had a reputation for violence and unpredictability. The underlying social order of its ancient cultures is easily overlooked. Even as its states come to the end of the second century of independence, much about them remains mysterious to outsiders. Yet the Latin American republics are now among the oldest in the world. Together with the new democracies of the Caribbean, they have led the Third World to demand full equality for its citizens and are destined to play a crucial role in the development of a New World Order.

This book is intended as a concise and up-to-date introduction for the general reader to the rich and exciting story of a family of nations, stretching from Mexico to Argentina.

Peter Calvert/Sue Calvert/Southampton 1992

1 Order and Progress

Many Latin Americans believe that theirs is the continent of the twenty-first century. South America alone is twice the size of the whole of Western Europe, and has a smaller population. As the legend of 'El Dorado' (actually modern Colombia) bears witness, it has long been seen as a source of almost limitless wealth and in terms of mineral resources this is true. The fortunes of the Spanish monarchy in Europe were based on the wealth of the Indies; Mexican silver funded the Napoleonic Wars. Yet today huge numbers of Latin Americans live in poverty such as Europe seldom, if ever, sees. As the twentieth century nears its end, the inhabitants of much of the region are divided into a wealthy few and a vast poverty-stricken mass, and the story of Latin America remains largely the story of the Third World facing the First and Second, the South versus the North.

In this book we shall look at the story of the states of the region in the second century of their independence. We shall be asking several questions. What lessons can the study of the region teach us? What is it, if anything, that makes Latin America different? How far have the states of the region achieved the goals of their founders, and how far have they fallen short? How is it that so many Latin Americans still suffer from a degree of poverty, underdevelopment and suffering almost unknown in affluent Europe? Why has insurrection been common, revolution rare? And, what will happen next?

HISTORICAL ANTECEDENTS

History is shaped by geography, and many of the main geographical features of the region are of great interest in their own right. Only in recent years has it been learnt how these in turn have been shaped by the geophysical forces of plate tectonics. The two American continents have long been moving westward away from the west coast of Africa, carried on the underlying American plate. Beneath the west coast of North America this is in collision with the Pacific plate carrying California, so creating the Rocky Mountains; but the Pacific plate is moving southward also with a shearing effect which will eventually separate California and the peninsula of Baja California from the mainland. The Pacific plate in turn is in collision with the Cocos-Nazca

1

plate lying off South America, where its impact with the American plate again creates the dynamic, upward moving cordillera of the Andes, the world's newest mountain chain and the earthquake prone highlands of Peru, Bolivia and Chile. The combined effect of these movements is to create the 'land bridge' of Central America, which is highly active volcanically, and a small zone of stability in the Caribbean.

The indigenous inhabitants of the Americas arrived from Asia in a series of waves over another 'land bridge' in the area which is now the Bering Straits. From about 40 000 BC onwards they spread out across the North American Plains and down into modern Mexico and Central America, where, shortly after the end of the last Ice Age, they domesticated maize and developed a highly effective pattern of subsistence agriculture based on the cultivation of corn, beans and squash. How they crossed the swamp lands of Panama into South America is not known, and it is probable they moved by water as it is still necessary to do today, for the characteristically South American crops of cassava and potato were still cultivated on Santo Domingo and Cuba in raised beds termed callampas when the Spaniards arrived.

From the point of view of navigation the Spaniards had enormous advantages over their European rivals, though they did not know it. The Caribbean Basin lies in the Trade Wind zone so that a ship setting sail from a southerly point in the Azores would be driven towards it; it was only necessary to sail north on the American side to pick up the Gulf Stream and favourable winds for the return journey. There were of course still some problems. It was natural to make the outward journey in the spring when conditions were at their best. Unfortunately the end of the summer in the Northern Hemisphere also coincides with the hurricane season, and hurricanes not only formed a major threat to early Spanish exploration but remain a major threat to homes and cultivation in the region even today.

The Discovery

The surprise is not that the Americas were 'discovered' from Europe. They were evidently 'discovered' on several occasions before 1492 without permanent effect. The surprise is that European contact and invasion came so late, and that the Chinese, who under the Ming Dynasty were sailing many thousands of kilometres to the south into South-East Asia and the Pacific, did not get there first. It was therefore left to Christopher Columbus, an Italian from Genoa sailing under the flag of the Queen of Castile, to make a landfall in what is now known as Watling Island in the Bahamas on 28 October 1492, still celebrated in many parts of Spanish-speaking America as 'the Day of the Race'. From Watling Island he sailed southward along the coastline of Cuba and Santo Domingo (which he named Hispaniola – 'the Spanish Island') and having boldly identified Cuba as Japan (despite the absence of Japanese) sailed for home to report his find.

The news came as a major diplomatic sensation in Europe, and with great speed Queen Isabella of Castile moved to reach an agreement with the only other major European colonizing power capable of challenging her right to the New World, namely Portugal. Disputes with Portugal over the Atlantic Islands had for more than a century been resolved by invoking the mediation of the Pope, and by a fortunate coincidence the new Pope, Alexander VI, was a Spaniard. It was proposed that a line (subsequently known as the Line of Demarcation) should be fixed one hundred leagues to the west of the Cape Verde Islands, land to the east of that was to be Portuguese and the West Spanish. At the request of the Portuguese by the Treaty of Tordesillas the line was moved westward by 270 leagues, to what is in modern terms the meridian 49° west of Greenwich. In consequence, when some six years later the Portuguese explorer Cabral came back and announced that he had found Brazil, it turned out to be on the Portuguese side of the line, and the conclusion is inescapable that the Portuguese had known about Brazil for some time (probably since the 1480s, when a ship standing out to the west to clear Africa could have sighted land) but had sensibly kept quiet about it.

By their agreement the two great colonizing powers sought not only to keep the peace between themselves but to close out rival empires. In the tradition of Roman Law the Spaniards were therefore to seek to gain control both over the land and the sea, and indeed to make the Caribbean a 'closed sea'. The Catholic King of France for one said that he did not see the clause in Adam's will that entitled the King of Spain to rule half the world, and from the early seventeenth century, as Spain's power in Europe began to wane, other powers began to move into the Caribbean, beginning in the British case with English settlement on the small island of St Christopher (St Kitts) in 1628. After a failure to establish another settlement on the Bay Islands off Honduras in the 1640s, England finally obtained Jamaica in 1655. From then on the expansion of rival empires in the Caribbean was determined by the succession of European wars and the rather random effects of the peace treaties that ended them. In 1763, for example,

Britain returned the important sugar-producing islands of Guadeloupe and Martinique to France in return for the whole of Canada, and the French thought they had the best of the bargain. (Now that Canada is independent it could be argued they probably were right). By the same Treaty Cuba, which had been captured in 1762, was also returned to Spain.

This was a crucial decision, for it was Cuba that was the key to the Caribbean, and shortly after independence Havana had been established as the centre from which Spanish control of the Western Hemisphere was to be maintained. Several years of exploration were needed to determine that there was no sea outlet to the Pacific, Columbus himself having died still believing that he had found the true East. The name of 'the Indies', however, stuck, even if the material returns remained disappointing. Only with the conquest of Mexico in 1519 by Cortés and his followers did the legendary wealth of the Indies become an accomplished fact. In 1538 Pizarro's conquest of Peru brought even greater wealth from the mines of Peru and Upper Peru (modern Bolivia). Spanish settlements on the coast of modern Colombia were built into fortresses to afford protection from attack and the fortress of Nombre de Dios in modern Panama secured the shortest overland route to the Pacific. The entire Spanish presence in the area came to rest on sea power and on maintaining the chain of communication by which the wealth of the mines was brought to Panama, carried across the Isthmus, and finally shipped for safety in a single convoy which made a rendezvous at Havana before setting out for Cadiz and Seville. And Spanish political control of the region worked in reverse, by the orders of the King through the Council of the Indies at Seville, arriving via Havana for the consideration of the Viceroys of New Spain (modern Mexico) and Peru. It was from Peru that the first settlements were made in Chile and in the north-west of modern Argentina in the late seventeenth century. For a brief period between 1582 and 1640 Portugal itself and with it Brazil was part of the dominions of the King of Spain and forces from Brazil played an important role in regaining Portuguese independence and recapturing Angola for the Portuguese crown. Yet in the eighteenth century Spanish power continued to expand in North America. The oldest town in the United States (St Petersburg, Florida) was founded in 1513 by Spanish settlers. Florida remained a Spanish possession until the end of the colonial period, but in the meantime, Spanish control was consolidated in the military frontier districts (Provincias Internas) of the Californias, Sonora, Sinoloa, Coahuila, Nueva Viscaya, New

Mexico, Arizona and Texas, and was extended to the Louisiana territory west of the Mississippi, which was transferred to Spain from France in 1763. To this day far up into modern (Upper) California the traces of Spanish missionary activity and colonization remain in placenames such as San Diego, Los Angeles, Santa Barbara, San Francisco and Sacramento. The implantation of the Catholic faith was the great work of the Spanish Crown and overrode where possible merely secular preoccupations. It sought to incorporate an uncharted and heathen wilderness and was, thus, the justification of Spain's right to rule. Where, as in Mexico, Central America and the Andes, there were substantial indigenous populations, their conversion was the task of missionary orders such as the Franciscans. Monasteries, schools and universities were founded under royal and pontifical patronage, and the full apparatus of secular and regular clergy paralleled the complex and cumbersome civil administration of the Empire. The Spaniards gave the Indies the best that their culture had to offer; its limitations were that their culture was itself rather old-fashioned in European terms, and the dominance of the Inquisition (although it took a milder form in the Indies than in Spain itself) checked the growth of new and important ideas. Nowhere was this more marked than in the field of science. After the initial excitement of discovery, which brought us the potato, the tomato, the turkey, chocolate and quinine, had died down, reports by Spanish scholars were buried in the royal archives and it was left to a Frenchman, Louis-Antoine de Bougainville, and a German, Alexander von Humboldt, to re-awake Europe to the beauty and fascination of the flora and fauna of South America.

Independence

With the consolidation of peace and Spanish culture in the Indies it was natural that in such a vast continent men and women should dream of independence. But the Enlightenment was slow to reach the Indies. The Inquisition was very hostile to the new ideas of rationalism and scientific progress. The Crown was easily persuaded that the new ideas were dangerous – the expulsion of the Jesuits from the Spanish dominions in 1753 was largely the result of their inconvenient habit of asking questions. In any case, the educated were a small élite and many of them were members of the clergy. But it was, nevertheless, from among this small élite that the precursors of independence came.

Their aims and ambitions were initally very different. In such a vast area the spirit of nationalism was slow to develop. Two early nationalist leaders, the Brazilian nicknamed 'Tiradentes' ('the toothpuller') and the descendant of the Incas who called himself Tupac Amaru II and raised a revolt in the Andes in 1780, were before their time and their suppression was so severe that Brazil and Peru were areas of relative quiet in the struggle which was to come. It was once again events in Europe that precipitated the long and ultimately successful struggle for independence in Latin America, most notably the outbreak of the French Revolution. The message of the Rights of Man and of the Citizen directly provoked the outbreak of a slave revolt in the sugar plantations of Haiti, then the richest territory of the French Empire, in 1794. In turn Haiti acted both as a beacon and a refuge to exiles such as Miranda of Venezuela and Bolívar, whom later generations were to hail as the Liberator of northern South America. It also acted as a dreadful warning to many conservatives in the Indies of the need for absolute resistance to change to forestall for as long as possible the threat of an Indian revolt. For a long time the conservatives were to be in a majority among the élite, and this meant that they were often reluctant to accept independence when it was thrust upon them. It was the forces of conservatism which fought boldly and successfully against two tentative attempts by British forces to detach Buenos Aires from the Empire in 1806 and 1807.

The break-up of empire therefore came not from the Indies but from Europe, as the result of Napoleon's invasion of the Iberian Peninsula in 1807. King Carlos IV and his son the Crown Prince were brought before Napoleon himself at Bayonne and forced to abdicate in favour of Napoleon's brother Joseph. The Spaniards themselves rose in revolt, and as the news filtered through to the Indies the separate kingdoms of the Spanish Empire took measures for their own defence. The Napoleonic forces, however, reached Lisbon 24 hours too late to stop the King of Portugal sailing on a British warship for Rio de Janeiro, which thus became the temporary capital of the entire Portuguese Empire. When the wars in Europe ended the Crown Prince was to refuse to return to Europe and it was he who in time led the peaceful assumption of independence by Brazil in 1822.

The titular King of Spain, however, remained a prisoner in French hands while, in the name of Fernando VII, the leaders of the colonies tried to decide what to do. The worst fears of many of them seemed to be justified when in 1810 a priest, Father Miguel Hidalgo y Costilla, called his Mexican Indian congregation together and called on them to revolt and overthrow their Spanish masters. The revolt was put down but the Spanish *criollos* blamed the ideas of the revolutionary leaders in Spain itself, whom conservatives termed 'Liberales'. When in 1813–14 the French were driven out and peace began to return to Spain there too the conservatives were in the ascendant, and in the years after Waterloo every attempt was made to stamp out dissent. Parts of the Indies were already irretrievably lost, inland Paraguay being the first to go (1811) followed by Buenos Aires and the inland provinces of what is now Argentina (1816). In 1818 General José de San Martín led his epic march over the Andes to free Chile at the Battle of Maipú. Finally in 1820 a liberal revolution ocurred in Spain itself, and once again events there had their consequences overseas. The Mexican conservatives adopted independence (1821), as later did their opposite numbers in Peru (1824) and Bolivia (1825), where the rival claims of San Martín and Bolívar were resolved by the self-sacrifice of the former to the leadership of the latter. Only the major islands of the Caribbean remained Spanish and even there Santo Domingo, though fearing Haitian domination, was ultimately to go its own way in 1844.

Bolívar was briefly both President of Colombia and Dictator of Peru (and, incidentally, received no pay for either job). He died, depressed at the failure of the continent to unite, in 1830. His famous statement of futility: 'He who tries to govern America ploughs the sea . . .' was long remembered, as his successors tried to grapple with the problem of creating stable states in the chaos that had been left by two decades of civil war and revolution. All four Spanish viceroyalties broke up into smaller units: some large but disunited (like Mexico), some relatively small (such as Paraguay and Uruguay). Only Brazil, under a hereditary monarch, remained united, ultimately to become by far the largest state in Latin America and substantially bigger even than the continental United States.

The Early National Period

The legacy of independence was a divided continent. Small élites tried to retain their privileges. In the absence of any tradition of general participation in government power fell naturally into the hands of military personalist leaders, termed *caudillos*. Some of these, like Bolívar himself, were enlightened men who sought to establish balanced constitutions for Republics in the Roman mould. And this influence, it must be emphasized, was remarkably permanent. To this day the ideal of democracy and popular sovereignty has proved notably resilient; springing up even in the most unfavourable soil whenever the dead hand of dictatorship has been lifted. But it is for military coups and dictatorships that Latin America has become notorious, since sadly all too many of the *caudillos* were ignorant or greedy men who sought to enrich themselves and their families at the expense of the people.

Dictatorship flourished in nineteenth-century Latin America, not because of any predisposition towards it among the local inhabitants, but because of the social and political cleavages that divided them. There were five principal cleavages which prevented the spread of national sentiment and the evolution of true democratic systems.

The first of these was the gap between the oligarchy and the people. Civil war destroyed such systems of education as had been inherited from Spain. In consequence the élite remained very small, and although in the early years of independence, under the influence of European liberalism universal manhood suffrage was an ideal which was sometimes written into Constitutions, later the vote was taken away from all those who could not read and write. Elections were frequently held, as with the disappearance of the monarch there was no other source of legitimacy for a government, but often they simply ratified deals made in advance. Where elections were significant, as in Chile after 1833 but in most other states not before the late nineteenth century, it was because the élite were prepared to use them to choose officeholders from among their own circle or to confer formal legitimacy on those who already held power. This dominance of an élite was quite compatible with the classical ideas of the early nineteenth century, it should be noted. Power, they believed, should only to be exercised by those who could use it properly. The Latin American states (except Brazil before 1889) were republics, but they were not democracies in the modern less limited sense.

Within the élites there were, however, further divisions. The division between liberals and conservatives stemmed from the nature of independence itself, and to it all other divisions were for a time tied. Liberals broadly believed in the perfectibility of man, the inevitability of progress, the spread of education and the broadening of the franchise to incorporate some new social groups as they knocked on the door and asked to be admitted. Conservatives believed in the old Hispanic values, the importance of tradition, and keeping power within the old élite. The two political traditions became the base of nineteenth-century political parties and in Colombia both the parties, and the divisions that gave rise to them, still survive. A split in the ruling élite was the foundation, too, for the two historic parties of

Uruguay, the Nationalists or Blancos (Whites) and the Colorados (Reds).

By the late nineteenth century the liberals tended to be federalists, in the sense of seeking regional autonomy, as opposed to the conservative tendency to be centralizers. In Central America the conflict was so severe that the state disintegrated into the five states of today: Guatemala, Honduras, El Salvador, Nicaragua and Costa Rica. Likewise in South America, Ecuador, Venezuela and Colombia, and Peru and Bolivia, each went their separate way, though in some of them the struggle was renewed at the provincial level. Where it ended depended on the balance of forces in each case and the time at which a compromise was eventually accepted. The fact that Argentina, Brazil and Mexico are nominally federal states today derives ultimately from the liberal tradition, although liberalism had confronted the forces of federalism during the chaos of the post-independence period in Argentina at least. The liberals who overthrew Juan Manuel de Rosas in 1852 wrote the Argentine Constitution of 1853 under North American example; US influence also can be seen to a limited extent in that of Mexico in 1857 which is largely reproduced in the present (1917) Constitution. The unitary constitution of Colombia (1886–1991), on the other hand, reflected conservative influence at the time at which it was completed, and from 1860 onwards so did the successive constitutions of Peru. Since constitutions were the product of factions, so many were produced (Venezuela has had 21) that few ever succeeded in gaining a fraction of the general respect accorded to the Constitution of the United States. This lack of agreement on 'the rules of the game' was to continue to be a major problem in the present century.

Bitter as the struggle between federalists and centralizers was, it was as nothing compared with the debate over the role of the Church in most, if not all, of the new states. Given the immense significance of religion in the Hispanic tradition, it is perhaps surprising that the issue of secularization should have become a major one. But it has to be remembered that the very nature of the universal Church meant that in many places its hierarchy was identified with support for Spain against independence. Nationalists therefore feared and distrusted it. In addition liberals feared its ideological control and under the influence of the French Positivists increasingly saw it as the most serious obstacle to economic progress. They sought to disestablish the Church to reduce its wealth, its support for the conservatives and its hold on the people. The contest was a bitter one. Again at times it led to actual civil war, as in the Three Years War in Mexico (1857–60). But by the end of the nineteenth century the new social ideas of Leo XIII, set forth in the encyclical *Rerum Novarum* (1891), began to percolate into Latin America and the old conflicts began to die down, though their power to provoke passions even now is not dead – the Argentine Liberator, San Martín, as a Mason, was buried outside the consecrated area of the Cathedral in Buenos Aires and to this day the President of Argentina (like the President of Paraguay) has to be a Catholic.

In the struggle for leadership in the new states the nineteenth century saw the decisive advantage of military officers over civilians. The armed forces were small, weak and disunited by European standards. But they had led the fight for independence and provided the sole effective political authority and protection from banditry in the countryside. They had gained through their special relationship with government the resources to become effectively an armed political party, and once in power identified their role with patriotism and national prestige. Though there are some major exceptions, South America was in general spared in the nineteenth century international wars between states. South American armed forces were too weak and the distances and obstacles between them too great for them to mobilize enough troops to fight large-scale battles. Fighting, where it occurred, concerned remote frontier regions in dispute. On the other hand frontiers were still very fluid. National rivalry remained a potent support for military rule. It should, be emphasised, however, that in this respect South America and the Caribbean area were already going different ways. In Central America national conflicts were indistinguishable from international ones. Mexico had a different fate from either. As we shall see later, its leaders not only lost Central America, but came into conflict in turn with the rising power of the United States and the imperial ambitions of France, in each case with catastrophic consequences.

THE STABILITY OF LATIN AMERICA AT THE CENTENARY OF INDEPENDENCE

In its first half-century of independence Latin America had not developed economically, but (with the exception of Brazil) had fallen behind the position it had held at independence. In the 1790s Mexico was technologically as developed as Spain, and its School of Mines was one of the leading training institutions in the world. Artists and craftsmen worked with the same materials and to the same standards as in Europe. Great aqueducts led potable water into the expanding capital city. A five-storey colonial residence, the Palacio de Iturbide, still stands where modern steel-framed buildings have been levelled by earthquakes. The viceregal capital was linked to the northern frontier territories by a paved road, the Camino Real, which ran far up into modern California. Yet whereas the first railway engine ran in the United States in 1828 it was not until 1854 that the first railway in Latin America was to be built, and that was in Peru, which with the sole exception of Bolivia was the least sensible country in the region in which to build railways. Mexico had to wait another ten years until (under the French intervention) Mexico City acquired its first rail link to the port of Veracruz. The capital of Honduras in Central America, Tegucigalpa, has yet to see a train – there are railways in Honduras, but they are up on the north coast around La Ceiba, Tela and San Pedro Sula, where they exist to carry the banana crop down to these ports for shipping to the United States.

In the late nineteenth century Latin America began a period of economic development which by the end of the first century of independence in 1910 seemed well established and promised more to come. Most conspicuous was the great expansion of Argentina's rail network after the unification of the country in 1862. The development of the meat-packing industry, accelerated by the introduction of the refrigerated ship in 1876, spurred Roca's so-called 'Conquest of the Desert' three years later and turned the pampas into vast ranches. Immigrants flocked into the country to share the wealth and did so to some extent, though they found the land already owned by others. Uruguay and later southern Brazil reproduced the same pattern. Chile with nitrates, Peru with copper, Brazil with rubber and Colombia with coffee seemed similarly to have found the secret of success: large-scale production for the swelling export markets offered by an industrializing Europe. Europe's industrial surplus would also provide much of the funding necessary for the development of South America's productive infrastructure.

Until recently it was generally assumed that economic development was a series of stages that countries would go through in turn. Like aircraft on a runway reaching the point of 'take off' (the analogy used by the US economist W. W. Rostow) the Latin American states would therefore come to industrialize as their European counterparts had done earlier. In the immediate post-war period it was argued, notably by the UN Economic Commission for Latin America (ECLA), that it was the duty of the advanced industrialized countries to help the less fortunate to follow their example. Only from 1960 onwards was it increasingly argued not only that this might not be possible, but that the very fact of development of Europe and North America had so affected the Latin American economies that they had been distorted into a condition of dependency and their potential for autonomous growth had been stunted. Dependency meant that these countries were not in the economic sense free to choose their own way; they were in effect forced by the terms of the world market to produce low-value primary products for export, while at the same time their economies were invaded by large multinational corporations (MNCs) which prevented capital formation by remitting their profits abroad. The dependency theorists (dependentistas) argued that dependency was a necessary condition of the existence of the world capitalist system and from it Latin America could only break free as a result of social revolution.

Technological development does depend on certain things being available. Cheap and abundant raw materials are the first requirement. In Britain the right sort of deposits of coal and iron ore were available and lay close together. In the United States they were still more abundant, and the development of railways could bring them together. In the rest of the Americas nature, though generous, had been less helpful. In 1900 only Mexico was known to have significant deposits of both coal and iron ore and even there they lay on opposite sides of the Sierra Madre. Nevertheless, Mexico began to build up a significant native iron industry in the early years of the twentieth century. Venezuela, rich in iron ore, had oil but not coal; Colombia had coal but not iron ore; hence the development of the Venezuelan iron and steel industry had to wait until the open hearth process was developed and the country could utilize its huge hydroelectric power potential.

In Britain capital which had been generated through the commercial and agricultural revolutions was available for investment in industry. The United States benefited from the wealth of its land, but until 1914 was a debtor nation, industrializing with the aid largely of British investment. Thereafter, as the European nations threw away their wealth in armed conflict, it became the world's largest creditor, with extensive investments in the Caribbean and South America. Unfortunately towards the end of the nineteenth century the élites of Latin America seem to have become very reluctant to invest in their own countries, and where they did so they were soon bought out by foreign companies. Thereafter they preferred to hold their wealth in more reliable investments overseas, in the United States and advanced industrialized countries, which thus benefited from it. Above all, in Europe the growth of population accompanied industrialization, and it was industrialization that gave rise to the growth of the new industrial cities. In Latin America the Spaniards imposed the pattern of urban living in colonial times. It was already well advanced long before industrialization began to provide the necessary jobs by which a rapidly growing population can be supported. At the beginning of the century no Latin American country was far advanced down the road to industrialization, but the expectation generated already existed. Industrialization, where it existed, tended to be concentrated in mining, as in Chile or Bolivia; in railways, as in Argentina, or in relatively simple processes directly related to agriculture; sugar mills or conversion of raw latex to sheet rubber. None of these activities, by their nature, provided employment for the inhabitants of the expanding cities. When industrialization expanded later it borrowed technological modes developed to suit the capital-rich, labour-poor situations found in more developed nations. Unemployment is therefore a key problem for nations with massive labour surpluses such as Brazil, especially so if their populations are growing rapidly. Today half the population of Brazil, the largest country in South America, is under the age of 16, and hence consuming and not yet contributing significantly to the resources needed to maintain a developed modern society with an adequate range of social services.

In continental Europe the state performed a significant role in linking together and providing resources for new forms of economic activity. From independence onwards, on the other hand, all Latin American states faced the problem of filling out the national territory. So vast were the areas involved, and so limited the resources which these governments controlled directly, that borrowing abroad seemed to many early statesmen a necessary first step in establishing a state machinery capable of enforcing some sort of order in the provinces. This was a disastrous move. As faction fought against faction, scarce resources were wasted and the new governments were saddled with substantial debts. Attempts to increase taxation led to rebellion – and in some states they still do.

Expanding the power of the state brought another risk, the possibility of international conflict. Most of the new states had no agreed boundaries. It was not until 1849 at the Congress of Lima that the assembled delegates agreed to recognize between themselves the Spanish administrative boundaries as at 1 January 1810 – and by then hardly any of those boundaries were still intact. No orderly transfer of power took place in Spanish America. Spain (unlike Portugal) refused for many years to recognize the independence of its former colonies and made determined efforts to hold on to the Caribbean islands and to reconquer Mexico and Peru. The baleful legend of Napoleon and the true story of independence both fostered dreams of military glory.

These dreams were to be a direct cause of the most serious military conflict of nineteenth-century South America: the War of the Triple Alliance, known in Paraguay as 'the National Epic'. It began in 1865 when the young Dictator-President of Paraguay, Francisco Solano López, in response to conspiracies, plots and counterplots, declared war on Uruguay and sent troops through Argentine territory, thus bringing on a conflict in which Paraguay was ranged simultaneously against Argentina, Uruguay and Brazil. It ended in disaster in 1870 when Paraguay, its male population reduced by nine-tenths, and its President dead on the battlefield, was defeated and occupied and forced to cede half its national territory to Brazil and Argentina.

Nearly a decade later, in 1879, Chile protested against the treatment of its nationals in the nitrate fields of Antofagasta, the coastal province of Bolivia. Bolivia, trusting in its so-called 'Secret Treaty' with Peru, resolved to fight. Chilean ships destroyed the Peruvian navy, occupied Lima, and seized not only Antofagasta, but the Peruvian provinces of Tacna, Arica and Tarapacá. The War of the Pacific, as it is known, made Chile very wealthy indeed for a generation. It confirmed the status of Chile as a power to rival Argentina in the Southern Cone, ended any possibility of a reunification of Bolivia with Peru (which had already lost half its national territory) and cut Bolivia off from the sea.

The abortive Congress called by Bolívar at Panama in 1826 in retrospect can be seen to have represented the last point at which unity among the Spanish-speaking states of South America could still seriously be considered. By the Congress of Lima it had been hoped at least to maintain the peace. After the War of the Pacific Argentina and Chile did agree on a common boundary which was greatly to the advantage of Chile, at least in the far south of the continent, but it was left to a citizen of the United States, Secretary of State James G. Blaine, formally to propose and in 1889 to preside over the formation of the Pan-American Union with a secretariat in Washington, DC. This in turn was to become the foundation of the series of conferences and collection of agreements which we know historically as the inter-American system, and which after 1945 was to be transformed into a regional organization of the United Nations, the Organization of American States (OAS).

Other trends combined to make the 1880s and 1890s for most states the Indian summer of the nineteenth century, in which as the great issues of the post-independence period reached uneasy compromises, in the oligarchic republics two party systems coalesced and civilians came to the fore. With the power and influence of the Church restricted in many places, the dominant intellectual influence was that of Comtean positivism. Comte taught the possibility of scientific understanding of society. As railways, gas and electric light spread across the continent the new knowledge seemed to offer a certainty about the future that secularism had taken away. In Brazil positivism permeated the army, which in 1889 overthrew the unique monarchy and placed on the national flag the Comtean motto 'Order and Progress'. In the same spirit the 'Generation of 80' in Argentina and the civilistas of Peru sought to manage their societies free from excessive interference from the masses.

New social movements and political ideas were, however, already stirring and, as events proved, could not be ignored indefinitely. Latin America had long been a place where anarchist communities sprouted in hope, free for a time at least to experiment away from the power of the European state. Now, as the steamship brought immigrants and even migratory workers, termed 'swallows', from Spain, Germany and Italy to Argentina and Uruguay, new ideas of trade union organization and various forms of socialism arrived with them. In Argentina such ideas initially contributed to what would later become a distinctive if vague and ill-defined movement, Radicalism. But at the turn of the century there was no clear trend even there, and elsewhere the influence of the US-based International Workers of the World (IWW) was to be the dominant influence on one stream of labour organization, notably in Mexico, with Catholic teaching always an important contrasting factor.

It is easy either to underestimate or to overestimate the early influence of the United States in Latin America. Until 1898 the US had very little naval or military power and hence little direct influence in the region. For a generation after its own Civil War it hardly involved itself with the affairs of its neighbours, preoccupied as it was with its own growth and expansion westward. What was clearly important was its example as a stable state which was rapidly becoming an industrial giant. The US in fact can in some important respects be regarded as a Latin American country which happened to speak English. It had confronted successfully many of the same problems that the South American states faced, and it had done so successfully. But at the same time its success provided not only a model to emulate, but also a focus for resentment, especially so after the 1898 US defeat of Spain, which would lead to the development of hispanicism (*hispanidad*) and increase Latin American opposition to the United States.

THE EXPANSION OF THE US INTO THE CARIBBEAN REGION

'Westward the course of Empire takes its way', wrote the poet, and it is a common misconception, beloved of poets and politicians, that the United States had an inevitable tendency to expand westward. In colonial times its tendency was to expand to the south, as the names of the colonies show: Virginia (Elizabeth I), the Carolinas (Charles II) and Georgia (George II). Then came the Napoleonic Wars and with them in 1803, the Louisiana Purchase, by which the United States doubled its original size. The break-up of the Spanish Empire was next accelerated by the conquest of Florida, which secured the southeast flank of the Union and confirmed the new status of the United States as a Caribbean power. The acquisition of Cuba was seriously considered but Spain was in no mood to sell.

By the early 1820s it was clear that the Spanish Empire on the mainland was on the point of dissolution. In Europe the British Foreign Secretary, George Canning, and in the United States President Monroe and his Secretary of State, John Quincy Adams, were concerned that this process should not be stopped. They particularly feared that France might help Spain to reconquer part of the Indies, and in Washington there was also concern that Russian sailors from Alaska might extend Russian power into the west of Mexico and so establish a new continental Empire to replace the old. North American fears were embodied in Monroe's message to Congress on 2 December 1823 in which Adams set out what later was to become known as the Monroe Doctrine.

Monroe's message was threefold. The United States had no interest in Europe and would not interfere with existing European colonies (the non-intervention principle). But it would oppose any new colonies in the Western Hemisphere (the no-colonization principle) and would as far as its power allowed oppose the transfer of colonies from one external power to another (the no-transfer principle). In fact its power had very little to do with the outcome; the message relied on the known fact that Canning held similar aims and the Royal Navy would and did enforce them. There was a price, of course. The United States could not directly enforce the Doctrine against Britain, which extended its foothold in Belize (so-called British Honduras), established its sovereignty over the Falkland Islands (1833) and successfully for a time asserted a protectorate over Mosquitia (the Mosquito Coast of what is now Nicaragua) and the Bay Islands. But it could use Canada as a bargaining counter to secure a gradual acceptance of a status quo which after 1865 Britain did not seek to challenge.

Meanwhile in the United States as early as the 1840s growing ambitions to conquer the whole Northern Continent, the spirit which became known as Manifest Destiny, led to the rediscovery of Adams' principles. They became fundamental planks of US foreign policy, and such important ones that politicians and the public alike lost sight of the fact that they had never been more than a unilateral statement of policy. They were not, though they were often represented as being, principles of international law accepted by the world community at large, and at the beginning of the twentieth century the United States had still to find the power to make the Doctrine effective. Yet in the meanwhile it had become a continental power, with all that that was to mean for the future.

It began the year after Monroe's message when American settlers under Stephen Austin obtained permission to move further south into that area of northern Mexico we now know as Texas. Within a decade the English-speaking settlers outnumbered the local inhabitants, and in 1836 the Republic of Texas successfully asserted its independence under the Lone Star flag. In 1845 the election of an Ulster Scot, James Knox Polk, to the Presidency of the United States cleared the way for the annexation of Texas. Polk provoked a Mexican attack by sending United States troops down below the de facto frontier, the Rio Grande, and in the conflict that followed, known in the United States as the Mexican War and in Mexico, rather inaccurately, as the War of 1847, a US party seized Upper California while US forces under General Winfield Scott occupied the Mexican capital and dictated peace terms. At the Treaty of Guadalupe Hidalgo Mexico lost more than half its national territory, including the modern states of California, Nevada, Arizona, New Mexico, Texas, the southern part of Colorado and part of Oklahoma. To rub salt in the wound, only weeks later gold was discovered in California and the great Gold Rush of 1849 was on.

The United States was to pay an unexpected price for its glory. Southward expansion had been held up from 1820 onwards by the growing rivalry between North and South. Westward expansion renewed the question of balance in a new and more urgent form. As Texas entered the Union with full statehood and California received statehood within months the question of the incorporation of new states in the Union could no longer be postponed, and the ultimate result was to be the American Civil War. Meanwhile the acquisition of California had already demonstrated the future importance of Central America and the Isthmus of Panama as a sea link between the East and West coasts of the continental United States. Panama, the traditional route, was then a much less healthy place than Nicaragua, and it was there that Commodore Vanderbilt set up a shipping line linking New York and San Francisco while William Walker, the 'gray eyed man of destiny', with the aid of southern 'filibusters' (soldiers of fortune) attempted to carve out an American protectorate. But the Civil War cut short US interest in control of the Isthmus region for a generation.

Between 1868 and 1878 civil war raged in Cuba as what began as a slave revolt assumed nationalistic overtones. Peace returned to Spain and with it control over Cuba. Then in 1895 the poet José Martí landed in Cuba to restart the movement for independence. He was captured and shot, but the revolt continued and as the Spanish General Weyler rounded up the local inhabitants into concentration camps (*campos de reconcentración*) opinion in the United States became increasingly restive. Fanned by the work of William Randolph Hearst, it erupted into anger in 1898 when the USS *Maine* exploded while it was moored in Havana, and the United States declared war on Spain.

The Spanish American War signalled the arrival of the United States as a Great Power and brought four hundred years of Spanish rule in the Indies to an end. Cuba and Puerto Rico were occupied. The United States had promised to give Cuba independence. This was accorded in 1902, though under the Platt Amendment with conditions that made it a virtual American protectorate: US financial control and the right to intervene to restore democracy if invited to do so. No promise had been made with regard to liberating Puerto Rico, which was annexed, while US forces consolidated their control of the Philippines and so pushed forward the boundaries of the American Empire in the Pacific (Hawaii, a Republic since 1892, was also formally annexed in 1898). It was the very scope of the victory that created a new problem. The United States had taken a great risk in fighting a two-ocean campaign with its fleet divided; its success highlighted the unique value to the new Great Power of an Isthmian canal.

Three routes had been surveyed in the early 1870s. One, across the Isthmus of Tehuantepec in Mexico, was regarded as technically feasible but very expensive; a British-owned railway had just been completed there and it was not seriously considered. The second, across Nicaragua, using the waters of Lake Nicaragua and the San Juan River (Commodore Vanderbilt's old route), was the next nearest to the United States and could be built at sea level, avoiding the need for locks. The third, across the Isthmus of Panama, involved the shortest crossing but was furthest from the United States and needed locks. The arguments in favour of the Nicaraguan route were very strong. Members of the US Senate preparing to vote on the Nicaraguan proposal were circulated by the Panama interests with sets of postage stamps recently issued by Nicaragua. These showed the beauties of Nicaragua and in particular the volcano Momontombo. The Senators, as they were intended to do, drew the conclusion that if they chose Nicaragua the canal would be blown up by volcanoes. This left Panama, but the government of Colombia, of which it was a province, held out for more money. This problem was solved when a spontaneous revolt for Panamanian independence broke out in 1903. While US ships stood off the coast to prevent Colombian forces arriving to suppress it, the United States recognized the independence of Panama within three days and signed a treaty with the new state. By this treaty, Panama immediately ceded to the United States perpetual sovereignty over a ten-mile wide strip of land on either side of the route of the proposed canal and signed over the right to build, operate, fortify, collect tolls and generally do anything needed to make the new canal a reality. Work began the following year and the Canal was opened in 1914, three days after the outbreak of the Great War.

Theodore Roosevelt did not conceal the active role he had played in the whole business. In his re-election campaign in 1904 he declared proudly: 'I took Panama'. But he and his successors were soon to find that becoming an imperial power brought problems as well as rewards. The new Canal had to be defended, and the sea routes leading to it kept clear. Yet the very fact of the surviving European possessions in the region meant that the United States was surrounded by rivals, to which could now be added Imperial Germany. And continual pretexts for intervention were given when the smaller independent states of the region, as they so frequently did, suffered involuntary changes of government and defaulted on their debts. The events that were to lead the United States even further down the path of intervention initially had nothing to do with financial considerations. In 1903 Germany, Britain, France and Italy joined in blockading the mouth of the

Orinoco to insist that the then dictator of Venezuela, Cipriano Castro (President, 1899–1908) treat their nationals justly and protect them against attack. In the first century of its independence the homeland of Simon Bolívar had not seen a single President who had succeeded in completing his term of office, and not surprisingly the rule of law was conspicuous by its absence.

In the United States it was wrongly believed that the intervention was a debt-collecting expedition. With the Press becoming militant, Roosevelt responded to the popular mood. But he chose his ground carefully – it was with the case not of Venezuela, but of the Dominican Republic in mind that in 1904 he enunciated what was to become known as 'the Roosevelt Corollary [to the Monroe Doctrine]', which essentially meant that since the United States could not countenance intervention by others it would have to intervene itself, both for its own debts and as a trustee for those of the European powers. In 1905 President Carlos F. Morales of the Dominican Republic was per-suaded to issue an executive decree which confirmed the de facto receivership the US had been operating since 1900 over Dominican customs duties – the government's chief source of revenue. More than half the revenues were confiscated for distribution to creditors. The reasoning was that by removing the chief prize of political revolution from contention in this way, stability of governments could be increased and the risk of foreign intervention eliminated. Things did not go quite as planned: Morales himself was overthrown in 1906, but his successor, Ramón Cáceres, assented to a Treaty which was enacted in 1907 and financial trusteeship was re-established, to last in one form or another down to 1940, despite the ending of a relatively peaceful and prosperous period in 1911 with the assassination of Cáceres.

Roosevelt is famous for his use of the African proverb 'Speak softly and carry a big stick', and the evocative phrase 'the big stick' suggests the use of force. But Roosevelt himself was slow to use force, and though in 1906 he did answer the call of the Cuban government and sent troops there to re-establish orderly government, no further armed intervention took place during his Presidency. Instead his Secretary of State, Elihu Root, encouraged the Central American states to settle their disputes through a Central American Court (1907), the first such international body for the peaceful resolution of disputes. William Howard Taft, President 1909–13, took a different tack, trying to avoid the pretext for European intervention in the region by substituting American capital investment for European. This policy, known as 'Dollar Diplomacy', annoyed the Europeans without solving the problem. Matters came to a head in Nicaragua where what Roosevelt called the 'furtive meddling' of his successor assisted in the fall of the nationalistic dictator José Zelaya, but fell short of providing a satisfactory successor government until in 1912 US Marines were landed. With the American nominee Adolfo Díaz in office Nicaragua with its competing canal route became a virtual American protectorate.

Woodrow Wilson, President 1913–21, came to the Presidency with little knowledge of international affairs, but with a strong belief in the duty of the United States to give a moral lead. The Great War in Europe, though it left intact the colonial empires of the victorious Powers, fatally weakened their financial resources and left the United States by default the dominant power in the Caribbean area. This was paralleled by a direct increase in physical control. By the Bryan-Chamorro Treaty of 1913 the United States finally acquired the rights to the rival Nicaraguan canal. In 1914 American forces were landed in Mexico to help overthrow the dictatorial regime of General Huerta, and when its President fled in despair troops were also sent to the Dominican Republic, which became a new protectorate. In 1915, when the fifth president of Haiti to hold office that year was torn to pieces in the streets of Port-au-Prince, US forces landed there too. Another protectorate came into existence. In 1916 a punitive force under General Pershing (the Pershing Expedition) was sent into northern Mexico, where all central government had broken down, to capture 'Pancho' Villa and bring him to justice for his raid on Columbus, New Mexico. It was withdrawn in 1917 shortly before the German offer to Mexico in the Zimmermann Telegram of the return of their 'lost territories' brought the United States into the European War. In the same year, fearing a German invasion of Denmark (which fortunately never took place), the United States bought the Danish Virgin Islands, now an American tourist resort. Finally, between 1917 and 1919 the United States exercised such pressure on the military ruler of Costa Rica, Fernando Tinoco, that he was forced to resign. Wilson did not support the Central American Court, which collapsed in 1918. But he did adopt the cause of a League of Nations to which all states would belong. He remains a complex problem for historians: an idealist who sought to uphold the rule of law and often found himself using the very methods he criticized in others. His successors were often to be much less scrupulous, and only occasionally more effective.

Other imperial powers in the region acquiesced in the new US dominance because they had no alternative, and because the United

States was, Monroe Doctrine or not, becoming a force in European politics. The entry of the US into the War was reluctant, but its status as an Associated Power protected the colonies of the victorious British and French empires in the Caribbean for a generation. The Dutch, who had been neutral, kept their possessions also. For the first time in three hundred years the end of a European war resulted in no transfer of territory in the region.

What was the real importance of the Caribbean to the United States? For many years now, Latin American and Caribbean Marxists have sought to explain the rise of US power in the area in terms of economics: markets, plantations and multinational corporations, they say, were the driving forces in American expansion. However, before 1920 US interests in the region, with the major exception of Mexico, were surprisingly limited, and strategic considerations dominated American policy. They did not do so consistently, and in the nature of the American political process individual entrepreneurs were able to gain the ear of the President and individual political appointees made a lot of money, the more easily since in the United States itself capitalism was far from being seen as a crime. As the region entered the 1920s, however, it was already clear that US influence was going to increase further. What was not yet clear was how far the new financial involvement of the United States would come to dominate South as well as Central America.

2 Land and Liberty

THE LAND QUESTION IN LATIN AMERICA

Latin America is the product of conquest. Conquest is the seizure by others of the sole basic economic resource, land. Without access to land, hunters and gatherers cannot find food and crops cannot be grown. But land is clearly not a standard product of uniform quality. Its value depends on its nature and composition, the prevailing climate and its proximity to markets. The conquerors, as far as their limited technical knowledge allowed, took the best land for themselves. The indigenous inhabitants were left with land of poor quality, mountain or forest land far from 'civilization', desert land lacking water resources or areas where excess rainfall and tropical diseases made colonization unattractive. The distribution of land, therefore, has been and remains a major theme in the story of Latin America in the twentieth century.

Land inequality in itself is not an adequate measure of the problem. Nor does it tell us anything about its political consequences. It is true that the Latin American countries which have suffered from agrarian unrest and dictatorship have some of the most unequal land distributions in the world. But so too does Australia, a relatively egalitarian country with a stable democratic system. Until 1950 many Latin American countries, in fact, had very large tracts of 'unoccupied' or underutilized land. Nor were these just the larger countries: as late as 1954, for example, more than half of Honduras in Central America did not 'belong' to anyone. With so much land apparently going begging it was difficult for governments of such countries to realize that a problem existed, and it was tempting for them to avoid more difficult political decisions by land-colonization schemes which soon foundered for lack of resources.

The problem was that from colonial times onwards, possession of large tracts of land has been the most public and effective affirmation of political power. Outside the cities, landownership *was* power. In the early national period, governments did not rule in the countryside; they made deals with local landowners (*caudillos* or *caciques*) which enlisted their support in return for maintaining their interests. Such governments simply did not have the power to act against the interests of the landowners. Yet the interests of the landowners were in many ways hostile to the interests of central government, not least since they had little or no concept of economic efficiency. Their great estates existed mainly for show; they operated mainly on a subsistence level, producing little more than was needed to support the family and their retainers. Moreover, as long as they did so they paid no taxes.

Taxes were levied on trade and commerce, so if the estates were to pay their share they would have to produce crops for export, and this in the later nineteenth century they began to do, producing a new and higher level of affluence for their owners, many of whom became virtual absentee landlords. In Mexico, for example, the landowners of Yucatán built large houses on the outskirts of Mérida, the state capital, with wealth drawn from the sisal plantations which were used as a penal colony by the government of Porfirio Díaz (President, 1877–80 and 1884–1911); the landowners of Morelos, a small state adjoining the Federal District, lived in the capital on the proceeds of their sugar estates and, like their opposite numbers on the pampas, took vacations in Europe. As their ambitions grew they used the law, backed by the armed force of the rural police (*rurales*), to annex land from neighbouring villlages and add it to their own. By 1910 many rural inhabitants had been born and worked all their lives on *haciendas* (plantations), but some still lived precariously in Indian villages on the edges of the great estates, selling their labour when and where they could to local landowners. In Morelos one of these, a young man called Emiliano Zapata, who was noted for his skill with horses, had already briefly worked in the stables of a big landowner in the capital before returning to his native village to help them in the struggle to preserve its freedom. As elsewhere in Latin America in the late nineteenth century, positivist ideas of progress and liberal economics had led to the passage of laws allowing landowners to take over so called 'unoccupied lands'. The area of land in common ownership was remorselessly shrinking as the demands for access to it grew with the expanding population.

In the Southern Cone, in Argentina, on the other hand, huge tracts of land in Patagonia became available for settlement as a result of the Indian wars of 1879, the so-called 'Conquest of the Desert'. But though the Indians were speedily exterminated by modern weapons, or driven over the mountains into southern Chile, and for the first time the southern frontier of Argentina pushed south of Viedma-Carmen de Patagones, new immigrants in the 1880s and 1890s found that no land was available to them. It had simply been distributed amongst existing large landowners, military officers and other friends of the governnment. Immigrants, therefore, were driven into an urbanized way of life, creating both a new entrepreneurial middle class and a large mass of urban workers.

The land question, in short, was already set to become one of the major themes of twentieth century Latin American history. But the fact that it was Indian land that was threatened by Europeanizing ideas of progress was to form another. Class structure was inextricably linked with race, except where, as in Argentina and Uruguay, no significant element of the indigenous population had survived the Indian wars of the latter half of the nineteenth century. Elsewhere, though with the revival of learning intellectuals were beginning to become aware of the importance of the Indian heritage, access to political power was still denied to all but a few Indians. Social advancement for them was a rare accident, and invariably meant giving up any characteristically Indian features of their life-style. At least two routes of upward mobility, the Church and the armed forces, had existed since colonial times. Overcoming the barriers had always been possible for those with sufficient money – in eighteenth century Peru strict rules precluded access to the highest ranks of society for people with non-Spanish blood, though money could purchase a certificate of whiteness from the Viceroy. But by the beginning of the twentieth century failure to succeed in material terms was more critically regarded. Under the influence of what had come to be known as Social Darwinism, the ruling classes regarded the position of their social inferiors as a sign of their unfitness to rule, and this view had consciously or unconsciously come to be accepted quite widely by those they ruled.

STIRRINGS OF SOCIAL CHANGE

It is not surprising, therefore, that new doctrines of social change should have come in the first instance from Europe and been accepted among that sector of recent immigrants who did not share the assumptions of the old colonial society. For them, social advancement was a matter not of race but of class. Hence the new impact of radical ideas from Europe in South America came first in countries such as Argentina, Uruguay and Chile which had most successfully adapted themselves to the Europe-dominated world and sought to integrate themselves more fully into it. Elsewhere socialism in particular tended to be an intellectual creed, lacking any substantial workers' organization on which it could be based, its impact was easily lost as warring sects competed to offer their own interpretations to a mass that was still essentially uninterested. For them masses were to be aroused or mobilized, not to be consulted. The success of the Russian Revolution and the formation of the Third International (Comintern) in 1920 split the new socialist movement irrevocably.

Argentina was the most obvious place for the new ideas to take root. Strikes and labour unrest in the early years of the century demonstrated the extent to which they had become accepted among the new immigrant masses. The second government of President Julio A. Roca (1898–1904), hero of the Conquest of the Desert, was, however, above challenge, and it was regarded as a measure of enlightenment when in 1912 the Sáenz Peña Law established universal suffrage and brought the native-born element of the new masses within the scope of the 1853 Constitution. The immediate result was a steep rise in support for the Radicals, and in 1916 the election of their leader, Hipólito Yrigoyen, to the Presidency (1916–22).

Yrigoyen, a figure of undoubted charisma despite his opaque style and ill-defined ideas, used power as ruthlessly as any of his predecessors. The federal power to 'intervene' in the provinces was employed wherever necessary to consolidate the hold of the Radicals, and in Tragic Week (La Semana Tragica, May 1919) labour unrest was confronted as in the past by military force. In 1922 power passed to Marcelo T. de Alvear (1922–28) who, though also a Radical, was a product of the old oligarchy and a much more practical political leader. Argentina was at the height of its prosperity, and though already the distinctive sound of the tango, with its message of hopelessness and futility, had spread out from the bars and brothels of working-class Buenos Aires to capture the imagination of a generation, confidence reigned supreme.

Neighbouring Uruguay, geographically almost a province of Argentina, shared in the prosperity brought by the combination of immigration and the rise of the chilled beef industry. A much smaller country, its wealth was spread much more evenly. It was the impact of one man, however, that was to give it the enviable reputation of 'the Switzerland of South America'. For Uruguay the nineteenth century had been a period of almost continuous political upheaval punctuated with periodic military interventions. In the generation after the War of the Triple Alliance the Colorados had gained ascendancy over their rivals the Blancos. But the small state, which had gained nothing from the war, remained internally unstable and in addition had to be continually wary for possible threats from its large neighbours. Thus there was nothing unusual when in 1904 President José Batlle y Ordóñez preempted a military revolt by ordering the corralling of the would-be insurgents' horses. What was different was that, having gained the upper hand, he negotiated a peace treaty with his opponents (1904), and then in two terms in the Presidency (1903–7, 1911–15) he began a major programme of social reform, believing correctly that equality and participation were the key to political stability. This work, however, important as it was in establishing schemes for universal education, social security and the extension of roads and railways, would not be complete until the spectre of militarism was exorcised. It was his successor, Dr Feliciano Viera (1915–19) who was to carry these changes into effect by carrying through the Constitution of 1918, weakening the power of the executive president and allowing both parties a say in government through the creation of a nine-member Council of State on which the minority would have three representatives.

The First *Colegiado*, or period of collegial government, received the support of the Blancos and, as they had hoped, their party gained strength from their new role in government. Concerned that they might lose their dominant position, the Colorados in 1924 pushed through a major change in the electoral system. The unique system they adopted, the invention of a Belgian named Borély, is known in English as the 'double simultaneous vote' because it enabled the elector at one and the same time to vote for a party and for a specific faction or *lema* within that party. It thus combined a primary election and a general election in one; in itself a good idea. Its distinctive feature was that the votes for all the lemas were added up and credited to the winning faction of that party, thus ensuring that a larger but more divided party, such as the Colorados, could maintain their supremacy over a smaller but less divided one, such as the Blancos. Again for Uruguay the 1920s were to be a period of great prosperity, in which stock-raising became even more efficient and more profitable than in Argentina, thus supporting the growing structure of Batlle's welfare state.

Chile's experience was very different. Isolated as its central valley was from the rest of South America, Chile had been able to establish a stable oligarchy after 1833 and, as we saw above, to expand at the expense of its neighbours. Conflict came when in 1890 Congress refused to ratify the budget presented by the then President, José Manuel Balmaceda (1886–91), who had become increasingly unpopular with the big landowners because of his insistence that the time had come for reform. The President used his prerogative to proclaim it in force by decree but in the civil war that followed in 1891 the Congressional forces, based on the Navy, defeated the Presidential forces, based on the Army. Balmaceda committed suicide and the victorious Congress established a semi-Parliamentary regime, in which a President continued to play a figurehead role but a Prime Minister and cabinet responsible to Congress actually governed, and the domination of the small group of big landowners linked to foreign commercial interests was prolonged for a further generation.

In 1893 arrangements for the plebiscite which was to determine whether Tacna, Arica and Tarapacá should remain Chilean or be returned to Peru broke down as Chile sought to ensure that its outcome would be favourable. Relations with Peru remained cool, and it was more than a decade after the Civil War that even part of Chile's mineral wealth was safeguarded by the long-awaited boundary treaty with Bolivia, by which Chile's right to Antofagasta was recognized in return for Chile guaranteeing transit rights for Bolivian products. Already, however, the domination of the Chilean economy by the nitrate fields was having significant internal consequences. There was no country in the region so dependent on good labour relations in a single key industry, and the early years of the century were punctuated by a series of severe and often violent strikes before the Parliamentary republic began to enact laws protecting the rights of workers to organize and to defend their interests. Slowly Chilean industry began to diversify but not, as it proved, fast enough.

The nitrate boom lasted until the First World War, when demand for Chilean nitrates exceeded all expectations. The slump, when it came, was all the harder to bear. Cut off from outside sources of supply, chemists in Imperial Germany had devised the modern method of manufacturing artificial nitrates, by fixing nitrogen directly from the air. With the peace, the price of nitrates on the world market fell steeply. One politician stood out both for the breadth of his support and his confidence in his ability to deal with the crisis. He was Arturo Alessandri, the candidate of the Liberal Alliance, of Italian descent and known to his supporters as 'The Lion of Tarapacá' because he came from one of the poorest of Chile's provinces. He failed to gain a clear majority but was chosen as President nevertheless by a 'Tribunal of Honour' appointed by Congress in 1920.

The problem was, of course, that he lacked a Parliamentary majority. He sought to gain one through the ballot box, but was unsuccessful. In 1924 his opponents sponsored a military coup to remove him from office, but six months later a counter-coup by his supporters recalled him from exile and placed him briefly at the head of a new government while a new Constitution was prepared, restoring the powers of the Presidency. The vast majority of Andean or Central American peasants had no vote, no role in the political system except as victims. In Mexico, the government of Porfirio Díaz, himself a pure-bred Zapotec Indian, passed laws prohibiting peasants from entering the national capital in their native costume of large hat and floppy white pyjamas. In Guatemala peasants had before the liberal reforms of the nineteenth century been subject to forced labour for local landowners; now a system of work cards was introduced to punish 'idleness' and ensure a plentiful supply of cheap labour for the landowners. In Bolivia, Peru and Ecuador peasants could keep their freedom at high altitudes where the thin air and the biting cold made all but subsistence farming impracticable, but in the lowlands they were displaced by large estates and everywhere by economic pressures forced them to leave their lands and try to get work in the mines or in the cities.

Some of the educated classes, to their credit, did see that the degradation of the Indian was a national disgrace. By 1900 the first stirrings existed in Peru of *indigenismo*, the grouping of political ideas that place at the centre the rehabilitation of the Indian. Socialism and *indigenismo* came together in the writings of Mariátegui, founder of the Peruvian Communist Party, who died in 1928. Peasant insurrection would be, he wrote, the 'shining path' leading to socialism. The Mexican Revolution was to give rise to a similar movement, which in turn was to feed back into Peruvian politics when the young student leader, Víctor Raúl Haya de la Torre, founded the Alianza Popular Revolucionaria Americana (APRA) while in exile, and then returned to his native country in 1930.

BRAZIL: THE OLD REPUBLIC

Brazil, with its very different inheritance, faced not only the problem of the future of the Amazonian Indians, but also the complex inheritance of slavery. In Brazil, with its classical tradition, slavery was a civil status and not a mark of race. There were white slaves as well as black, and slaves could and did own slaves in their own right. On the other hand, as in other slave states, slavery was regarded as a taint in the blood. The institution itself had lingered for a generation after the American Civil War, while landowners pleaded economic necessity and politicians the immense complexities of doing anything. But the ending of slavery in 1888, and the consequent collapse of the monarchy in the following year, was not accompanied by any measures to integrate the numerous freedmen in a modern social order. Many had in fact remained in the same employment and virtually the same conditions as before emancipation. The difference was that many had not, and they formed a substantial landless, unemployed underclass for which no-one was willing to take responsibility.

The governments of the 'Old Republic', as the period from 1889 to 1930 is, often nostalgically, known, were dominated as in other Latin American states of the period by the landowning oligarchy, for whom politics was a game played among themselves. The two parties of the Empire had become four, and from 1891 onwards the Republican Party dominated, but otherwise little had changed, and the Republic consolidated the gains of the Empire and basked in the glory brought by its success in doing so. Power passed constitutionally as a result of democratic elections and the Presidency alternated between representatives of the two leading states, São Paulo and Minas Gerais. The last thing that seemed to be a problem in these years was the land question.

The main achievement of the first decade of the century, moreover, was the series of boundary settlements negotiated by the Baron of Río-Branco with all of Brazil's neighbours but one, in which he established the Republic's position as the world's fifth largest country, and the would-be future Great Power of South America. Río-Branco had no practical experience of diplomatic service overseas except a brief period as Vice-Consul in Liverpool, which gave him an abiding distaste for the United Kingdom which he was never able wholly to overcome. But during the 1890s the expansion of settlement into the interior had continued, led by the *bandeirantes*, pirates of the 'inland sea', whose campaigns became epic in Da Cunha's *Os Sertões*, consolidating a new national self-consciousness. Behind them stood a powerful if indolent government and Army, and ahead of them fanning out into the Amazon basin, more freebooting entrepreneurs hunting for new supplies of a unique product, rubber. A range of uses had been found for rubber since it first became available in commercial quantities in the mid-nineteenth century, and the Empire had prohibited the export of its seeds. But the invention of the pneumatic tyre by the Belfastman John Boyd Dunlop had transformed rubber from an amusing curiosity to a major commodity in world trade, and the free ranging rubber

tappers of the early twentieth century roamed vast tracts of the upper
Amazon in which Brazil vied for sovereignty with Colombia, Peru and
Ecuador. Brazil had the advantage, however, in that wherever it was
gathered, the crop had to be shipped out down the Amazon, which the
government of the far-sighted Dom Pedro II had opened to free
navigation in 1867. Millionaires congregated in a new imperial city at
Manaus, crowned by a vast Opera House where Jenny Lind appeared
at the height of her fame. The dark side of this prosperity was revealed
to the world only in 1911, when it emerged in a report commissioned by
the British Government from Sir Roger Casement that in the
Putumayo region of Peru, where a boundary dispute with Colombia
had nearly brought the two countries to war, the local boss had
established virtually an independent state, where his agents coerced
the Indian rubber-tappers into greater and greater exertions by threats
of flogging and physical mutilation; threats that were all too often
carried out.

Under Nilo Peçanha (President 1909–10), Brazil's first President of
black ancestry, the first steps were taken to protect the Amazon
Indians by establishing the Brazilian Indian Service. The rubber
boom, however, collapsed soon afterwards. Seeds, taken from the
country by an Englishman, had been successfully grown at Kew and
seedlings planted out in the Malay States. Scientifically farmed, this
new source not only destroyed the Brazilian monopoly but brought
about a sudden collapse in the world price. Fortunes fell away as fast as
they had been made, Manaus, in the steamy heat, began to crumble away
into obscurity, and in 1914 military and civilians banded together to
find a single Presidential candidate to cope with the national crisis.

Unlike Argentina and Chile, Brazil did not benefit economically
from the Great War, though during it the foundations of another great
economic boom were laid as coffee advanced to first place among its
export crops. Instead Brazil became the only South American state to
be drawn into the conflict, when in 1917 the declaration of unrestricted
submarine warfare by Germany led to a Brazilian declaration of war.
Subsequently Brazilian troops served for the first, but not the last time,
in Europe, on the Entente side in Flanders and the Ardennes
campaign. Brazil, unlike the United States, subsequently became a
founding member of the League of Nations, though its ardour for the
new organization rapidly cooled when it learned that it would not be
granted a permanent seat on the Council. On the centenary of
Brazilian independence, in 1922, as the bones of the last Emperor,
Dom Pedro II, were brought home for honour and reburial in the

Cathedral at Petrópolis, Brazilian nationalists felt that they could justifiably be proud of their country.

Political weaknesses were becoming evident, however, as new social groups rose to claim prominence. Inevitably this threatened the orderly succession to the Presidency. In 1918 ex-President Rodrigues Alves was chosen for a new term, but owing to illness was unable to take office. His Vice-President, Delfím Moreira da Costa, served in his stead, and when he died a special election was held in accordance with the Constitution. It returned Dr Epitácio da Silva Pessoa, former senator from the State of Paraíba, who thus broke the traditional dominance of the two great states. It was further disrupted in 1922 when instead of a Paulista another Mineiro was chosen as official Republican candidate. Marshal Hermes da Fonseca and his son led a revolt among the Navy to prevent the inauguration of the new President, Arturo da Silva Bernardes (1922–26). The revolt was unsuccessful, and in 1926 the claims of São Paulo were again recognized by the choice of the experienced Paulista Governor, Washington Luiz Pereira de Sousa, to serve for the Presidential term 1926–30. But the breach in continuity paved the way for Getúlio Dornelles Vargas, a politician from the extreme south of the country, to advance the claim of his state, Río Grande do Sul, and his *gaúcho* supporters to be admitted to the circle of power. The revolt showed them the way to do it.

The early 1920s were rife with revolt among the junior officer ranks, commonly known loosely if somewhat inaccurately as the *tenentes* (subalterns). Between 1924 and 1927 Captain Luiz Carlos Prestes led a guerrilla revolt in the interior in the name of the forgotten masses. The government responded with a state of siege, and Prestes sought refuge in Argentina. Already the great coffee boom was under way, doubling foreign trade in less than ten years. In 1924 the large coffee growers banded together to form an association to hold up price levels on the world market, and incidentally to support the continuing growth of the acreage devoted to coffee, which accounted at the height of Brazilian prosperity for 70 per cent of all exports. Foreign bankers were impressed, and both the federal government and private interests found them ever willing to lend. In July 1929 President Washington Luiz announced that he had chosen a fellow-Paulista, Dr Júlio Prestes, to succeed him and to continue his policies. But within weeks the slump came and the shallowness of Brazil's prosperity was laid bare. Brazil in 1930 had planned to grow more coffee than the entire world consumption of the day. Yet with the foreign debt standing at the then unprecedented figure of $1 181 million, servicing the debt required more foreign currency than the country's exports could supply. As confidence vanished overnight, Vargas, a charismatic political figure with strong local support, contested the election of 1930 as the candidate of the Aliança Liberal (Liberal Alliance). He and his party polled almost three-quarters of the votes cast for the official candidate, but as ever there had been extensive fraud. Vargas launched a revolt and when the President resigned in October 1930, the military junta that had taken power offered him the Presidency, which he speedily accepted. His new regime marked a sharp break in continuity in the political order and a new departure in Brazilian nationalism.

PERU: THE EXCLUSION OF APRA

Peru at the beginning of the twentieth century was a land of largely Indian population ruled by the descendants of the Spanish conquerors, a white skinned, bearded oligarchy whose power was based on their ownership of the fertile lands of Peru's narrow coastal strip. It was they who controlled the remaining wealth of the nitrate fields, which had been nationalized in the 1880s, and their dominance was assured by their alliance with the inland aristocracy of the *sierra*. As the century opened, the peaceful transition of power, if only within the narrowly circumscribed ranks of the Europeanized ruling class, following the retirement of the enlightened Nicolas Piérola, suggested that Peru was to become one of the stable democracies of the region. This seemed to be confirmed by the victory of the Civilista party in the elections of 1904, benefiting from the rubber boom in the Peruvian Amazon region, which was only nominally under the control of the central government.

It was from within the ranks of the Civilista party that there emerged the first challenge to this assumption of emergent stability. Augusto Leguía, President 1908–12, was a tiny, reclusive lawyer, over-shadowed by the personality of his Vice-President, Guillermo Billinghurst, descendant of an English naval officer who had fought for Peru in its war of independence. Billinghurst ran for the rival Democratic Party and was swept to victory in 1912 on a platform of social reform and public welfare, funded by heavy borrowing abroad. Within two years he had been deposed by the armed forces, who, despite twice having been defeated by civilians in their chosen profession of armed combat, thus returned to power. From then on, though from time to time they were to retire to the wings, the armed forces have never ceased to play a major role in Peruvian politics. It is hardly coincidence that this followed the decision to adopt universal military service and to employ foreign instructors to upgrade the armed forces, though unlike most other Latin American states of the time Peru looked to France and not to Germany for its instruction.

General Oscar Raimundo Benavides, the promoter of the coup, in the military tradition of the period held power only briefly while new elections were held. With Billinghurst disposed of, the way was open for a second term for the Civilista José Pardo (President, 1904–08 and 1915–19). His rival Leguía was then elected to succeed him, but overthrew his predecessor prematurely, alleging that Pardo was plotting to prevent him assuming power. Once in office, with military support, he established a personal dictatorship which was to last until 1930. All radical groups were suppressed and a strict press censorship established. Political opponents went underground or, like Haya de la Torre, were driven into exile. It was in Córdoba in Argentina that Haya had acquired his reforming zeal, but in Mexico in 1924 that he founded what, ambitiously enough, was to be not just a party for Peru, but a political movement for the whole of what he termed 'Indo-America', the Alianza Popular Revolucionaria Americana. When Leguía fell in 1930, Haya brought APRA back to his native country.

Leguía's fall followed from his very supremacy. By 1929 50 years had elapsed since the War of the Pacific, in which Peru had lost three provinces to Chile, and Leguía had become so confident that he agreed to sign a Treaty, the Treaty of Ancón, recovering Tacna for Peru, but yielding Arica and Tarapacá to Chile and guaranteeing in effect the permanent exclusion of Bolivia from its former coastal province. Younger officers were dissatisfied, and the impact of the Great Depression spurred them to action. The new coup was led by a young *cholo* (mestizo) colonel, Luis Sánchez Cerro, who had sprung to prominence in the 1914 coup, when as a mere sergeant, his forces stalled at the palace gates, he flung a bomb at them, rushed through, and, though wounded in the attack, secured the victory. Like Billinghurst, he spoke in the name of the many who as yet had taken no part in public life, and within a year he was confirmed as President, but he wanted to hold power, not to change the system, and his supporters were rapidly disillusioned when he failed to fulfil their expectations.

APRA, with its radical nationalism, indigenista flavour and

grandiose if vague ambitions, similarly appealed to a new, wider constituency, and, by organising workers into a potentially powerful force, soon came into conflict with the army. A clash between soldiers and Apristas in 1932, which cost many dead on both sides, left a legacy of bitterness in the armed forces, who with the conservative instincts of their profession, feared that the new movement would prove uncontrollable. When Sánchez Cerro was assassinated by an Aprista in the following year, Benavides returned to power, and in 1936 Haya was excluded from the election by the simple expedient of removing his name from the ballot. Instead the Presidency passed to the safe hands of a reliable and diplomatic civilian member of the oligarchy, Manuel Prado y Ugarteche (President, 1939–45), and in the new liberal climate of the times APRA was again legalized and began to operate as a normal political party.

It was not until 1948 that the armed forces, now under General Manuel A. Odría, again took fright at the prospect of APRA gaining power. They deposed the elected incumbent, and for eight years (the *ochenio*) Odría sought to carry out what he termed a regeneration of the fatherland, to extirpate Aprismo and make the country safe for the coastal oligarchy. APRA was, of course, immediately banned. Haya himself had taken refuge in a building which served as an annexe to the Colombian Embassy. This was in the Latin American tradition, enshrined in a late nineteenth-century agreement recognizing the right of Embassies to offer sanctuary to exiles. Haya would normally within days have been given safe conduct into exile, but instead the building was surrounded by armed guards and when he was finally released, five years later, in April 1954 he was a broken man, heavily overweight, with much of his revolutionary fire gone. He was apparently willing to think well of the United States, which he had formerly denounced as an alien influence in the Americas. Indeed, in a *volte face* of staggering cynicism, he was even prepared, when Odría's successor, the inevitable Manuel Prado, allowed him to return but not to contest an election, in 1962 to do a deal with his former jailer, Odría, and support his candidature in return for his allowing Apristas a share of representation. The Left were outraged but the Army was eerily consistent. If Haya was for Odría, they were against him. Once more they intervened. After more than 30 years, Apristas had yet to get a chance to change a system that kept power in the hands of the few, denied illiterates the vote and in the revolutionary climate of the early 1960s, looked as if it might succumb at any moment to a well organized pro-Cuban revolutionary movement led by the Peredo brothers.

CHILE: FROM SOCIALIST REPUBLIC TO COLD WAR

Isolated from the rest of South America by mountain and desert, Chile pursued an idiosyncratic course. Before 1970 it was widely seen as a prosperous and peaceful country, a model of civilian-dominated political development for the rest of Latin America. Yet despite 80 years of civilian government, the fall of Alessandri in 1924 was the beginning of eight very unstable years for Chile, and the experience was to prove prophetic.

Three thousand miles long and never more than 200 miles wide, Chile, in fact, comprised three parts. The bulk of the population lived in the middle third, a fertile zone but one in which there were still sharp differences of wealth. Strong working class movements were growing up in the nitrate fields and mines of the north, and in the cold south, which breaks up into many large and small islands as it nears Cape Horn, lumberjacks and fishermen worked hard to earn a living and had developed independent political views. Militarism had been slow to develop because of the dominance of the Navy – the Chilean Navy is probably the only navy that has ever defeated its own army, in the civil war of 1891. But from the turn of the century it received a powerful impetus from the fear of Argentina, which in turn led to universal military service in ranks drilled by German military instructors. Today the Prussian 'goose step' is still seen in Chile.

Alessandri, recalled to power in 1925 by the lower ranks of the Army under Colonel Ibáñez del Campo, was almost immediately forced to resign, and elections were held. But Ibáñez was dissatisfied with the choice of the capable Emiliano Figuero Larraín (President, 1925–27), deposed him, and established himself as a military dictator. His reforms, notably the establishment of the state nitrate monopoly COSACH, were fortunate in their timing, in the short-lived boom of the late 1920s. But as Depression struck, rioters appeared on the streets and the armed forces constrained Ibáñez to resign. For months there was no stable government, and in 1932 a group of three junior officers, Carlos Dávila, Arturo Puga and Marmaduque Grove, proclaimed Chile a 'Socialist Republic' but were soon forced out by their more conservative colleagues. Alessandri, though a shadow of his former self, was recalled to office, if not to power, and served out his term, retiring in 1938 with substantial public support freshly evident. Not the least of the reasons for his success was fear among the middle classes of the Left, which drove many to look more favourably on the rising power of the Nazis. But when the socialists and communists allied in 1938 in a 'Popular Front' behind the candidature of Pedro Aguirre Cerda, working-class and the son of Basque immigrants, the Nazis supported it and he won handsomely.

But as this shows, Chile's political divisions were too numerous and too deep to allow radical departures, and the great earthquake of 1940 put a severe burden on an administration already riven with dissension. When Aguirre Cerda died prematurely in 1941, power passed to a conservative coalition which in varying guises was to underpin all the governments of the next 30 years, but Chile was left with the strongest left-wing movement in Latin America. Hence, though Chile was able to escape the stresses of the Second World War by remaining neutral almost throughout, and benefitted handsomely from demand for both copper and nitrates; and then declared war on Japan, and so secured the approval of the United States and membership of the United Nations for the minimum of exertion; it not only failed to recognize the risks posed by the Cold War, but embraced it with an ideological fervour which was ultimately to prove its undoing. In 1948 under US influence, President González Videla, who had already joined forces with rival Argentina to press his Antarctic claims against Britain, expelled the communist members of his coalition government and aligned himself firmly with the Right. The opportunity for major social reform had been lost.

NATIONALISM AND ANTI-AMERICANISM

A new sense of national identity was bound to fuel nationalism, but not all the new nationalisms of the twentieth century were to have indigenista roots. The nationalism of Martí in Cuba, where no indigenous population had survived, was Hispanic and romantic. After the crisis of 1906, when the hero of independence, Tomás Estrada Palma (President, 1902–6), sought re-election and the Conservatives rose in revolt, three years of US occupation made anti-Americanism a dominant theme of Cuban politics. Though in 1909 self-government was resumed with the election of José Miguel Gómez (President, 1909–13), resentment grew at the continued presence on the island of US marines, and was increased when, at a time when the United States was anxious to avoid European intervention in the region, they protected Mario García Menocal (1913–21) in his bid to achieve re-election in 1917. Unlike Latin Americans, Cuba's overlords had no prohibition on re-election – Roosevelt himself had been re-elected in 1904 and Wilson achieved the same feat in 1916, though by a wafer-thin majority which anywhere else in the region at that time would have resulted in an immediate civil war. In 1920 the United States sent an official mission to Cuba to oversee the elections which returned the official candidate, Alfredo Zayas (1921–25). Not surprisingly there was considerable unrest, which flared into open revolt in 1925 when Zayas in turn sought a second term.

The Republicans had returned to power in the United States in 1921 and initially under President Harding had sought to mend their fences in Latin America. But Coolidge, who succeeded Harding in 1923, became increasingly entangled. He chose not to oppose, and in consequence the US was to be blamed for the rise to power of General Gerardo Machado y Morales, who dominated Cuban politics from 1925 to 1933. Under his dictatorship a new generation came to adulthood fired with nationalistic fervour and a hatred both of the regime and of the United States, whose intervention in Haiti and the Dominican Republic, however well intentioned, provoked very similar reactions among the educated élite.

The fact was that American investment everywhere in the region was already shaping national economies into complementarity with the vast economy of the United States. A symbol of this growth was the emergence in the early 1920s of one giant corporation, the United Fruit Company of Boston. This vast organization, with its 'Great White Fleet' of specially built banana boats, was the creation of the freebooting entrepreneur Samuel Lee Zemurray, building on the earlier work of Minor C. Keith, who from banana growing in Jamaica, saw Central America as the last great area of the world in which to build railways. The railways would carry bananas and bananas would provide the revenue for the railways. Within a decade his rail network, International Railways of Central America, later a subsidiary of United Fruit, linked Guatemala, Honduras and El Salvador, though in Honduras, as noted above, the bulk of the railways were built in an enclave on the north coast. At the same time, United Fruit ('La Frutera') became the largest landowner and greatest financial power in each of these states. In the mid-1920s the four northern states each linked their economy to the US dollar, while Costa Rica, whose large number of small landowners gave it a very different sort of economy, became no less dependent on the US market for sales of its coffee.

Further north, in Nicaragua, the Byran-Chamorro Treaty of 1913, ratified by the US Senate in 1916 in the year that the Conservative Emiliano Chamorro became President, made the country a virtual protectorate. Neighbouring El Salvador complained that the Treaty was a violation of the agreements of 1907, and submitted the Treaty to the Central American Court, which ruled in its favour. It was the fact that Nicaragua simply ignored this decision (1918) that destroyed the Court, but it would not have done so had it not been able to count on the support of the United States, which maintained its 'Legation Guard' of US marines in Managua until 1925. In that year they were withdrawn as an economy measure. Immediately Chamorro began to extend his influence, first forcing the minority of Liberals out of the government and then claiming the Presidency for himself. At this point, when revolt broke out, the US refused to accept Chamorro, enforced an armistice between the contending parties and supervised new elections which resulted in the choice of the Liberal José María Moncada (President, 1928–33).

Since the US troops did not then leave the country, a dissident Liberal General, Augusto Sandino, took to the hills. An outstanding military leader who defied all attempts of the US occupation forces to capture him, Sandino did not come down from the hills until the Americans had gone. In the meanwhile he had built a substantial peasant-based nationalistic movement. Despite his later importance as a nationalist hero, it does not appear, however, that he personally had very strong views on social reform. A traditional liberal, he fought to free his country from foreign domination and believed that once a democratic order was established people would be able to choose for themselves.

Though Panama is still seen as part of South rather than Central America, in both its size and its dependence on the United States its history has been very similar to that of its northern neighbours. Constitutional rule was formally established in 1904 with the Presidency of Manuel Amador Guerrero (President, 1904–8). The construction of the mighty Canal made the US presence very conspicuous, however. The forces stationed in the Canal Zone for its protection were inevitably from the outset a major force in Panamanian politics, and their role an active one. US intervention took place in 1908, 1912 and 1916 to guarantee the outcome of the Presidential elections. Meanwhile, the choice by the ruling élite of Pablo Arosemena (President, 1910–12) established a dynastic tradition which was to mark Panamanian politics for some 60 years.

As in Cuba the 1920s saw a massive influx of US investment into Panama, and a government newly aware of its insecurity sought in addition to revise the 1903 Treaty to give the United States airport facilities, radio communications and the right to joint control of all military operations in Panama in the event of war. In face of the influx of new wealth, Rodolfo Chiari (President, 1924–28) confronted challenges from both sides: in 1925 the San Blas Indians went into revolt, and two years later, amid demands for the seizure of the Canal, the Congress refused to ratify the new Treaty. So great was the feeling that Chiari's Conservative Party was defeated in the 1928 elections, and replaced by a Liberal administration under Florencio Harmodio Arosemena (President, 1928–31). The forces that had been liberated, however, were not to be so easily contained.

In all the countries of the Caribbean region the educated middle class was very small. The sense of belonging to an élite rather than any identity as a class was what was important. So small were the numbers involved that US intervention inevitably had a deep cultural effect which went well below the superficial evidence of 'coca-colonization'. To this day, for example, Nicaraguans of all political persuasions learn American English, watch American movies and play baseball. Even where until recently there has been no US presence, as in the former British and Dutch colonies, US culture has established itself. The one factor resisting US influence, because of the association of the United States both with Protestantism and with the lax morals of Hollywood, has been the Church.

It is therefore no coincidence that in the larger states the awareness of US power established at the beginning of the century by the secession of Panama has been associated with a traditional style of politics and the continued dominance of the Church. Nowhere is this more so than in Colombia itself, where the 'War of a Thousand Days' at the beginning of the century, which had weakened Colombia in face of the US demands, resulted in the ascendancy of the Conservatives, the clerical and centralist party. For more than two decades they were to watch events to the North with foreboding and trepidation, resisting any move to change the existing order of things. Elsewhere nationalist aspirations were associated with the Army, as in Peru, where in 1914 the attempts of Guillermo Billinghurst to strengthen the country's economy by inviting in foreign investment were terminated by the intervention of General Benavides. There and in the rest of South America, however, the United States as such was not yet seen as a major threat, and indeed for many years after that time lacked the capacity to intervene except through the use of naval power. For intellectuals its symbolic importance was considerable, and the war of 1898 marks a dramatic change in their attitudes towards it. In 1900 an

Uruguayan, José Enrique Rodó, made the definitive statement of what was subsequently to become known as 'Arielismo' – the view that the United States (Caliban) embodied gross materialism, against which the Latin Americans could and should oppose a greater and higher spirituality (Ariel). But whether or not this view was true (and there are many who would argue that the twentieth-century United States has a very vigorous cultural life), it was all too easily converted into an excuse for inaction in face of the growing economic and social problems of the region.

THE MEXICAN REVOLUTION

In Mexico the 30-year dictatorship gave way to a great social revolution, one of the few such revolutions which, despite all that has happened since, would almost universally be recognized as such. In its violence it ranks with the American Civil War; deaths from epidemic disease, including the great influenza epidemic of 1919, add to the total, but the best estimate is that some half a million people died. In its train it brought profound social changes and established a stable regime that has lasted to this day. The impact on Latin America was incalculable. And because it shared a common frontier with the United States, its relationship to the United States was also very significant.

The apologists for the regime of Porfirio Díaz had argued that dictatorship was necessary if the new scientific understanding of society brought by positivism was to be applied to making Mexico a modern nation. In his last years, the old man had himself come to believe that he was laying the foundation for a democratic society in his country, and in 1908 he told an American journalist that it was his intention to allow free elections in 1910.

One man, Francisco I. Madero, son of a wealthy family of Coahuila, took this seriously. With other Mexican liberals, he formed an Anti-Re-electionist Party and contested the election of 1910. The strength of his support alarmed the government, who locked him up for the duration of the poll, but he subsequently escaped to the United States and called for a nationwide revolt, which, despite a government attempt to pre-empt it, finally broke out in November 1910. Within a few months the aged Díaz had left the country and Madero was elected President (1911–13). But the forces that had been unleashed were too great. Early in 1913 Madero was overthrown in the course of a military coup by his own Commander of the Army, General Victoriano

Huerta, who like many of the old guard believed in the policy of the 'strong hand'. When Madero and his Vice-President were vindictively 'shot trying to escape', however, they became martyrs to the cause of constitutional government. Led by the Governor of Coahuila, Venustiano Carranza, as First Chief of the Constitutionalist Forces, the whole of northern Mexico was soon in revolt.

For the next three years civil war raged unchecked. The United States under Woodrow Wilson tried to intervene to secure the removal of Huerta, but found that given the strength of Mexican nationalism no Mexican politician was prepared to work with them. Carranza was careful to distance himself from US support, but was in any case unable to impose his authority. In August 1914 Huerta fell. A Convention of Revolutionary Chiefs met at Aguascalientes and appointed an interim President, but he was unable to impose his authority. Similarly Carranza, although he was able to disrupt the Convention, also could not gain its support, though one of his generals, Alvaro Obregón, leading the Army of the North-West, remained loyal when Pancho Villa (born Doroteo Arango) and the agrarian leader of the State of Morelos, Emiliano Zapata, met in Mexico City and formed a temporary alliance which controlled the central part of the country. From Veracruz, Carranza's temporary capital, the Constitutionalist government issued an historic decree ordering a start on land reform and masterminded the slow rebuilding of political alliances and the recapture of the capital. At Querétaro in 1917 a new Constitution embodied guarantees both for the agrarian reformers and for the industrial workers who had supplied 'Red Battalions' for Obregón's armies. It also established the principle of 'no re-election' to any public office which with one exception has been observed ever since.

Carranza as President form 1917 to 1920 failed to maintain the momentum generated by the Revolution. He was already an old man, an essentially conservative figure, who had little sympathy with the young leaders and their radical forces, and was seen as such. Hence when in 1920 he tried to nominate a weak civilian successor, revolt again broke out, and, as he tried to flee to Veracruz by train, he was captured and killed by his political enemies. Constitutionally elected to succeed him, Obregón (President, 1920–24) established a socialist regime, ruling with the support of the Labour Party and the workers' central organization, the CROM. Under the leadership of the writer and publicist José Vasconcelos, a major education drive was launched in town and country, literature was harnessed to the service of the Revolution and the walls of public buildings given over to the Mexican school of muralists. The first serious programme of land distribution was begun in 1920 under the interim government, and continued under Obregón. His successor, Plutarco Elias Calles (President, 1924–28), also from the northern state of Sonora, depended even more on the support of organized labour and as a socialist and an anti-clerical came increasingly into conflict with the traditionally-minded Church hierarchy. In 1926 open revolt broke out and for three years church services were suspended while the Cristeros (so-called from their war-cry, 'Cristo Rey' – Christ the King), based mainly in the western states, fought a bitter guerrilla war against government troops. As the war consumed scarce funds, the distribution of land again tailed off and, though he established the first credit agency to fund agricultural development, Calles himself began to have considerable doubts about the economic consequences of breaking up the old estates. The problem was that while they were being reorganized production fell off steeply, and a growing population needed food.

Though the Revolution had begun as a struggle against re-election, the Constitution was now amended and in 1928 Obregón was re-elected, only to be shot at his victory banquet by a religious fanatic. As Mexico trembled on the verge of even more conflict, a political compromise was hastily arranged. Calles went abroad at the end of his term, an interim President was appointed, the Cristero War was ended through the good offices of the American Ambassador, Dwight D. Morrow, and a new official ruling party, the Party of the National Revolution (PNR), was created, funded by a charge on the salaries of all state employees. When the expected military revolt broke out in 1929, Calles was recalled to lead the government forces. But though he continued to dominate politics from behind the scenes until 1935, the structure of the party he had helped to create and for a time led proved strong enough to unite pro-revolutionary interests behind a new and radical programme of social change, the First Six Year Plan (1933–39), and a new and youthful president, Lázàro Cárdenas (President 1934–40), who had been formed by the Revolution and whose name has become synonymous with the social changes the Revolution brought about.

Unlike other great social revolutions the Mexican Revolution (a term which covers the whole period from 1910 through to 1940) was late in developing an official ideology, and for this reason it is often wrongly believed that its proponents did not have one. The difference lies in the nature of the regime that it overthrew. The regime of Porfirio Díaz had an ideology – the positivist belief in authoritarian rule by an élite to develop and modernize the society they controlled.

The leaders of the revolutionary period were brought up in this tradition. They found it easy to agree that they should decide what was to be done. What divided them was what they should put in the place of the old order. The new Constitution, with its advanced guarantees for peasant and labour interests, was however already in place by February 1917, a month before the fall of the Tsar in Russia. The destruction of the institutional power of the Church in the 1920s was equally striking: all church lands and buildings were nationalized and seminaries, monasteries and convents dissolved. The large-scale distribution of land began in 1929, a year before Stalin's collectivization of agriculture, and under Cárdenas some 20 million hectares of land were distributed, mostly in the form of co-operative farms called *ejidos*. In the 1930s and 1940s the example of the New Deal in the United States was gradually to help move the course of the Revolution away from European-style socialism, but as the first major social revolution in the Americas it continued to have a powerful effect.

The influence of the Mexican Revolution was not limited to the domestic context. For Catholics abroad it became both an example (as for the separation of Church and State in Chile in 1925) and a dreadful warning (for Evelyn Waugh and other Catholic publicists in Europe and the United States). For social reformers it had diverse meanings, influencing the group of students that surrounded President Grau San Martín in Cuba in 1934, the makers of the civilian and democratic revolution in Costa Rica in 1948, and the rise of the MNR in Bolivia in 1952, which implemented an important if modest land reform programme. Its most powerful influence, however, was on the rise of economic nationalism, both within Mexico and abroad. The nationalization of the foreign-owned oil industry in 1938 by Lázaro Cárdenas is still celebrated in Mexico by an annual public holiday as a virtual declaration of economic independence.

THE FIRST OIL BOOM AND THE TRANSPORT REVOLUTION

Natural seepages of petroleum are common in the Mexican south, especially in the Isthmus of Tehuantepec, and the Aztecs used the black, sticky substance in their religious rituals. The English contractor, Sir Weetman Pearson, who saw these seepages during the construction of the Tehuantepec Railway, and inspired by reports of oil strikes in Texas, in 1901 secured extensive concessions from the

Mexican government to drill for oil. In the meanwhile the American oil magnate, Edward L. Doheny, had bought up large private tracts for the same purpose and in the same year brought in his first small well. Until 1884 all subsoil resources had, in the Spanish tradition, been owned by the government, but in that year the Díaz government had changed the law and given the rights to the landowner in order to attract foreign firms into the country. After the first major fields were discovered in 1910 it became clear that these resources were very valuable, but during the Revolution the oil continued to be extracted to help fuel the war in Europe and in the prevailing state of turmoil the succession of changing governments gained little or nothing. Worse still, in the early 1920s production fell steeply as fields drained by hasty and inefficient exploitation began to run dry. The part-British Royal Dutch-Shell group embarked on a large-scale exploration programme which by the early 1930s began to bring results. Their US counterparts held back, so that production overall remained static. They were distrustful of the powerful oil workers union, which was a major part of the coalition that supported the new ruling party. As part of his moves to consolidate his position, and to outflank Calles, Cárdenas encouraged the union in its claims for better pay and working conditions. Matters came to a head when in 1937 the government intervened in a strike at the request of the head of the labour confederation to order the companies to give their workers a substantial pay increase and promote Mexicans to managerial positions. When they refused to comply, Cárdenas decreed the nationalization of the companies' assets in Mexico and set up a new state oil enterprise, Petróleos Mexicanos (Pemex), to run the industry. Despite a boycott of Mexico by the companies, which drove the administration for a time to seek barter agreements with Fascist Italy and Nazi Germany, President Roosevelt eventually pressured them into accepting the compensation offered. The British government under Neville Chamberlain, however, refused to do the same, and diplomatic relations were severed. Though they were restored in 1942 when Mexico came into the Second World War, Britain has never regained the position in the Mexican market which it thus foolishly lost, while the principle which Cárdenas was one of the first to assert successfully, that a national government has the sovereign right to the control of its soil and sub-soil resources, is now generally accepted not only by Third World states but also by the major powers.

Three other Latin American states developed their oil potential during this period: Argentina, Venezuela and Bolivia. In each a very different approach was adopted. In Argentina as early as 1922 Yrigoyen established a state oil enterprise, Yacimientos Petrolíferos Fiscales (YPF). Under the leadership of General Mosconi, appointed by President Alvear, it established itself as sole marketing and distribution agency within the country, and along with the Argentine railway syndicate Ferrocarrilera took the lead in exploration and drilling. After 1929 production by independents almost ceased and the importation of crude oil fell off steeply, leaving Argentina essentially self-sufficient in energy resources.

In Venezuela, Castro's seizure of power in 1898 ushered in half a century of 'Andean ascendancy'. The new rulers, like those of the nineteenth century, were backed by military force. They were not, however, the old caudillos, but praetorians, generals backed by the power of a modernizing army. Juan Vicente Gómez, who seized power in 1908 while President Castro was in Europe for medical treatment, ruled the country until his death in 1935 regardless of who held the Presidency. He laid the foundation for his country's future prosperity when he did separate deals with foreign concessionaires, but drove a hard bargain which ensured that at least part of the profit was ploughed back into economic development, even though then and later much Venezuelan crude was refined on the Dutch West Indian island of Aruba. His tyrannical rule, accompanied by a personality cult, was financially successful but untainted by any zeal for the public welfare, and at his death his family were attacked and his home destroyed. Nevertheless he left Venezuela financially stable and the policy of 'sowing the oil' (*sembrar el petróleo*) was to be continued by his military and civilian successors.

In Bolivia, still cut off from the sea, the development of energy resources became a matter of national survival when in 1932 war broke out with Paraguay. Bolivia had long disputed with its neighbour possession of the Chaco Boreal, or northern Chaco, part of an upland plain which stretches from Brazil in the north southward across the Río Pilcomayo into northern Argentina. The area is one of featureless semi-desert which turns to swamp when the rains come, stretching from the foothills of the Andes to the Río Paraguay. To avert the threat of Bolivian troops being stationed on the other side of that river, close to Asunción, the national capital, the Paraguayan Army had built forts in the Chaco to assert its claim to possession and the Bolivians had done the same. All might yet have been well had not oil been discovered around Camiri in the eastern Bolivian province of Santa Cruz in the early 1920s, leading to the belief that a large extension of this oilfield might be found under the Chaco. Bolivian oil became in this way both the cause of war and the means by which it could be waged.

The discovery of oil had been accompanied by a major transport revolution which was even then beginning to open up parts of the continent that previously had been almost inaccessible. First to benefit were the existing railways. Initally in Mexico and then in Argentina steam locomotives were converted to burn fuel oil. Then came the car and the diesel engined bus or truck. Petroleum supplied both the fuel and the surface on which the new vehicles ran. Mexican asphalt was laid on the Paseo de la Reforma to turn it into Mexico's first all-weather road in 1908. Outside the capital, however, dirt tracks remained the norm, and during the Revolution the major campaigns were fought out along the main railway lines using rail transport and the destruction of both track and rolling stock was very heavy. Only when the fighting of the revolutionary years came to a halt in 1920 was it possible to make further progress. In that year the interim President-elect, Aldolfo de la Huerta, took nine days to reach his capital from the north-western State of Sonora. Zapata rode to his assassination in 1919 on a black horse; Villa, a pensioner of the Obregón government, was shot in his car in 1923.

Mexico City was linked to the United States by an all-weather road only in 1928. By that time buses had begun to reach the outlying districts which had never before been regularly accessible, and by 1940 an amazing assortment of decrepit purpose-built vehicles, hand-me-downs from the United States and converted trucks formed a nationwide network which enabled schools and health centres to flourish in the most remote areas. But it was not until the 1950s that an all-weather route connected Mexico City to the Yucatán Peninsula, or to Guatemala.

The progress of urbanization was greatly accelerated in the early years of the century by the growth of municipal transport. The Canadian entrepreneur, Fred Stark Pearson, pioneered streetcars in both Mexico City and Rio de Janeiro. In Buenos Aires the British-owned surburban railway line to Tigre was electrified as early as 1925, and the *Subte* (underground railway) constructed.

THE CHACO WAR

The Chaco War (1932–35) was the most serious conflict to break the peace of Latin America this century. Ironically the two countries involved, Bolivia and Paraguay, had much in common. Both had been the victims of wars in the nineteenth century, in which they had lost strategically important territory and had sacrificed lives needlessly to no effect. They were both land-locked, dependent on trade routes running through the territory of watchful neighbours. They were both poor, though Bolivia's position as one of the world's few producers of tin, then at the peak of its industrial importance for preserving food, gave it both a source of wealth and a leverage on the world community which its subtropical, agricultural neighbour lacked. It was a bitter irony that they turned their attention inward toward one another and failed to make a common stand against their powerful neighbours and the world.

It was Paraguay that began in the weaker position. After the disaster of the War of the Triple Alliance the inland state, deprived of some one third of its national territory by Brazil and Argentina, took two generations to recover a semblance of normality. The Liberals, who had been left after 1870 with the task of clearing up the mess, had been shunted aside and the Army dominated politics, ruling in the interest of the conservative landowners. Economically Paraguay, three days from Buenos Aires by rail and even more remote by river transport, was still essentially a backward province of Argentina.

In 1904, following a series of military coups, the Liberals returned to power after three months of civil war, brought to an end by the Pilcomayo Agreement. Under this the Liberal nominee for President, Professor Cecilio Báez, took office and held an election which chose the Liberal leader, General Benigno Ferreira, as President (1906–8). It was Ferreira's nominee, Colonel Albino Jara, as Minister of War, who was charged with the task of eradicating military influence in politics. Jara soon found, however, that his President, once in power, was not giving him the support he needed. In 1908 he led a revolt in which gunboats in the river shelled Asunción, until a rising in the garrison at Concepción enabled the rebels to carry the day, instal a new President and allow Jara to carry out his programme to dissolve the Army and form a new one on the basis of universal military service.

Not surprisingly this did not solve the problem of militarism. Jara himself became impatient, swept aside the lawyer Manuel Gondra (President 1910–11), and seized the Presidency for himself, only to be deposed in a bloodless coup a few months later by moderates opposed to his authoritarian style of government. The radicals then planned a fresh assault on the capital. Their plans were betrayed by a telegraphist, and government forces sent a train loaded with dynamite down the track towards the village where the rebels were assembling. The dynamite exploded with tremendous force, blowing to pieces the village, the rebel troops and radical hopes. Jara himself was later killed in battle against government forces near Paraguarí. If radicalism was dead, constitutionalism momentarily seemed to have triumphed. The moderate Liberals remained in power, and Eduardo Schaerer (President 1912–16) was the first elected President of the twentieth century to complete his term, while Paraguay enjoyed a revival in its prosperity through trade with the outside world. In 1920 Gondra was chosen for a second time, but was again deposed in favour of the elder of the two Ayala brothers who dominated Paraguayan politics for more than a decade, and whose nominee, José Guggiari (President, 1928–31), had the unenviable task of preparing Paraguay for war with Bolivia.

The very magnitude of Paraguay's previous defeat was a powerful restraint on her leaders. Bolivia, on the other hand, had been relatively unscathed by the brief War of the Pacific, and an orderly succession of conservative governments suggested a deceptive stability. In fact its leaders, retaining a strong sense of grievance at being deprived of its natural outlet to the sea, strove to retrieve it, as if obsessed with this one objective to the exclusion of all others. They had some reason: the historic route through Peru by way of Lake Titicaca, the highest lake in the world, involving trans-shipment to and from the two lake steamers taken up there in pieces on muleback in the 1870s, was hardly a commercial alternative. Hence in 1904 José Pando, who had seized power in a military coup in 1899, signed away the Acré region to Brazil in return for the right to build a railway into Brazil and a cash indemnity of $10 million, and negotiated a Treaty with Chile, signed by his successor Ismael Montes (President, 1904–9). This treaty, the first Treaty of Ancón, did little to satisfy Bolivia's territorial claims, since by it Bolivia abandoned its claim to Arica and Chile merely admitted Bolivia's right to the Atacama Desert. But it provided the transit rights for the construction and operation of the Arica-La Paz Railway, which was completed in 1912 and made the development of tin mines possible. A brief period of prosperity was already under way in which important steps were taken to expand public education.

In 1913 Bolivia had been willing to share the region of the Chaco with Paraguay on terms that could have been quite satisfactory to both sides. By the 1920s things had changed. The optimistic belief that the new League of Nations would recognize Bolivia's claims to Arica were soon dashed. After a brief recession, Bolivia's mining industry began, during the term of Bautista Saavedra (1920–25), to expand more rapidly. But his successor was deposed following an unusually fraudulent election, and Hernando Siles (President, 1926–30) found himself in a very unstable political position. Hence he was unable or unwilling to control either the adventurist policy of the armed forces in the Chaco, or his Foreign Minister, who extended the Bolivian claim to the region far beyond anything that had been claimed before, beyond the line of 1913 and the actual line of Paraguayan defence. Both sides then built forts and sent out patrols, and the first armed clashes in the region began as early as 1928. War would probably have followed at once had it not been for two factors. Word of the reopening of negotiations between Chile and Peru on their boundary dispute aroused Bolivian hopes, only to dash them when they found that the Treaty of Ancón, signed in 1929, returned Tacna to Peru but provided that none of the land involved could be alienated to a third party (namely, Bolivia) by either country without the consent of the other. This effectively spelt checkmate to Bolivian hopes of regaining its sea coast. Then came the Great Depression and a steep fall in the world price of tin and in 1930 Siles was deposed by a military coup, which was followed by a further period of provisional government.

In the meanwhile a military coup in Argentina had placed a military government in power there, and the Paraguayan government were therefore able to count on their tacit support and on the diplomatic skill of the new Argentine Foreign Minister, Carlos Saavedra Lamas. Paraguay sought to bring the question of the Chaco before the League. They were, however, frustrated by the fact that the United States, not being a member of the League, favoured a Pan American alternative, but with Argentina favouring Paraguay and Chile supporting Bolivia, the major Latin American states were divided so the Pan-American Conference was unable to work out a satisfactory formula. While skirmishes continued in the disputed zone the best possibility seemed to be a return to the status quo ante.

However, news reached Paraguay that the Bolivians were making strenuous efforts to increase their military strength, and that arms were reaching Bolivia through Chile, which was itself almost in a state of civil war. In a desperate attempt to forestall an invasion, the Paraguayans opened hostilities in mid-1932 by attacking a Bolivian advance guard on the near side of the Chaco. They hoped other states would then follow the usual practice and cut off all military aid to both sides. They were sorely disappointed. What happened instead was that the League branded Paraguay an 'aggressor', and, after a time, its obsession with the question of who fired the first shot led further to the arms ban being raised in favour not of Paraguay but of Bolivia. Fortunately for them, by the time that happened, superior Paraguayan training and preparation had prevailed, with the Bolivians being driven back into the foothills of the Andes. With his troops not only in a worse position than when they started the conflict, but further away from their objective than any line of demarcation that had been proposed since 1879, the Bolivian President, Daniel Salamanca, was overthrown in December 1934.

In their victory, the Paraguayans were helped above all by the physical conditions of the Chaco. The difficulty of communications across the swamp and desert meant that the Bolivians began by fighting at the end of an over-long line of supply. But the same factor in turn forced the Paraguayans to stop short of the Bolivian heartland in 1935. A truce was then hastily agreed by the Bolivian government, and the Paraguayans were prepared to make a reasonably generous peace, until a military coup overthrew the victorious government of Eusebio Ayala (1931–36). It was replaced by a short-lived military government under General Rafael Franco (1936–37), while in Bolivia the defeated government of Salamanca's Vice-President and successor, José Luis Tejada Sorzano, was also overthown in 1936 by a revolt led by Germán Busch, and replaced by a Fascist-style government under José David Toro (1936–37). Both countries, it semed, had acquired dictatorial regimes devoted to the reconstruction of every aspect of national life. Both attempted by the imposition of rigid controls on the people to develop the economy and military infrastructure, especially through the nationalization of key industries. But in neither case did they last long, though in Bolivia there were long-lasting consequences of this brief experiment. Busch overthrew Toro, while in Paraguay Franco fell to a bloodless Liberal coup and was replaced by the constitutional regime headed first by Félix Paiva (1937–39) and then briefly before his untimely death in an air accident by the Chaco war-hero Marshal José Félix Estigarribia (President, 1939–40).

By then Saavedra Lamas had fallen from office in Argentina. He had done more than anyone else to prolong the Chaco War, so that Paraguay might gain, and so was rewarded with the dubious honour of a Nobel Peace Prize. Peace was at last signed in 1938. The concessions made by each side were disguised as a so-called 'arbitral award', the terms of which had in fact been agreed in advance. An unfortunate effect was to strengthen the myth of inter-American co-operation, of which the war had in fact been the negation. Another effect was seriously to damage the reputation of the League at a critical moment.

3 Depression and Dependency

THE IMPACT OF THE GREAT DEPRESSION

At the end of the 1920s virtually all of the Latin American states were enjoying a degree of prosperity and political stability under civilian rule. In 1930 this changed abruptly. The governments of the Dominican Republic, Bolivia, Peru, Argentina, Brazil and Guatemala were in turn overthrown by their armed forces. The following year, 1931, those of Panama, Chile, Ecuador and El Salvador fell also, while in 1932 Chile suffered forcible changes of government no less than four times. And in 1933 the President of Uruguay gave himself extraordinary powers, the dictator of Cuba was overthrown and the President of Peru assassinated. Military regimes became as much a feature of the 1930s as civilian ones had been in the previous decade.

As more research takes place on the complexities of the period, however, reservations have to be made about the nature of the relationship between the economic crisis and the political consequences. That there was a relationship is not in doubt. In economic terms, 1930 marks a watershed in Latin American history; the crisis destroyed the old assumptions on which economic policy had been conducted. The effects were both direct and indirect. Directly the sudden end of the boom years and the collapse of prices on world markets meant a crisis for the great estates and all those who worked on them, for the mining industry, and for the financial interests who had lent money to Latin America and were now faced with the familiar prospect of default. The indirect effects were more complicated. First and foremost the crisis gave a new urgency to social problems that had long existed and oligarchic governments suddenly lost credibility as the protectors of popular interests. Secondly a new wave of nationalism swept the hemisphere, fanned by the evident intention of the United States to protect itself against the crisis by raising new tariff barriers against imports, thus in the end exacerbating its own difficulties and delaying the recovery. A similar tendency in the United Kingdom brought Imperial Preference, so that Argentina, which was economically though not politically part of the British Empire, could only continue to sell beef to the huge UK market if it accepted the terms of the so-called Roca-Runciman Treaty (1933), the purpose of which from the British point of view was to assure a supply of cheap food for its turbulent industrial population. The Depression, therefore, not only led many to question the value of economic association with democracies, it also led to questioning of the practical value of democracy itself.

In the long term the Depression was to focus attention on the economic relationship between the developed countries and the less developed ones and ultimately to give rise to a distinctive Latin American perspective, dependency theory. Dependency theory is a system of ideas developed in the 1960s within a Marxist framework which sees events in Latin America (as in other parts of the developing world) as being determined by the subordinate role of Latin America in the world capitalist system. That system, the *dependentistas* argue, has as its centre the developed capitalist states of Europe and North America. The developing countries are on the system's periphery. Development in the periphery is not independent, but conditional on the nature of development in the centre. Hence the countries of the periphery are by the nature of the system relegated to the role of primary producers, providing cheap raw materials from which the developed countries earn their huge profits. Peripheral economies are then encouraged to re-import the manufactured goods produced by developed nations at vastly inflated prices. Hence their development is arrested. Worse still, it is distorted and deformed, expanding further and further the primary export sector and making the country concerned more and more dependent on its overseas market, in which, because of the abundance of supply, prices are generally low and fluctuate wildly according to the needs of the developed countries.

Economic dependency is underpinned and assured by political dependency. Though no longer formally colonies, the dependent states are so closely linked into the system that they operate as if they were. The way in which this happens is that the local business and financial interests find if more profitable to do business with foreign companies than to invest in productive enterprises in their own country; they sell out and put their money in foreign securities where they can reap a steady and safe profit. Foreign capital does indeed spur development in mines, trading companies and estates, but it is development directed not towards the good of the dependent area but towards that of the foreign investor and foreign businessmen. The government can no longer control its own economy, for foreign corporations hold the whip hand. The corporations operate in so many different countries at the same time that they can evade the controls which the dependent governments try to impose on them, using devices such as transfer pricing to minimize the amount of taxes they pay locally, and in the last resort threatening to move production elsewhere. Further development towards a self-sustaining economy is checked, and the huge burden of foreign debt crushes any attempt at local initiatives to break out of the trap. Effectively, therefore, the government cannot exercise its political independence, it is constrained from both inside and outside its national boundaries to act in the interests of foreigners.

It was the Great Depression that helped create this sense of national powerlessness in Latin America, and it is no accident that it is especially in Argentina, where the myth of national greatness and economic prosperity was so abruptly ended, that dependency theory was later developed and refined. At the time the effect in the Southern Cone generally was to promote political extremism both on the Right and on the Left. There has been a natural tendency in both Europe and North America to see much of this extremism as imported from Europe, but this is to overstate the case. The Depression was certainly associated with the conditions that led to the fall of the Spanish monarchy in 1931, and the Nationalist rising against the Republic in 1936. The successful stabilization, both political and economic, of Portugal after Dr Salazar had become Prime Minister in 1932, further strengthened the appeal of nationalism, and in Argentina, Brazil and Chile, where there were many Latin Americans of Italian origin, new significance was attached both to the economic success of Italian fascism (which had been achieved in the 1920s) and the military adventures on which the regime was to embark thereafter. Benito Mussolini (Prime Minister of Italy, 1922–43) had been named after the hero of Mexican liberalism, but it was not his vague and often inconsistent ideological positions that mattered to the outside world so much as the example he gave of brutal power. The rise of Hitler in Germany further called up echoes among the substantial German communities in the same countries, and stirred support for fascist solutions not only there but in Paraguay, Bolivia and Guatemala as well. If the trappings of fascism were imported, however, its popularity among the armed forces derived from the extent to which it gave a new justification for forms of military intervention that lay already to hand. Democracy being discredited, they now had the opportunity that many of them had long sought.

On the Left, on the other hand, the rise of Stalin, with his grandiose schemes for the industrialization of the Soviet Union, caught another part of the imagination. By 1931, as the Western world appeared to be grinding to a halt, the Soviet Union was 'giddy with success' at the collectivization of agriculture, the true cost of which in starvation and human suffering was not to be known for decades. The notion of economic planning and the primacy of the state were something that Latin Americans had known since colonial times; the veneer of liberalism acquired in the late nineteenth century was easily peeled away. The Left, however, suffered from a weakness that was to prove very difficult to overcome; the very nature of underdevelopment in Latin America meant that workers' movements were small and still to a large extent craft-based. Hence though the 1930s were to see an important extension of left-wing sympathies amongst intellectuals, their impact on practical politics in the decade was very small and confined to those countries in which economic circumstances gave particular weight to workers' power blocks.

As it proved, moreover, the 1930s were also to show one important triumph for democracy: the New Deal in the United States. The proximity of the United States to the Latin American states meant that in the end this example was to be far more important than any other. But this too led in the direction of greater powers for central government and more state intervention in the economy, so in the Latin American context the example of the New Deal was often used by figures who had very poor democratic credentials. But not always.

COLOMBIA

There were not many exceptions to the rule that Latin American states in this period underwent military intervention. Even in Uruguay President Gabriel Terra in 1933 terminated the 'First Colegiado' by proclaiming a state of emergency and ruling by decree. Colombia, however, was an important exception. There the election of 1930 brought the Liberals to power peacefully. Despite Conservative opposition, placated to some extent by public works schemes and grants to coffee producers to replant, Enrique Olaya Herrera (President, 1930–34) established laws giving labour the right to organize and introduced a social security system and so softened the impact of the Depression.

Unfortunately his administration immediately became embroiled with Peru in a dispute about Colombia's right to access to the headwaters of the Amazon at Leticia. Such a right, which effectively gave Colombia, which apart from Mexico is the only major Latin American state with direct access to both the Atlantic and the Pacific, a third 'sea coast' in the interior, was of potential economic importance. As so often in boundary disputes its symbolic importance was of even greater significance, and though Colombian diplomats, despite having no effective naval or military forces in the region, were highly successful in gaining their point and securing Peru's agreement, the incident caused the Conservatives to accept the leadership of the intransigent Laureano Gómez, and he in turn made the first blunder of his disastrous career by inducing the Conservatives to boycott the election of 1934. The result, as might have been foreseen, was that the enlightened and able Alfonso López Pumarejo (President, 1934–38) was returned with an all-Liberal Congress, and so was able to carry through a timely and comprehensive programme of legislative and social reform.

A new constitutional code of civil rights gave the new administration extensive powers to intervene in economic matters. An income tax was established to give the government a consistent and reliable source of funds. Enactments carried through long overdue Liberal reforms, including toleration for all religious persuasions and the introduction for the first time of a national system of secular education. López handed over power peacefully to his successor, Eduardo Santos, who in his second term, between 1942 and 1945, became the President who led Colombia into the Second World War. But as demands for further change were not met, the Liberal Party split, and when López resigned in 1945 and handed over power to his Vice-President, Alberto Lleras Camargo, the radical faction under Jorge Eliecer Gaitán split away. On a minority vote the Conservative candidate, Mariano Ospina Pérez, was chosen as President in 1946.

DICTATORSHIP IN VENEZUELA

Unlike its neighbour, Colombia, where military rule had been almost unknown, the birthplace of Bolívar had been almost continuously subject to dictatorship. Between 1899 and 1935 power had been held continuously by two military leaders from the State of Táchira. And after the death of Gómez in 1935, power passed constitutionally to his son-in-law and Minister of War, a third military President from the same state, General Eleázar López Contreras. Having served out his predecessor's term, López Contreras was elected constitutional President for the term 1936–41. Though in 1937 he sharply restricted the freedom of the opposition, he did not thereafter return to the tyranny of his predecessors.

In fact, with the resources inherited from Gómez, López Contreras was able to carry out significant reforms, including a measure of land reform, before becoming the first President in Venezuelan history voluntarily to hand over power to an elected successor. The successor he chose, General Isaías Medina Angarita, also from the State of Táchira, continued the gradual extension of civil liberties, legitimizing political parties and allowing trade union activity. Breaking off diplomatic relations with the Axis powers on 31 December 1941, Venezuela became a major supplier to the Allied war effort and prospered accordingly.

Despite these moves, desire for greater democratization grew as the war came to an end and expanded within the armed forces. In October 1945 Medina was overthrown by a military coup which established a civilian-military junta. The new junta was led by Rómulo Betancourt, founder of a social democratic movement called Acción Democrática (AD). Betancourt had been one of a small group of men exiled by Gómez who met in 1931 at Barranquilla, Colombia, to organize left-wing opposition to the dictatorship. Between 1935 and 1937 they tried to put together a Popular Front government, but in 1937 left-wing activity was proscribed and Betancourt's nationalist group went underground until 1941, when it re-emerged under its present name. By that time there was certainly nothing in its programme that had the Marxist flavour so often attributed to it by its enemies, and its first aim, successfully carried through, was to hold elections by universal suffrage and establish a new Constitution (1947). But the undemocratic way in which it had come to power was to frustrate its intentions of establishing a truly democratic government.

AD was at the same time a reforming movement and Betancourt himself, as interim President, carried out several major changes. Above all in 1947 he established the principle that for the future the revenue of the government from the exploitation of the nation's oil resources should at least be equal to that gained by the oil companies – the so-called 50:50 principle. He ended the practice of granting new concessions and proposed the formation of a national oil company. A major programme of ploughing investment back into agriculture and industry was also begun, doubling electricity generating capacity and starting middle-cost housing schemes. In 1948 Betancourt handed over power to a constitutional government under Rómulo Gallegos, which passed an Agrarian Reform Law and established the Instituto Agrario Nacional (IAN) to administer it. Gallegos, a distinguished novelist and thinker who in his *Doña Bárbara* had written a telling critique of dictatorship in the guise of fiction, and subsequently served as Minister of Education under López Contreras, got four times as many votes as his nearest rival, Rafael Caldera of the Christian Socialist Party (COPEI). But before he could carry out the programme foreshadowed by his successor, in the new climate of the Cold War, the permanence of left-wing rule that his election implied brought about a successful revolt by the armed forces. The coup, led by yet another soldier from Táchira, Lieutenant Colonel Marcos Pérez Jiménez, established a military junta and AD was dissolved. But the junta did not and could not bring peace. In 1950 its military head, General Carlos Delgado Chalbaud, was kidnapped and murdered in circumstances that cast considerable suspicion on his colleagues. Under a civilian, the junta then held fresh elections, but the armed forces refused to accept the verdict which went to the candidate of the anti-military Unión Republicana Democrática (URD), and in the name of the armed forces Pérez Jiménez assumed dictatorial powers (2 December 1952).

His seizure of power was ratified formally by a rigged election, but the intimidation that accompanied it was a foretaste of a new kind of dictatorship, backed by a secret police whose refined tortures were designed to spread terror among opponents of the regime. Yet Pérez Jiménez ('good ol' P.J') was very popular with foreign financial and business interests, especially those of the United States, as he seemed to them to promise stability and end the threat of nationalization. His policy was a forerunner of the military developmentalism of the 1960s and 1970s, which gave short-term prosperity to the élite and those who did business with it but none to the masses. In 1956 he opened the country up to a new round of oil concessions, the proceeds of which nearly doubled the national budget. As time went on, he spent more and more of the nation's oil revenues on megalomaniac building programmes that left Caracas a showplace of super-highways and expensive buildings (the Officers Club was a byword in the hemisphere for luxury). But this showplace was surrounded by some of the worst shanty-towns imaginable, and much of the proceeds went corruptly to his family and associates. Excluded from real power, military leaders seized their chance when it became apparent Pérez Jiménez dared not risk an election and tried to extend his term by plebiscite. Army and Air Force officers conspired in secret and in 1958 deposed the dictator with the connivance of AD leaders in exile.

DICTATORSHIP IN THE CARIBBEAN

For the rest of the Caribbean, however, the withdrawal of the United

States from direct involvement to concentrate on its own economic recovery had the unintended effect of leaving its polities open to would-be dictators. The effect was most marked in the case of the island states of the Caribbean.

The history of the Dominican Republic has been determined directly or indirectly by its geographical location. Although occupying the larger and more desirable part of the island of Hispaniola, the Dominican Republic (then often termed Santo Domingo, more accurately the name of its capital) spent much of the nineteenth century either under the occupation of its neighbour Haiti, or resisting further invasions. This led to that desperate search for foreign protection which began with the unfortunate experience of a brief further spell of Spanish rule and was followed by overtures to the United States. A US protectorate was effectively established immediately after the Spanish-American War, when the US government took control of Dominican customs receipts and undertook to distribute them to foreign creditors. However, internal chaos continued, inviting increasing US control and this in turn caused growing domestic opposition. The year following the start of the nearly 20-year US occupation of Haiti, in May 1916, the US Marines arrived and the unpopular eight-year period of direct rule from Washington began. As in Haiti, the US instigated various modernizing public works programmes, though without the forced labour used in Haiti. Three main roads were built, public health facilities and hygiene were extended and some schools opened, though the schemes were severely limited and acted incidentally to increase the Dominican Republic's foreign debt.

The most important legacy of the US occupation was the establishment of the constabulary which would in due course become both the Dominican police force and the Dominican Army. The latter had become the key force in politics by 1930 when its commander, General Rafael Léonidas Trujillo, led a coup against the government and emerged as the chief power broker. (US professionalization and training of the Haitian Army may have helped the military in their political role there too and have contributed to the rise of the Duvaliers, but there the sequence is much less clear and the process more protracted.) Shouldering aside his nominal leader (whom he made Vice-President), Trujillo emerged as the leading candidate for the 1930 elections. As the campaign proceeded other candidates withdrew or died suddenly of bullet wounds until on polling day, as sole remaining candidate, Trujillo won with more votes than there were eligible electors. Unemployment was already spreading as the US market for Dominican products was hit by the Depression and the effects, compounded by hurricane damage to Santo Domingo in

September 1930, was to give the new President the pretext to extend his constitutional powers without much domestic opposition. His position was confirmed when his newly formed political party, termed simply the Dominican Party (PD), won the 1934 elections easily, not surprisingly, perhaps, because it was the only party allowed to stand. Politically the Trujillo regime was a personalist dictatorship. All officials were obliged on appointment to tender the dictator their undated resignations. Government workers paid for his political organization, the Partido Dominicano, through a compulsory deduction from their salaries. The press was controlled and such local administrative autonomy as had previously existed was destroyed. Some labour organizations were suppressed, others were adapted and tamed. After 1931 Congress ceased to function. The shadow of the secret police, the Servicio de Inteligencia Militar (SIM), stilled criticism for fear that it might be picked up by the ubiquitous microphones or reported by one of the numerous informers (*orejas*). Soon the people were, on the contrary, being whipped up into ever greater extravagances of enthusiasm for Trujillo, 'the Benefactor of the Fatherland'. In 1936 Santo Domingo, the oldest Spanish city in the New World, was renamed Ciudad Trujillo, the name it was to bear for the next 25 years.

In fact the PD was devoid of economic policies as such, and if the regime saw further expansion of sugar plantations, the beginning of Dominican industrialization and the revival of mining (gold had been found in the islands rivers by Columbus, but had not been exploited effectively in modern times), it was for a very simple reason. Insofar as there was a policy, it was that Trujillo, his relatives and the friends who comprised the leadership of the PD, should benefit from his rule. Indeed, Trujillo and his family amassed incredible wealth, amounting to more than half of the nation's agricultural and industrial assets. The value of these assets was fortuitously enhanced by the Second World War, which increased Dominican prosperity. The US receivership ended in 1940 and by 1947 Trujillo was in a position to pay off the entire remaining foreign debt 20 years before it was due – a grandiose gesture which was unthinkingly praised by the Democratic administration in the United States.

By then the brutality of the regime should have been well known abroad. Only US support for the regime, and its payment of more than half a million US dollars in compensation, prevented an international outcry when in 1937 Trujillo ordered the massacre of some 15 000 Dominicans of Haitian origin. Fear of Haitian rule, a common feature among the Europeanized Dominican élite, probably explains this, just as the desire to increase the proportion of whites in the population is suspected of being the real reason for Trujillo's flamboyant offer at the end of the War to accept 100 000 Jewish refugees from Europe. Opposition to Trujillo first began to organize covertly in 1939 with the formation of the Partido Revolucionario Dominicano (PRD) by Juan Bosch. In 1949 discontent was overtly expressed in an abortive revolt. But as opposition increased, so did repression. Trujillo's megalomania knew no bounds. He believed that all problems could be solved either by force or with very large quantities of money, and wherever he went he travelled with plenty of both.

Matters came to a head when in 1959 a small force of exiles landed in the island to try to repeat Castro's success in neighbouring Cuba. Trujillo saw in this the hand, not of Fidel Castro, but of their mutual personal enemy, the newly-elected democratic President of Venezuela, Rómulo Betancourt. In return he sponsored an assassination squad who detonated two suitcases full of explosives by the side of the road in Caracas in June 1960. Several people were killed but Betancourt himself survived with third-degree burns to his hands, and formally lodged a complaint with the OAS, who, reversing the policy of non-intervention inherited from the old Pan-American Union, formally censured the Dominican Republic. The censure did not stop Trujillo's irrational behaviour; he planned to assassinate the Pope and in May 1961 ordered the arrest of all his country's bishops. However, before this order could be carried out, on the evening of 30 May 1961 armed men intercepted Trujillo in his light-blue Chevrolet Belair as he sped out of Ciudad Trujillo on his way to visit his mistress, and riddled him with bullets as he stepped out into the road, whether to shoot back or to negotiate was never discovered.

Events in the Dominican Republic after the death of Trujillo were of the greatest possible concern to Washington. In February 1960, General Eisenhower asked whether the CIA's planning body, the Special Group, had personally approved contingency plans to aid a coup in the Dominican Republic to depose Trujillo if the situation there should continue to deteriorate. He had in mind the danger of a possible invasion from Cuba, but the landing that had actually taken place, on 14 June 1959, had been known to the SIM well in advance and the rebel contingent, under the veteran Major Enrique Jiménez Moya, were sitting ducks. Most were slaughtered; the survivors, trussed head and foot, were taken to San Isidro Air Base and subjected to ingenious tortures by Trujillo's son Rafael Trujillo Jr (known generally by the operatic nickname 'Ramfis'). Only three survived.

The episode had led to an outbreak of plotting previously unimaginable. The SIM watched and waited until it learnt of a plot to blow up the dictator on 20 January 1960. It was the spectacular round-up by the SIM of literally thousands of suspects, many of them the sons and daughters of the leading members of Dominican society, that triggered President Eisenhower's concern. In the Dominican Republic, the local CIA station now gave its protection to various exiles and seriously considered backing the assassination attempt that actually succeeded. However, for fear of the possible consequences if it went wrong, Washington had withdrawn its support and failed to supply the weapons needed. The conspirators had therefore acted on their own initiative and in desperation, in fear of the retribution that might follow premature disclosure of their plans. They had banked on the assumption that General José Román Fernández, the Secretary of the Armed Forces, their chosen candidate, would assume power, but they knew he would only do so when he had irrefutable evidence that the news was not another of the dictator's tricks. Hence they stuffed Trujillo's body in the boot of their car and drove around the capital looking for General Román. Unfortunately for them, the news broke before they had succeeded and both car and the body were abandoned. Román changed sides, and when Ramfis returned from France he was allowed to seek vengeance on the killers and their relatives, many of whom were captured and systematically tortured by beating, burning and the electric cattle-prod. But the popular opposition could not be contained, and prevented him assuming power, the formal position of President being already held by a 'front man', Trujillo's protégé Joaquín Balaguer. Mob unrest led to the dissolution of the PD and the exile of Balaguer and of Ramfis, whose last act before leaving the country was to take a machine-gun and personally kill the six conspirators remaining in custody at the Hacienda María. The still complaisant press reported that they had tried to escape.

BRAZIL UNDER VARGAS

The Great Depression marked the end of the 'Old Republic' in Brazil. During the first three decades of the twentieth century a system of regional co-optation from within the Republican Party ensured peaceful transfers of power from one President to the next. National leaders were selected alternatively from the powerful states of São Paulo and Minas Gerais. The main federal government use of the military was against regional élites temporarily out of power. By the late 1920s regional differences had deepened to prevent state governors achieving any consensus on the succession and in July 1929 President Washington Luiz (a Paulista) announced his proposed successor as Dr Júlio Prestes (also from São Paulo). The Brazilian élite not only faced problems resulting from the increasingly outmoded political system, but also those generated by the Great Depression. The economic crisis had a particularly severe impact on the coffee market and coffee comprised some 70 per cent of Brazilian exports, but it also hit other exports. Brazil already had a high foreign debt which made its situation still more vulnerable, though it was not obliged to default until September 1931. Thus the old mercantile and coffee élite was much weakened by the changing economic climate.

When Prestes 'won' the 1930 Presidential election against Getúlio Dornelles Vargas, the candidate of the main opposition grouping, the Liberal Alliance, he was supported by the important states which felt excluded from access to power, most notably his own, Rio Grande do Sul, and Minas Gerais, which objected to another Paulista President. Junior officers had been involved in several rebellions against the Old Republic in the 1920s, and Vargas was able to muster some considerable military support. As Vargas' troops moved on the capital, the loyalties of the rest of the Army evaporated. President Washington Luiz resigned in October 1930 and was replaced by a temporary military junta which then offered Vargas the Presidency. Thus began the Decada Getuliana, which would last until 1945 and would continue to play a major part in determining the future direction of Brazilian politics right down to the present.

Centralization was a strong theme of Vargas' presidency. As might be expected from someone who had himself risen to power on the strength of regional dissent, Vargas was a nationalist who enhanced centralized executive powers at the expense of Brazil's federal structure. He suspended Congress, state legislatures and local government, governed by decree and intervened in all states. Bitterness at this turn of events was particularly strong in São Paulo, and in 1932 a São Paulo separatist movement rose in revolt against the Vargas administration. During the three months rebellion, the Paulistas were, however, unable to stir up the support of either Rio Grande do Sul or Minas Gerais and Vargas was able to survive the revolt. It did, however, lead him to question the extent to which his regime was seen as legitimate and to call for elections in July 1934. These elections did not simply return Vargas as constitutional President, they also adopted a new constitution which he had proposed. This, as might be expected, had strong centralizing features, especially so in its removal of tariffs on inter-state trade. The new constitution also reflected Vargas' nationalism in another way, as it nationalized banking and insurance and placed restrictions on the operations of foreign corporations, limiting certain core areas of the economy to the prerogative of domestic business interests. Industrialization was a further feature of the Vargas government, and the one which was in the long run to make the greatest impact. The industrial capacity established in the 1920s had remained under-used, but now the demand shock of the Depression formed the basis for the rapid expansion of import-substitution industries and the development of new heavy industries. Two major landmarks were the establishment of Petrobrás (Petróleo Brasileiro) to replace foreign domination of the discovery, extraction and marketing of Brazilian oil and the encouragement given to the domestic steel industry, which by 1945 was the only one in Latin America capable of producing the huge steel plates from which ships are manufactured. This rapid industrial development was naturally accompanied by the forging of an industrial working class. To Brazil's burgeoning masses Vargas brought new benefits: improved social security and child welfare provisions, more public works and a new labour code to protect the wages and conditions of workers. The Constitution of 1934 mobilized these new sectors in support of the regime. Provided they were neither illiterate nor itinerant, all men and women over 18 were given the vote. By making some representation in Congress a function of occupation rather than geographical area, he enhanced the role of corporate interests, especially the trade unions. Many workers in the new industries were enrolled in state-controlled unions and enlisted in Vargas' support.

Nor was agriculture forgotten. Brazil played a leading role in creating an international regime for its two main export crops, coffee and sugar, in order to secure price stabilization on the world markets. In each case this had significant domestic consequences, since to operate such a regime the position of the domestic growers organizations had to be strengthened. This enlisted the support of these organizations for the government, but the imposition of quotas in the domestic context not only formed an important weapon of patronage in the hands of government but also inevitably strengthened still further the power of the larger growers, and of the workers whom they could deploy at election times, against the smaller, independent growers, who had much less political leverage.

The mobilization of the Brazilian masses, albeit contained within a framework determined by the state, brought right-wing opposition to Vargas' policies. But, at the same time, he was challenged by the far Left, who, though disappointed in the events of 1930, saw in his reforms a starting point for social revolution. This challenge was met by a very harsh reaction from the administration. Martial law was imposed, Congress again suspended, political parties prohibited. The elections scheduled for 1937 were postponed and yet another new Constitution was promulgated by which Vargas could succeed himself as President. At the same time Vargas proclaimed the Estado Nôvo, or 'New State'; the idea derived from Mussolini's Italy, its name from Salazar's Portugal, but taking up and furthering themes already evident in Vargas' rule. The Constitution of 1937 was certainly more authoritarian than that of 1934: powers of federal intervention were increased, as was central government control over education, the Presidential term was extended to six years and government by decree was made easier. At the same time the corporatist elements became more prominent. Congressional powers were reduced, though, as it happened, this did not have any effect since Congress did not meet again until after Vargas was ousted in 1945. Instead it was replaced by a National Economic Council with legislative powers in which sat representatives of industry.

The increasingly authoritarian state which the 1937 Constitution heralded rested on press censorship by the Department de Imprensa e Propaganda (DIP) and the use of the secret police (Departamento de Ordem Político e Social – DOPS) and the National Security Tribunal (Tribunal de Segurança Nacional) to watch and detain opposition elements. Such moves, were initially supported by key military factions seeing communism as a more potent threat than Vargas. Later a combination of military dislike of corruption, exemplified by the nepotistic appointment of the President's brother as chief of police, and pressure on legalist officers by middle-class groups rushing for elections to justify Brazil's wartime support for the Allies, changed the dominant orientation of the officer corps. From 1943 Vargas began again to retreat cautiously towards constitutionalism. By the end of the war, the very features which had been associated with strength earlier, had become associated with fascism, with the corruption that had left the Braziiian Expeditionary Force humiliated in the face of the enemy, and hence with defeat, and led to a non-violent coup on 29 October 1945.

General Enrico Gaspar Dutra, the power behind the successful coup, was elected to the Presidency and held office for five years from January 1946. His emphasis on development, embodied in the ill-fated SALTE Plan (meaning a 'leap [forward]' but an acronym formed from the Portuguese words for health, food, transport and power) not only continued traditional military policies but was specifically intended to supplant Vargas' continuing support among the masses. However, Vargas' popularity was such that he was elected to the Senate only a few months after being displaced as President. He was able to stand as a candidate in the 1950 Presidential elections and won easily with the support of a coalition of labour groups behind his Brazilian Labour Party (PTB).

In Vargas' second term (1951–54), the trappings of dictatorship were missing, but so too, sadly, was the keen mind and the sense of priorities. An entourage characterized by corruption and intrigue contributed to a growing sense of disillusion, led by the sharp-tongued Carlos Lacerda. When an attempt was made on Lacerda's life, in which an Air Force Major was killed at his side, suspicion fell on Vargas' entourage, and the President himself admitted he was standing in 'a sea of mud'. Following Air Force demands for the President's resignation, Army officers joined in the clamour for Vargas to resign and on the morning of 24 August 1954 sent him a final ultimatum. Instead he retired to another room and shot himself, leaving a brief political testament reminding Brazilians of the many benefits they had obtained under his leadership. 'I gave you my life', it said. 'Now I offer my death. Nothing remains. Serenely I take the first step on the road to eternity as I leave life to enter history.'

Initial fears of unrest proved unfounded; the armed forces contained the succession crisis in the short term. However, the expectations aroused by the Decada Getuliana have proved more problematic in the long term. The chief legacy of Vargas was a mobilized, and partially organized working class, and the military intervention of 1964 owes as much to the actions of Vargas in the period 1930–45 as it does to the actions of his protégé and former Minister of Labour, João Goulart, in the period after 1955.

THE GOOD NEIGHBOR POLICY AND THE INTER-AMERICAN SYSTEM

A North American, James G. Blaine, was responsible for the formal creation of the inter-American system in calling the First Conference of American States at Washington in 1889. The Second Conference did not take place until after the Spanish-American War. It was held in Mexico in 1901–2. At it delegates agreed that in future Conferences would be held every five years, and the Third and Fourth Conferences, therefore, were held at Rio de Janeiro in 1906 and Buenos Aires in 1910, the latter to coincide with the centenary of the start of independence. These early Conferences were primarily about the promotion of trade and cultural contacts. It was not until 1914 that the United States first invited other American states, the so-called ABC countries (Argentina,

Brazil, Chile), to join it at a special conference at Niagara Falls, to take part in an exercise in regional peace-keeping by mediating in the conflicts of the Mexican Revolution. The conference broke up when it became apparent that the United States was primarily interested in securing its own objectives – an ominous sign of what was to come. During the Great War no further meetings took place. Then for a time it looked as if the League would supersede any regional organization, so it was not until 1923 that the Fifth Conference was held at Santiago de Chile. At this meeting the United States, which had not joined the League, threw its weight behind negotiations for the first inter-American peace treaty, the Pan-American Treaty for the Pacific Settlement of Disputes, usually known as the Gondra Treaty, after its sponsor, the ex-President of Paraguay. In the next five years, however, the United States was to resume its intervention in the Caribbean, and the Sixth Conference, held at Havana in 1928, following a tour of Latin American states by President Coolidge, was marked by the first moves of Latin American delegates to try to establish the principle of non-intervention in their internal affairs. Its main achievement was to establish the Pan-American Union on a formal Treaty basis.

By the Seventh Conference in Montevideo in 1933 radical changes had taken place on both sides. In the United States, the election of Franklin D. Roosevelt had been followed by the formal declaration of the 'Good Neighbor' policy. Latin American delegates, who had seen the financial power of the Colossus of the North brought low were much less nervous than they had been about offending the United States, and they subjected US delegates to hours of harangues about their country's past wickedness. After the rise of Hitler in Europe, and the failure of the League to settle the Chaco War, Latin American rulers once again sought the help of their powerful neighbour, now that it was restored to health. In 1936 a special meeting of the Pan-American Union in Buenos Aires formally established the principle of consultation in case the peace of the continent should be threatened, and at the Eighth Conference of American States held in Lima in 1938 all states adopted the Declaration of Lima reaffirming the sovereignty of the various states and their determination to defend themselves against 'all foreign intervention or activities that might threaten them'.

LATIN AMERICA IN THE SECOND WORLD WAR

The Western Hemisphere was after all uniquely important to the security of the United States and even in the age of American isolationism the United States retained close ties with other American states. Isolationism in the inter-war period had reached a peak with the enactment of the three Neutrality Acts of 1935, 1936 and 1937, by which the US Congress metaphorically shackled itself, padlocked its shackles and then threw away the key. Americans criticized Britain and Chamberlain's policy of appeasement (they still do, and President Reagan did so in his 1980 campaign), but they did nothing themselves to help Czechoslovakia, or Poland, or France. When war broke out in Europe in 1939 the general tendency was to be thankful for their far-sightedness. Roosevelt, whose chances of re-election depended on his promise to keep Americans out of foreign wars, proclaimed the neutrality not just of the United States but of the Americas, establishing a so-called 'Hemispheric Safety Belt' – a 320-km (200-mile) wide zone round the two American continents south of Canada, violation of which the United States would regard as an attack on itself. However, despite the unilateral nature of Roosevelt's declaration, and the fact that some Latin Americans were disturbed by the assumptions it contained, at the Second Meeting of Consultation of the Foreign Ministers of the American States, held at Havana in 1940, the United States had little difficulty in obtaining support both for this action and for the establishment of a permanent Inter-American Peace Committee to concert action in the event of attack.

This was to have unexpected consequences. When the United States finally did enter the war on its own account, the smaller Central American and Caribbean states immediately leapt to its aid and declared war both on Germany and Japan, a psychological support which is often underestimated in Europe. Costa Rica, El Salvador, Guatemala, Haiti, Honduras and Panama declared war the day after Pearl Harbor, 8 December; Cuba and the Dominican Republic a day later. In turn American military instructors arrived to train their forces, bases were brought up to combat readiness and the dictators of the region began to think what they might ask in return – President Ubico of Guatemala, for example, put in a claim to be given Belize (British Honduras) in the event of a British defeat.

Meanwhile, as the 'Phoney War' came to its abrupt end in May 1940, the new Churchill government desperately needed to strengthen its naval defences and sought, quite legitimately, to purchase 50 over-age destroyers from the United States. The Administration, perhaps over-mindful of its critics in Congress, drove an incredibly hard bargain. They demanded the cession in perpetuity of a string of naval bases in British possessions in the Caribbean, and in their need the British government had to agree. The United States was thus able for the first time to close the ring of naval bases round the Caribbean in anticipation of the defeat of the Allies and the arrival of German forces in their home waters. It was nearly 18 months later before the Japanese attack on Pearl Harbor precipitated US entry into the war; months in which Britain, though not occupied, was to be so weakened that at the war's end it seems never to have questioned whether it should do other than accept American leadership.

The United States, however, entered the war at a bad time, and the support of their tiny Caribbean allies, though very welcome, was not enough. British forces had been driven entirely out of Europe and were now fighting directly only in North Africa, where Rommel and the Afrika Corps had driven them back almost to the gates of Alexandria. The Japanese attack in South-East Asia had been a stunning defeat for the British Empire and the threat to India made the situation critical. The Russians had yet to turn the tide at Stalingrad (now Volgograd). Once the decision had been taken to give first priority to Europe and hence to the North African theatre, the United States government had to get troops there as fast as possible. The obvious way was to fly, across the chain of US bases old and new in the Caribbean to Brazil, and thence across the North Atlantic to Dakar in Free French West Africa. The problem was Brazil, where Vargas, with his quasi-fascist ideology and corporatist 'Estado Nôvo' was widely suspected of being in league with the Nazis.

Vargas, however, was a realist. He was willing to enter the war, but the price that he demanded was considerable. Brazil would expect very substantial financial compensation and at the end of the war the resources to help its future development. It would also want to take an active part in the war, to be seen to be taking part. But it must do so on its own terms – Brazil was no mere client state, but the future Great Power of South America. In August 1942 the pretext for Vargas to declare war came, as in 1917, when a Brazilian vessel was sunk by a German submarine. An Expeditionary Force was prepared for North Africa. Unfortunately it did not arrive until the fighting had moved on to Italy, and there in the summer rains it became clear how badly prepared the Brazilians were for the campaign. In effect, the Brazilian Expeditionary Force had to be completely rekitted from top to toe by the Americans. Though they fought bravely and won many medals for gallantry, some of them never forgot the lesson, the bitterness of which was exacerbated when at the end of the war they returned home to find no heroes' welcome, simply an order from Vargas to disperse immediately in civilian clothes to their respective homes. The order itself was futile – Vargas was in any case to fall some six months later – but the bitterness remained and contributed in its own way to the events of 1964.

The other American state to take an active role in the war was Mexico. Mexico with its 2000 km frontier with the United States was still strategically sensitive. Even before the First World War, the story that Japanese fishermen were establishing a secret naval base in the Sea of Cortez, between Lower California and the mainland, had led to a furore in the United States. The Roosevelt Administration, however, had the good sense to see that Mexico's prime contribution to the war must be to see to its own defence. A by-product of this was an agreement between the two states that US citizens in Mexico and Mexicans in the United States would in each case be liable for compulsory military service. Mexico preceded Brazil by formally declaring war on the Axis, on 1 June 1942 after one if its oil-tankers had been torpedoed. The announcement caused great astonishment, many citizens being amazed to find themselves fighting with and not against the United States. Later Mexico provided an air squadron for the Pacific campaign.

The other Latin American states were encouraged by the US Administration to declare war on the Axis and become part of the United Nations. By doing so they would have a full say in any post-war settlement. But this enticing prospect did not have as much effect as was intended. A third large state, Colombia, did enter the war while its outcome was still very much in doubt, on 28 November 1943, though it did not take an active part. The remaining states remained neutral until the fighting was nearly over and it became apparent that Germany had been defeated. Their primary role in the conflict had been to maintain the flow of essential raw materials for the war effort: oil from Venezuela, copper from Chile and Peru, tin from Bolivia, as well as coal and iron ore, chromium, manganese, vanadium and tungsten, sulphur and bauxite.

But if they had not been actively involved, they had nevertheless been profoundly affected. The principles of the Atlantic Charter and the Four Freedoms for which the Allies were fighting seemed to many to have as much relevance to the military dictators with which they were endowed as to Hitler, Mussolini and the Japanese warlords. Freedom from want, freedom from fear were seen as essentially achievable, and as the war went on it became harder and harder to see why Latin America should be denied them. In May 1944 the dictatorship of Maximiliano Hernández Martínez in El Salvador fell when civilians refused any longer to obey orders and started a general strike. On 1 June it was the turn of Jorge Ubico of Guatemala to resign. Anastasio Somoza García of Nicaragua held on to power by force but prudently yielded his office to a nominated successor (whom he in turn deposed a few days later) in 1947. The following year a democratic revolution ousted the President of Costa Rica. The 'shirt-sleeve' President of Honduras, Tiburcio Carias Andino, though also challenged, was able to retain his position until 1948, when he sensibly made way for an elected successor. Unlike the others, his tall and commanding form could still be seen walking unescorted and unarmed round his former capital a decade later.

ARGENTINA: THE 'INFAMOUS DECADE' AND THE RISE OF PERON

The period 1880–1930 in Argentina is frequently characterized as one of increasing prosperity as a result of integration into the world economic system and developing political democracy. Thus the economic and political problems Argentina has experienced since have suggested that 1930 constituted *the* turning-point in its economic and political development. This view is far too simplistic.

Certainly the coup that ousted President Yrigoyen in 1930 coincided with the Great Depression, but it must be seen as having had other, non-economic causes too. From the economic point of view, Argentina began experiencing a round of problems consistent with previous cyclical movements in its economy in 1928, before the Wall Street Crash, but despite a bad harvest in 1929–30 did not feel the full force of the global recession until after General José Uriburu has assumed the presidency. But the same period was far from harmonious in the social and political spheres and elements contributing to military intervention were discernible long before the event.

The effects of the wave of immigration which brought millions to Argentina in the late nineteenth and early twentieth centuries were partially mitigated by the high rates of social mobility experienced by immigrants. Many of the earlier immigrants were able to get middle-class jobs or to establish entrepreneurial activities as Argentina's economy expanded. Their sons and daughters became citizens and frequently supported the Radical Party. Nevertheless, there remained many for whom Argentina provided less opportunities and for whom the experience of overcrowded tenement housing in the *conventillos* of

Buenos Aires was radicalizing. These immigrants brought with them anarcho-syndicalist ideas from Europe and, being excluded by their non-citizenship from formal political participation, they resorted to direct action in defence of their wages and working conditions. The apparent threat to public order was thus associated with the effects of immigration and in reaction a right-wing nationalist movement developed during the 1920s, influenced by similar currents in Spain and Italy, and was reflected in the ideological position of Uriburu himself, though not among all who supported his intervention. Congressional impasse and Yrigoyen's meddling in internal Army matters provided further justification for what has become known as the 'Cadets' coup', because Uriburu set out to seize power on 6 September 1930 leading a column of Army cadets, some carrying replica weapons.

Following the fall of Yrigoyen, ideological differences became increasingly noticeable amongst the forces that had combined to seize power. Right-wing Catholic nationalists like Uriburu proved less numerous and less influential than liberal internationalists who wished to restore the upper-class-dominated political system that had served them well before the expansion of the suffrage and the rise of the Radicals. Through fraudulent elections, the conservative political front they established, the Concordancia, retained power throughout the so-called Infamous Decade until 1943, though with increasing difficulties towards the end of this period.

Again they were helped by the fact that Argentina recovered relatively quickly from the effects of the Depression and experienced accelerated industrialization and urbanization during the years of Concordancia domination. Immigration had slowed down but internal migration, reflecting both displacement from the land and an increasing demand for industrial labour, sustained the rapid expansion of Buenos Aires. Despite its growth, the urban working class remained excluded from the formal political process. The main electoral opposition to the Concordancia was still the middle-class UCR and the Radical tradition of intransigence precluded joining with other political parties to form a coalition capable of overcoming conservative fraud and of representing the interests of the mass of the Argentine population. Although the level of organization amongst industrial workers was quite impressive, especially given the many obstacles placed in its way, the labour movement was small, politically inexperienced, internally divided and characterized by bureaucratic leadership. Some social legislation had been passed under both the Radical and the Concordancia governments, but it was rarely enforced and the Department of Labour had little influence either within government or over the employers.

Growing nationalism, in response to the Concordancia's internationalist ideology, military reluctance to enter the Second World War on the side of the Allies, the increasing unpopularity of the regime under Ramón S. Castillo (Acting President, 1940–42; President, 1942–43) and the even greater military dislike of his proposed successor, led in 1943 to military intervention. Secret lodges among Army officers had for some time been a feature of military life, and the coup was carried out by a lodge embracing most Army officers, the GOU (*Grupo de Oficiales Unidos* or *Grupo Obra de Unificación*). The Secretary to this lodge was Colonel Juan Domingo Perón, who was appointed to head the Department of Labour.

Reflecting the importance to twentieth-century Argentine politics of the rise of Perón, a long standing debate on the source of his support, beginning in the 1960s with the work of the eminent political sociologist Gino Germani, has still not been resolved. Germani's view that Perón was able to manipulate the unsophisticated internal migrants into becoming the backbone of Peronism has been subjected to severe criticism. The evidence for the debate is too complex to summarize here, but the present authors take the view that both in-migrants and the older industrial unions contributed to the development of Peronism, since Perón expressed the perceived interests of the whole previously-excluded working class and was not opposed by any large sector of it.

Perón was able to build up his position from within the 1943–46 GOU governments. Under his direction, the Department of Labour became a Ministry in its own right. Regional and provincial agencies were brought under its control and labour legislation began to be enforced. Wages and conditions of work improved, rents were controlled and the *aguinaldo* (thirteenth month bonus) was introduced. Moreover, labour leaders felt that they had direct access to and influence on policy-making through the person of the Minister of Labour, Colonel Perón, who was chosen as Vice-President in the political infighting that accompanied the accession to power of President Edelmiro Farrell in 1944. Hence union leaders were willing to mobilize their members in support of Perón when his rivals within the armed forces displaced him from office and he was confined to the island prison of Martín García in October 1945. (The part often romantically accorded to Perón's then mistress, Evita, in rousing the workers is sadly merely a Peronist myth based on her future role.)

Thus working-class support for Perón had a wholly rational basis, though other factors were also important in contributing to the extraordinary appeal this authoritarian leader had for his supporters. Perón, in classically populist manner, was a colourful figure who spoke to working people in a language they could understand. He presented himself as one of them, removing his jacket and rolling up his sleeves in the style of the Argentine working man. Perón offered not only a redistribution to the wage earning and industrial masses of the wealth accumulated in the form of huge credits during the Second World War, but enhanced status for the working class. He raised material expectations, stirred nationalist feelings, and, when displaced from office by a military coup in September 1955, left a legacy of a strong Peronist labour movement confronting the rest of Argentine society. The Peronist/anti-Peronist division has remained the key political dichotomy in Argentina since that time.

THE BOLIVIAN REVOLUTION

The most dramatic response to a combination of the effects of the international economic crisis and unique national circumstances in the period after 1930 was the Bolivian Revolution of 1952. Bolivia was the second poorest nation in Latin America after Haiti. Despite its massive birth rate, population growth was relatively modest because its death rate was so high, especially among infants. Life expectancy at birth was a little over 40 years. Less than a quarter of Bolivians lived in population centres of more than 2000 people and less than a third of the population was literate.

Although nearly three-quarters of the economically active population worked either in agriculture or industries deriving directly from it, this sector accounted for only about one-third of the nation's Gross Domestic Product (GDP). The generally inhospitable, mountainous topography of Bolivia meant that most of its territory could not be farmed; in fact, only about 2 per cent of its land was under cultivation. The best farmland was controlled by a very few estate-owners. A feudal structure, the much resented *pongueaje* (personal service to the *hacendado* or land-owner in return for land), persisted despite its official abolition by the government of President Villaroel in 1945. Subdivisions of the smallest plots meant that these were insufficient even for subsistence and the availability of cheap labour minimized investment in larger units. Less than 10 per cent of the cultivated land was farmed with machinery, large landowners preferring to invest in urban property and commerce. A combination of absentee landowner-ship and a resentful peasantry meant that state coercion was needed to maintain the existing land tenure system. Nevertheless, the rural oligarchy, along with mining interests, had been able to dominate Bolivian politics from the 1880s to the 1930s.

These mining interests comprised mainly absentee tin bosses, among them the fabulously wealthy Simón Patiño, who found it much safer to live in Paris but still controlled local politics, though with declining ease. Three large companies, primarily national, dominated tin production. The tin industry had been stagnating since the 1920s, with low productivity and high costs. These problems were a consequence of little new capital investment as a result of declining world prices and exhaustion of the highest-quality ores. Yet the industry still accounted for a quarter of Bolivian Gross National Product (GNP) and more than three-quarters of its exports; it was the major, indeed virtually the only, source of foreign exchange. The mineowners, however, were having an increasingly difficult time coping with labour unrest. Conditions in the mines were disgusting. Half-starved miners worked deep underground in high temperatures and emerged into the thin, freezing air of the altiplano. Despite the practice of chewing coca leaves to inure themselves to the cold, mortality rates were appalling. Pay was so low that Bolivian miners were amongst the world's poorest industrial workers, and there was little or no legislation to protect their interests. As a result, the 1930s and early 1940s had seen the organization of powerful mining unions, encouraged by President Germán Busch, which had begun to challenge the status quo with violent strikes countered by no less violent government repression.

Disaffection of workers in the agricultural and mining sectors both paralleled and reflected growing dissatisfaction within factions of the élite itself. The Chaco War had done untold damage to the Bolivian economy, leaving more than 50 000 Bolivians dead and countless thousands wounded or captured. The old élite was discredited by its conduct of the war and Bolivian politics were irreparably changed in consequence. Indeed, the party was to achieve power in the 1952 Revolution, the National Revolutionary Movement (MNR), would later cite the effects of the war as the most important factor for the Revolution. Border disputes which had cost Bolivia more than half its national territory since independence probably also contributed to the growing nationalism of the 1930s, but more specifically it was the young, radical veterans of the war within the officer corps of the Bolivian Army, who seized power in 1936, who paved the way for the nationalist regimes with populist overtones of 1936–39 and 1943–46. Some nationalization including the expropriation in 1936 of Standard Oil assets without compensation (US pressure later produced a settlement), was accompanied by limited social legislation.

The late 1930s, then, had seen a cautious expansion of political participation accompanied by a radicalization of the middle-class. During the period new leftist political parties sprang up, the most important of which would be the MNR itself, formed from an odd amalgam of disparate groups ranging from fascists to communists. When President Busch committed suicide in 1939, senior military officers sought to turn the clock back, demobilize the emerging sectors and restore the traditional political parties to power. Weakened by debt and inflation, increasingly dependent on the armed forces to keep them in power, the old oligarchy was ousted by a coup in 1943. The flirtation of its leader, Major Gualberto Villaroel, with the fascistic elements of the MNR (later purged), made his presidency one of great violence, with force being especially directed against middle-class intellectuals. A popular revolt in 1946 ended with Villaroel being thrown out of a window and his body hanged from a lamp-post. There followed another attempt at a conservative restoration, even more dependent on repression than its predecessor. A military junta lasting a year resulted from conservative officers refusing to accept the MNR's electoral victory in 1951. The Revolution followed a repetition of those results and their aftermath in the wake of new elections held in April 1952.

Three days of heavy fighting followed between the military and civilians trained to some extent by compulsory military service, which had been extended throughout Latin America after the Second World War. The fighting brought the rebel seizure of La Paz, the collapse of the national government and the surrender of the Army to the MNR-led rebels. The rebels disbanded the Army and distributed its weapons to civilian militias which would remain the dominant military force in Bolivia into the 1960s. In the countryside, Marxist radicals distributed arms to the rural peasantry who used them against the landed élite. In all, 600 Bolivians died in the fighting. Among the young military officers captured by the rebel forces and later freed were two men who would nearly 30 years later figure significantly in the military attempt to liquidate the gains made by the Revolution: Lieutenants Alberto Natusch Busch and Luis García Meza Tejada.

The extent to which the 1952 Revolution was intended to change Bolivian economic and political power structures is still open to debate. As with other major social upheavals, historical events gather a momentum of their own and intentions are moderated as they give way to pragmatic responses. The MNR leadership was university educated, deriving mainly from the professional élite, but it had both strong working-class and middle-class support for its by then broadly socialist ideology. Certainly some military and police officers occupying key posts were briefed in advance by the MNR, but as an event the Revolution was a mixture of preparedness and spontaneity. It is plain that the rebels were surprised by the popular response which swept them along with the social revolution. The vigour of this response was emphasized when in 1953 workers took up arms to defend the new regime against a right-wing counter-coup. Afterwards MNR radicalism was tempered by reluctance to offend the new dominant power of the world, the United States, which recognized the new government only after three months. It happened that La Paz did not attract US political appointees, Bolivia was thus little understood. On the recommendation of career diplomats stationed at home US aid in the post-revolutionary period was massive, for fear that the alternative was communism. In return, the Bolivian government sought to protect private property and to attract foreign capital. By 1958 a third of the national budget was funded by the United States.

Although the MNR did not seek to implement a full socialist revolution and traditional class divisions remained untouched, the Revolution did succeed in reducing inequality. It raised the standard of living of the majority of Bolivians and extended access to education. The first administration of Víctor Paz Estenssoro increased political participation, extending the franchise to all Bolivians over the age of 18 and removing literacy requirements and property qualifications. In August 1953 it decreed an agrarian reform, much of which had already effectively occurred as a result of Indian land seizures in the previous year. The miners also initially benefited as the three largest tin companies were expropriated, the mines nationalized, a state mono-poly of mineral sales (COMIBOL) established and conditions for workers improved. The mining unions became more powerful, having the right to veto management decisions, as a new national labour federation was set up and labour was at last given representation in the Cabinet.

Perhaps the most important reason for the failure in the long term to consolidate the changes achieved by the Revolution has been the inherent weaknesses of the Bolivian economy, weaknesses exacerbated by the Revolution itself. Over the decade following it, per capita GDP dropped by a fifth. The agrarian reform enabled peasants to have access to the agricultural surplus and so consume it. On top of falling world tin prices, obsolete mining equipment and exhausted seams, industrial unrest in the mines, and the corruption and inefficiency of the new state agency led, by the 1960s, to a 40 per cent decline in tin production.

Corruption and inefficiency plagued other state enterprises too, not least the railways. The provision of desperately needed schools and hospitals was an expense the government could not hope to meet from its very limited resources. It therefore printed money. Massive inflation, running at nearly 1000 per cent per annum in the early post-Revolutionary period wiped out the savings of the urban middle-class and diminished their support for the MNR government.

Alongside this process, urban labour was alienated by the actions of the regime. Industrial unrest amongst miners snowballed into political conflict with the administration which, with US support, used the peasant militias to quell strikes and to suppress the miners' union. The peasants proved to be a conservative force whose goal of land reform had largely been achieved and which, under the influence of *caudillo*-style leaders, could be used against the aspirations of the miners. When the armed forces displaced the MNR in 1964, peasant support was easily transferred to the new regime.

The changing nature of class support for the MNR was reflected in the ideological and personalist factionalism of its leadership, which was to prove fatal. The more left-wing labour-based faction, led by the miners' union leader, Juan Lechín, became increasingly disaffected after 1956 when Hernán Siles Zuazo, representing the centrist middle-class wing of the MNR, assumed office. The selection of Paz as Presidential candidate for a second term in 1960 was expected to dissipate the tensions between the two wings of the Party and indeed it did just that, but not in the way foreseen and with very different consequences from those envisaged. Once back in power, Paz clamped down on the Left and started re-arming the military, who in addition began to receive counter-insurgency training from US forces. Intending to seek re-election for himself, Paz then changed the Constitution to make this possible. In doing so he united the two factions of the MNR against him, leaving only the unlikely combination of military and peasants as his support base. Soon after he had begun his third term as President, Paz was deposed by his Vice-President, Air Force General René Barrientos, who led the coup that restored the military to power and ended the Bolivian Revolution.

TRADITIONAL DICTATORSHIP IN PARAGUAY

Twentieth-century Paraguayan political history, on the other hand, has been characterized by authoritarian regimes. The 1954–89 regime differs from its predecessors more in the staying power of President

Stroessner than in any other aspect. Geographical isolation and unequal land distribution, dominated by large, inefficient estancias and small subsistence plots, have presented considerable obstacles to economic development until quite recently. The fierce competition of rival political groups and the violent succession process have also blocked progress.

Although most of the population were traditionally members of a political party and wore different coloured ties to signify their allegiance, politics has generally remained highly élitist. Of the 46 presidents who have assumed power since 1870, none has been freely elected. All have achieved office as a result of an illegal, often violent, seizure of power or in consequence of fraudulent elections. If they have retained office for a period of time, they have generally been able to do so only by coercion. Most have been ousted by force or the threat of it. There is no tradition of liberal democracy in Paraguay. Parties are not separated from each other by differing policy principles, although in theory the Liberal Party has been seen as less nationalistic and interventionist than the conservative Colorado Party. Rather, family and clientelist traditions have determined party membership, which is often quite simply hereditary. Both parties have suppressed their opponents when in power, thus contributing to the political intolerance reflected in unconstitutional activities.

Military influence has long existed at the highest levels in both the Colorado and the Liberal Parties, but rather it has been the factionalism, inability to compromise and, thus, relative weakness of the parties in government that has brought the military so decisively into Paraguayan politics. The period 1910–12, for example, saw seven presidents and in 1911 a military revolt. The breakdown of order in 1922–24 was such that it amounted to a civil war between the two main factions of the Liberal Party. In such circumstances and with a tradition of presidents assuming absolute powers, it is surprising that military rule remained indirect until 1954. In addition, Paraguay's historic need to defend its borders as a result of its geographical position has enhanced the role of the armed forces and led to one of the highest ratios of military and police to population in the world.

It was the Chaco War that ended the extended period of Liberal Party dominance from 1904 to 1936. The fighting was protracted and bloody and took place in an area in which disease was endemic. The soldiers 'lucky' enough to survive enemy action often met still more unpleasant deaths from natural causes. Despite their generally slow progress the Paraguayan forces were able to advance and win against Bolivia, not so much in consequence of superior military skills, as because the Bolivian

Army was mainly composed of Indians without a sense of nation fighting in hellish conditions for territory they did not value. By the 1935 cease-fire Paraguay had conquered the Chaco and under the 1938 peace treaty was awarded three-quarters of the disputed territory. The legacy of the Chaco War for domestic politics was, however, less advantageous. The War was seen by many who had fought in it as having been won *despite* the Liberal government of Eusebio Ayala. In the period immediately after the cease-fire, the social benefits, such as disablement pensions, that the veterans had asked for were not forthcoming. An anti-Liberal revolution led to the overthrow of the Ayala government in February 1936 by Colonel Rafael Franco and many prominent Liberals fled into exile. Franco had the support of the war veterans and became the leader of a motley selection of disaffected and/or ambitious young officers. He was a fine orator and a popular hero with an excellent war record. His policies were essentially nationalist and reformist. Although its tenure was too brief to achieve the labour legislation it had sought, the Franco government did manage to seize and redistribute some land. But Colorado support for Franco was lost through the fear that the Party would not gain, because Franco would establish a new and separate anti-Liberal political party. Alone, the Febreristas ('Men of February', as Franco's followers soon became known) were unable to resist the military rising against them. It is probable that Liberal conspiracies lay behind the fall of Franco in 1937, but the Febrerista movement survived.

After a two-year interim presidency, the Liberals succeeded in winning back the office in 1939 by using Febrerista tactics. They fielded their own war hero, none less than the victorious leader of the Paraguayan forces, Marshal José Félix Estigarribia. He was a reformist nationalist, popular with military and peasants alike. Nevertheless, Estigarribia's restoration of political freedoms was met with general unrest, including strikes, press attacks and conspiracies among some military cliques. He therefore declared himself a temporary dictator, repressed opposition and announced a developmentalist land programme which included land expropriation. Estigarribia proposed a new corporatist constitution, adopted by plebiscite in August 1940, which strengthened executive powers and allowed a president to serve a second term. He himself was not to benefit from these constitutional changes, however, as both he and his wife died in a plane crash on the outskirts of Asunción only three weeks after the Constitution was approved.

Estigarribia's Minister of War, General Higinio Morínigo, was selected by his fellow Cabinet Ministers to succeed to the vacant

Presidency. Initially Morínigo was seen as a reasonably benevolent autocrat who faced the unenviable task of balancing opposing political forces to retain control of the nation. In order to do this, he soon, like many of his predecessors, assumed absolute powers, restricting political activity and dissolving the legislature. In the Presidential elections of 1943, Morínigo was the only candidate. Eminent Liberals were forced into exile and Febrerista uprisings were suppressed. Until the end of the Second World War, Morínigo was able to coerce his opponents successfully because he had the funds to keep the armed forces sweet. These came from the US and Brazil, each determined to woo Paraguay away from the influence of neighbouring, neutral Argentina.

But the end of the War and the 1946 popular revolt in Bolivia, in which Villaroel died, caused Morínigo to realize that both the domestic and the international scene called for a changed approach. Exiles were allowed to return and a coalition government was established. In choosing some conservative Colorados as well as young, development-alist Febrerista officers to join his new government, Morínigo offended other factions of these parties and forced the four Liberals in his Cabinet to resign. From 1946 on there was an upsurge of violence. An attempted coup late that year was followed by the disintegration of the coalition government early in 1947. Declaring a state of siege, Morínigo formed a new military Cabinet; on the rebel side, Liberals and communists joined Febrerista forces led by Colonel Rafael Franco in a civil war which divided the armed forces, some 80 per cent of its officers defecting to the rebels. Since the Colorados backed Morínigo against the rebels, they came to dominate a much reduced officer corps when the rebels were finally defeated. One of the survivors, an artillery officer who had served in the Chaco and been decorated, and who at one point during the rebellion had hidden in the boot of a car to gain sanctuary in the Brazilian Embassy, found himself on the winning side and was rewarded with the command of the artillery. His name was Alfredo Stroessner.

Not only did the defeat of the rebels give the Colorados control of the Army, it also ensured Colorado domination of the political process. 1948 saw the restoration of the civilian presidency, but the sole candidate in the elections was the Colorado nominee, Juan Natalicio González. As President he was supported by al all-Colorado legislature; Paraguay had become a one-party state. But though Morínigo went into exile, factional in-fighting continued. There were uprisings by Colorado officers against the González government. Finally González, too, fled abroad, and another Colorado faction, led by Dr Federico Chaves, took power.

Despite plots against him, Chaves survived in power, presented himself as the sole candidate in the 1953 presidential elections and, of course, won them. He immediately made a grave error, from his point of view at least, by bringing Stroessner into his government as Commander-in-Chief of the armed forces. The economy, being closely tied to that of Argentina, was moving into crisis. As inflation rose, so did political opposition, and the conservative wing of the Colorado Party was in any case hostile to a nationalist and state interventionist government under the influence of Peronism. It was this latter problem, the disaffection of the Colorado Party itself, which inspired the intervention of the Commander-in-Chief of the armed forces. General Stroessner became the official Colorado candidate, and therefore the only candidate, for the July 1954 presidential elections.

The coup against Chaves was not immediately followed by the succession of Stroessner as the military reflected Colorado Party factionalism and many officers were not enamoured of Stroessner. Support by majority factions in both Army and Party, however, ensured electoral success, and, this gained, Stroessner lost no time in establishing a personalist dictatorship. Restrictions were placed on all political activities and the Febrerista and Liberal opposition groups were ruthlessly suppressed. A state of siege was imposed. It was renewed every 60 days to comply with constitutional niceties for over 30 years until 1988. But though the police were watchful, there was no secret police in Paraguay, and Stroessner himself, who liked to start work at 4.30 a.m., would walk freely around his small capital without the protection of armed guards. Foreign and domestic business interests were pleased, not only with the unaccustomed sense of order, but also with Stroessner's enthusiasm for the IMF austerity measures which by 1957 had stabilized the guaraní. In 1958, as the only candidate of the only permitted party, Stroessner was 're-elected' by plebiscite. Opposition continued, but for the most part it came from outside the national borders, and attacks from Argentina by exiles were repelled in 1959 and 1960.

Stroessner's strength in face of these attacks came from his command of the economy as well as of the armed forces. The 1960s saw the further development of traditional products alongside gradual industrialization. Increasing confidence led to some limited political activity being encouraged. Most importantly, perhaps, the pretence of democracy was encouraged by allowing a dissident wing of the Liberal Party, the Renovation wing, to stand in controlled legislative elections. In return for putting themselves up and allowing themselves to be soundly beaten, the Renovation Liberals were to receive one-third of the seats in the legislature. This did not in any way reduce the President's personal dominance of Paraguayan politics, as he controlled the ruling Colorado Party which still held the other two-thirds of legislative seats and personally vetted the selection of supporters who would be eligible to hold office. Thus, though the Colorados remained divided throughout the early 1960s, Stroessner gradually pared away the opposition. The dissident populist wing of the Party, the Movimiento Popular Colorado (MOPOCO), went into opposition and by 1967 the stroessnerites were the only Colorado faction left. In that year, the President saw fit to change the 1940 Constitution to allow himself legally to be re-elected to a fourth term (he had not bothered with constitutionality when he ran for and received a third term in 1963).

The transparently autocratic nature of the regime led to Church criticisms in the late 1960s and these inspired some popular unrest. However, the economic boom Paraguay enjoyed in the 1970s contained most opposition. The central feature was the joint development with Brazil of the vast hydroelectric project at Itaipú on the River Paraná, which brought vast quantities of construction work into the country and, likewise, many Brazilian settlers. The opening of road links into Brazil stimulated trade, and with it smuggling, for which Paraguay became a major centre. Although inflation was high, the latter half of the decade saw annual growth rates of more than 10 per cent. This growth came to an abrupt end, however, when the Brazilian economy went into crisis in 1982. Growth fell to 1.6 per cent per annum and, though work continued at Itaipú, the huge revenues that had been anticipated from selling Paraguay's share of its power to Brazil's developing south did not materialize.

Some opposition unrest was re-emerging, but the usual boycott of the 1983 election gave Stroessner a seventh term and an easy win, with 91 per cent of the vote. With the advancing age of the President, it became increasingly clear by the mid-1980s that a battle was brewing for the succession. Despite its modernization, Stroessner's rule, confirmed against all prediction by re-election to an eighth term in 1988, with a slightly reduced majority, was a very traditional Latin American dictatorship. For a Paraguayan leader, he showed remarkable endurance. The nation's lack of a democratic tradition, and its traditional poverty, may have made possible his rise to power, but his personal qualities, and, in particular, his skilled manipulation of the organization of the Colorado Party, enabled him to stay there. Early in 1989 he fell to a coup organised by his Army Chief of Staff, General Andres Rodriguez, who shortly afterwards was elected Constitutional President.

4 The Olive Branch and the Arrows

THE UNITED STATES A GLOBAL SUPERPOWER

The single most important influence on post-war Latin America has been the emergence of the United States as a global superpower. Nevertheless, the surprising thing is not that Latin America has been drawn into the sphere of the United States or involved in its confrontation with the Soviet Union, but that it has not been more involved and that the involvement came rather slowly. Yet this is not hard to explain. For the conflict was from the beginning a northern one, in which the two superpowers and their allies confronted each other over the Arctic. The remoteness of the South American continent from the scene of confrontation and the limited value of its states in terms of the world balance of power gave it a degree of isolation which enabled its leaders to indulge their own ambitions in largely rhetorical terms within a protected environment. When any serious challenge to US hegemony appeared to be on the way, Washington was not slow to act against it.

The groundwork for the future relationship between the United States and Latin America was laid in 1945 at a Special Conference of the American States held at Chapultepec Castle, former residence of the Viceroys of New Spain, overlooking Mexico City. At this meeting two divergent tendencies were to become apparent, with serious implications for the future. The United States, mindful of what it had spent, was concerned primarily about the restoration of its pre-war trade position. In institutional terms it saw the creation of the United Nations as the major guarantor of peace for the future, and expected the other states of the hemisphere to share this view. The Latin Americans, believing that by their support they had a claim on the financial help of the world's richest country, wanted funds for economic development. The United Nations, in their view, was too much as the creation of the Great Powers, and they wanted major changes in the structure of the organization. The changes sought foreshadowed positions later to be taken by other countries of the emerging 'Third World'. They included: two permanent seats on the Security Council, stronger powers for the General Assembly, an effective International

Court and greater provision for co-operation. Amid general goodwill it was somehow overlooked that no satisfactory arrangements had been made to reconcile these conflicting ambitions, and by the time the next meeting was held it was too late. The Cold War had begun, and the United States was for the time being concerned only with securing its strategic position.

The Act of Chapultepec did, however, establish a new basis for regular consultation. In future there were to be full conferences every four years, with annual meetings of Foreign Ministers when no conference was due. Resolutions reaffirmed the commitment of the American states to peace and the principle of non-intervention. Ironically in view of later events, it was the new democratic government of Guatemala that proposed Resolution XXXVIII, calling on the American states to defend democracy and oppose anti-democratic regimes.

Within two years events in Europe had transformed the scene to a degree that could hardly have been imagined in 1945. Taking part in the Second World War, for many Latin American states, had been their first contact with the Soviet Union. Communists were already a familiar if rather unimportant part of the political scene for many Latin American governments – in Chile, as a legacy of the Popular Front period, there were even communists in the Cabinet (they were ousted by González Videla in 1947). Now with the outbreak of the Cold War communism suddenly became the arch-enemy of democracy. The first step was also the most dramatic. In September 1947 at Rio de Janeiro the United States broke with Washington's tradition of avoiding 'entangling alliances' and signed the Inter-American Treaty of Reciprocal Assistance (in Spanish, TIAR, known colloquially in the United States as 'the Rio Pact'). By this was established a formal military alliance against the possibility of attack from outside the hemisphere, putting the Declaration of Lima of 1938 into written form in a fashion intended to meet the new conditions. By a series of bilateral military agreements with a number of countries, starting with Brazil, the United States proceeded on this basis to set up a permanent alliance system for the Western Hemisphere, analogous to that which in 1949 was to be established for the North Atlantic Treaty nations, including Canada.

The price of the alliance for the Latin Americans was economic co-operation, and early in 1948 the United States sponsored the creation of an Economic Commission for Latin America (ECLA, in Spanish CEPAL) to study the problems of the region and make recommendations. The theme for its work was set by the publication in the same year of Raúl Prebisch's *Economic Development of Latin America and its Principal Problems*. This, the first major attack by a Latin American economist on traditional ideas of development, was to be profoundly important.

THE BOGOTAZO

Colombia was an unfortunate choice to act as host to the Ninth Inter-American Conference in March 1948. It was one of the few countries in the region to have remained a democracy throughout the 1930s, and outwardly it seemed to have accommodated better than most to all the external stresses of the period. Unknown to the visitors, however, the internal stresses generated by social change were near breaking point, and it was already too late to avert the catastrophe that was to come.

The choice of President Ospina Pérez on a minority vote in 1946 coincided with the post-war depression in Colombia. Thousands who were thrown out of work, and many more landless in the countryside, were fired by the speeches of Jorge Eliécer Gaitán to become his followers. Though the Liberals remained divided, they hoped and expected that he would in due time be elected President, as López had been in the 1930s. But in April 1948, as the Inter-American Conference was meeting in Bogotá, Gaitán was shot and died in the street not far from the Cathedral. His assassin was immediately torn to pieces by the infuriated crowd, so that his motive has never been determined. For three days mobs ran amok in the capital, putting the visiting delegates in fear of their lives. They concluded, and it was widely accepted though without any shadow of evidence, that the rioting was the work of communist agitators.

Ospina Pérez, to his credit, kept his nerve and refused to be stampeded into resigning. On the advice of Gómez and other Conservatives, however, he then sought to save democracy in Colombia by totally destroying it. A state of siege backed by a curfew was imposed, Congress closed, all state legislatures and municipal assemblies forbidden to meet, public meetings banned, and censorship imposed on press and radio. The radical Liberals believed that there was no hope but in revolt. Fighting spread outward into the country-side until large areas were in a state of full civil war. Buses travelling from one area to another were ambushed and their passengers slaughtered; Liberals raided Conservative villages and Conservatives

Liberal ones; wearing the wrong colour tie (Liberals wear red, Conservatives blue) could mean death. Whole areas, notably the so-called 'Socialist Republic of Marquetalia' escaped from central control altogether. As for the Liberal leadership, they found even the Supreme Court precluded from ruling on the validity of the demobilizing measures, and in due course reluctantly decided they could not safely take part in the 1949 elections. The result was a foregone conclusion, the election of Gómez to the Presidency with this time an all-Conservative Congress.

The machinery of reform was immediately put into reverse. Gómez was not simply content to maintain the prerogatives of his office, as Ospina Pérez had done. He proposed a new Constitution to establish a corporate state under authoritarian leadership – his own. The President would no longer be accountable in any way either to the Congress or to the Supreme Court. To keep the Liberals out of power, the Senate would in future be appointed and not elected. But in June 1953, just two days before the proposals were due to be put to a Constitutional Convention, which being composed entirely of Conservatives seemed bound to accept them, Gómez was deposed by the Commander of the Army, General Gustavo Rojas Pinilla. He then offered the Presidency to other civilians, and when they did not accept it, assumed it himself.

LATIN AMERICA AND THE COLD WAR

After the Bogotazo in 1948 the badly shaken delegates to the Inter-American Conference had re-assembled. Whilst the North Americans blamed communist agitators, the Latin Americans blamed the prevailing poverty and misery of their continent. But the idea of a Marshall Plan for Latin America was rejected by none other than Secretary of State George Catlett Marshall himself. European recovery, he argued, in the mode of the then generally accepted 'trickle down' theory of development, was of first priority and in due course would ensure the development of Latin America also. The United States had established the Point Four programme to foster private investment in the region. The consequence of this was, of course, to increase Latin American suspicion of US motives, while Prebisch and his colleagues on ECLA were already in the process of demonstrating that the trickle down theory did not work. The Conference therefore broke up with little achieved except in one respect. The Pan-American Union was transformed into a new regional organization within the United Nations called the Organization of American States (OAS). Its Charter, it turned out, although it enshrined the principle of non-intervention, was in practice to allow the United States a measure of freedom within the hemisphere that it did not have and could not have had elsewhere.

So many things were going on outside the Hemisphere that Washington almost lost sight of Latin America and was to pay very little attention to inter-American affairs throughout the 1950s. The fall of Czechoslovakia, the Berlin crisis, the explosion of the first Soviet nuclear device, a communist government in China, came first, and in quick succession. At the outbreak of the Korean War the Latin Americans offered support for the United Nations effort, and troops from Colombia and Cuba were to serve in the peace-keeping force. Not surprisingly, given what had happened at Bogotá, there was little enthusiasm among the American states to act as host to the next Conference, due to be held in 1952, so it was postponed until after the return of the Republicans to power in the United States in January 1953. The venue was Caracas.

It would have been hard to think of a more unfortunate choice. Venezuela was then under the dictatorship of Marcos Pérez Jiménez. Spies (*orejas*) were everywhere and ex-Nazis were employed to use every refinement of torture to seek out opponents of the regime. In Venezuela there were many such opponents, but they kept very quiet. To North American businessmen 'good ol' PJ' was their friend, and the 'almighty B' (the Venezuelan currency, named after Bolívar, the Liberator) was the steadiest currency in the region. If the dictator himself was rich they saw this as a sign of his success, and with the palatial Officers Club as a sign of what the oil revenues could do for them, the officer corps of the Army were expected to continue to give him their loyal support. The decision to hold the Conference in such a place seemed to herald a return to the worst days of North American support for friendly dictators who gave favours to US business interests and those who thought so were, of course, right.

So the Conference began badly. To begin with, democratic Costa Rica refused to attend in protest against the regime, but the US paid no attention, rightly assuming that Costa Rica needed the US more than the US did Costa Rica. Then it became clear that all that the new US Secretary of State, John Foster Dulles, and the United States delegation were interested in was securing a strong resolution against communism aimed at the government of President Jacobo Arbenz in

Guatemala. Their original resolution the other delegates refused to accept, rightly recognizing that Guatemala was not a communist state nor anything like it. An alternative resolution, denouncing communism only in very general terms, was introduced and passed without support from Mexico and Argentina, and with reservations by Uruguay. Dulles then left without bothering to hear what the Latin Americans wanted to say. They wanted to talk about their economic plight. The end of the Korean war had left several of them in severe financial difficulties, as purchases of strategic raw materials tailed off. But the new Administration in the United States was not interested. The only country in Latin America that it was currently concerned with was Guatemala.

THE UNITED FRUIT COMPANY AND GUATEMALA

When Jorge Ubico resigned the Presidency of Guatemala in 1944 he did so in favour of the three officers his secretary found sitting in his ante-room. One of them, Colonel Federico Ponce Vaidés, tried to assume leadership of the junta but failed to recognize the strength of the democratic pressures that had carried him there, and the assassination of an opposition journalist and congressman spurred a new revolt amongst the junior officers. On 20 October 1944 two of them, Major Francisco Arana and Captain Jacobo Arbenz, led a coup, and with the aid of students and other civilian supporters, gained control of the capital though only at the cost of more than a hundred lives. Together they then formed a junta with a prominent civilian landowner and businessman, Jorge Toriello Garrido, to oversee elections and support the civilian candidate for the Presidency, Dr Juan José Arévalo Bermejo. Arévalo, a teacher who had written textbooks widely used in Guatemalan schools, had spent the previous 14 years in exile as Professor of Philosophy at the University of Tucumán in Argentina, and so was untainted by any association with the Ubico regime. In the full flood of democratic enthusiasm he received 85 per cent of the popular vote in the December elections.

Arévalo described himself as a 'spiritual Socialist' but the substantial reforms with which he attempted to modernize his country were essentially pragmatic ones and the major ideological influence on the regime was clearly that of the New Deal of Franklin D. Roosevelt. The Social Security Law of 1946 and the Labour Code of 1947 created the basis for a small but loyal labour movement, and preliminary steps towards agrarian reform, including the registration of land, the distribution of some of the land confiscated from German owners during the war and the Law of Forced Rental of 1949, generated support in the countryside. Their success was evidenced by the fact that Arévalo served out his full term (1946–51) despite more than 20 attempts to overthrow him. In 1949, however, the rivalry between Arana and Arbenz as to who was to succeed Arévalo came to an abrupt end when Arana, driving back to the capital from Amatitlán, was shot down when his car was held up at a narrow bridge. The assassins, who had used a car said by some witnesses to have been that of Arbenz's wife, were never found. In the 1950 elections Arbenz obtained 63 per cent of the vote; the candidate of the right-wing Redemption Party, General Miguel Ydígoras Fuentes, coming second with only 18 per cent.

Arbenz made his main task carrying through the long-promised land reform. The Agrarian Reform Law (Decree 900 of 27 June 1952) was a modest measure: it empowered the government to expropriate only the uncultivated portions of large estates, exempting all farms of less than 90 hectares and all farms over that size that were fully worked. Compensation was to be paid on the land's declared value for taxation purposes in May 1952 in 3 per cent government bonds payable over 25 years. What gave the measure its political significance was the fact that a major loser would be the US-owned United Fruit Company of Boston, which claimed that the 156 640 acres they would be required to surrender were needed as a reserve against disease and that the compensation offered bore no relation to the true value of the land. Instead of asking why the declared value of the land had been too low, the incoming Eisenhower Administration in the United States authorized the Central Intelligence Agency (CIA), then under Allen Dulles, to go ahead with a clandestine operation to depose Arbenz, while Dulles' brother, Secretary of State John Foster Dulles, who had previously served as counsel to the United Fruit Company, denounced the Arbenz regime as 'communist'. Hence the resolution he secured from the Tenth Inter-American Conference of the OAS stating that the domination of any government in the hemisphere by the 'international communist movement' constituted a 'threat' to the whole hemisphere was not as it then seemed a diplomatic move to put pressure on the Guatemalan government to conform, but a pretext for intervention which was already being planned. The opportunity to intervene came when on 15 May 1954 the Swedish freighter *Alfhelm* docked at Puerto Barrios with a cargo of weapons that the Guatemalan government had bought from Czechoslovakia. A month later the force of Guatemalan exiles the CIA had been training in Honduras crossed the border into Guatemala. Their numbers inflated in propaganda by a 'rebel' radio station run by the CIA, Arbenz was unable accurately to gauge the situation and eventually decided as in 1944 to distribute arms to the workers to defend the government. The Army refused to obey. On 27 June Arbenz resigned, though not before making his successor, Col. Carlos Enrique Díaz, promise never to negotiate with Col. Carlos Castillo Armas, the right-wing Catholic whom the CIA had selected to head their rebel movement.

With the encouragement of the US Ambassador, John L. Puerifoy, Díaz was, however, speedily ousted by military officers who would deal with the 'rebels', and a junta was formed from which the other officers were subsequently persuaded to resign, leaving Castillo Armas in sole charge. The United States poured some $80 million in aid into the country in two years, much of which went to drive the peasants off the land they had been given and restore the big plantations. The United Fruit Company was similarly favoured, though it found it expedient to give some of its land back to the government. But Castillo Armas was never popular, even with the middle classes, and he did not risk holding elections, only a plebiscite. In 1957 he was assassinated by a palace guard. A year later General Ydígoras was elected president. A more engaging figure than Castillo Armas, he was also more unpredictable, but he had the popular support that his predecessor always lacked and he knew how to gain the confidence of United States officials with a vigorous public profession of anti-communism.

NIXON'S TOUR

In 1958 President Eisenhower sent his Vice-President, Richard M. Nixon, on a goodwill tour of Latin America. Nixon was glad to accept the commission, since it offered him an important opportunity to show himself as an international statesman, in preparation for his own bid for the Presidency as Eisenhower's successor. Latin America had, however, been virtually ignored by the ailing Dulles since 1954 and the tour was in trouble almost at once. The crisis came in Venezuela, which had just returned to democratic rule after the tyranny of Marcos Pérez Jiménez, whose regime had been closely identified with the United States. On the streets of Caracas the Vice-President's motorcade was stoned and spat upon, and at one stage, as he describes in his account of the tour in his *Six Crises*, it was touch-and-go as to whether the security forces could hold the crowds back for long enough to enable him and his wife to escape their fury.

Nixon's report on the tour recognized that only a massive effort by the United States could meet the needs of Latin Americans, and that economic aid, consistently blocked by the arch-conservative Secretary of the Treasury, George Humphrey, was essential if the Left were not to win by default. The test for this new policy came in Cuba before its true significance was realized and any steps taken to implement it.

THE CUBAN REVOLUTION

It was also in 1957 that the enterprising US journalist Herbert L. Matthews secured an interview with Fidel Castro in the mountains of the Sierra Maestra, and informed the world that a previously almost unknown band of guerrillas were fightihg to depose the Cuban dictator Fulgencio Batista.

Batista had come a long way since 1933, when he had risen from sergeant to Commander of the Cuban National Guard in a mere one hundred days. In the 1930s he had made and broken governments as he saw fit. In 1940 he had become President in his own right under a new semi-parliamentary Constitution with a prime minister acting as head of government. In his first term (1940–44), and the terms of his two successors, Ramón Grau San Martín (1944–48) and Carlos Prío Socarrás (1948–52), constitutional government continued with free competition between the two branches of the old Liberal Party, the ruling Partido Revolucionario Cubano founded by Grau, known as the *Auténticos* and the Partido del Pueblo Cubano, known as the *Ortodoxos*. These were years of great prosperity for Cuba, which according to most standard indices of development ranked fourth or fifth of the most developed countries in Latin America. But there was little industrial base to the economy, and the affluence of the swollen capital, Havana, came from tourism, prostitution and crime including the illegal operations of the great gambling syndicates who used Havana to 'launder' their money.

With the onset of the Cold War the government became increasingly harsh in putting down strikes and concern rose about possible subversion within the Army. In 1952 Batista had promised a free and fair election. Instead he became impatient and shouldered aside the government he had helped create in a military coup that was a classic of its kind. It began at precisely 2.43 a.m. and was all over by breakfast time. In his second term, and the third to which he was elected in 1956, Batista became increasingly clearly identified with the welfare of the great crime syndicates from which much of the wealth for his and his friends' conspicuous expenditure derived. Constitutional guarantees lapsed. Yet the regime, though often brutal, was not systematically repressive. When in 1953 a group of young men tried to seize the Moncada barracks in Santiago de Cuba, they were gaoled for only a year before being released under a general amnesty. Even the leader of the group, Fidel Castro, who had been sentenced to 15 years, was freed. Afterwards it was claimed that he had been able to make an impassioned speech at his trial. Various versions of this, entitled 'History will absolve me!' were subsequently circulated. Though by his own admission the definitive version was carefully composed (almost certainly well after the event), it shows that at this stage he had little if any ideological awareness of any kind.

Fidel Castro Ruz was born at Mayarí in Oriente Province on 13 August 1926. His father, a wealthy sugar planter, had emigrated to Cuba from Galicia in northwest Spain, and Fidel was his second son and third child by his second marriage. In his childhood and youth he went walking and hiking in the mountains of the Sierra Maestra, which gave him some awareness of the terrain. However, he was educated as a boarder at a Catholic primary school in nearby Santiago de Cuba and later at the Colegio Belén, a Jesuit college in Havana, where, despite the reputation for stupidity that *gallegos* have throughout Latin America, he graduated in the top third of his class, and went on in 1945 to study law at the University of Havana. A keen sportsman (he played basketball and baseball) and a good orator, Castro took an active role in both student and national politics, and was elected vice-president (and became president) of the student governing body. Like other student activists he was a follower of Eduardo (Eddy) Chibás, founder and presidential candidate of the newly formed 'Ortodoxos', who became and remained one of his heroes for his stirring advocacy of clean government and social reform. But even in those days, Castro preferred action to debate; in 1947 he joined an expedition to overthrow Trujillo in the Dominican Republic and had to swim three miles to shore to escape when the force was intercepted by a Cuban naval patrol.

When he qualified as a lawyer in 1950, thus gaining the title of 'Doctor' which significantly he has since the Revolution shunned in favour of the military rank of 'Major', he was soon busy defending poor clients and continuing his political activities. In 1952 he had been adopted as a candidate for Congress by the Ortodoxos in the election Batista forestalled. Chibás had committed suicide in 1951 but his cause lived on. In a dramatic move Castro, the newly qualified lawyer, brought a petition against the government calling for Batista's imprisonment. No reprisal followed, but neither did action, hence Castro's fateful decision to organize a revolt. It was natural, in the circumstances, that unlike earlier abortive revolts, which had occurred in Havana itself, it was based in the part of the country he knew best, Cuba's second city, Santiago, but it was still a disaster and its failure brought catastrophe to the city. By the time Castro himself was captured, Batista's forces had rampaged through the city faithfully carrying out their orders that for every soldier killed at Moncada ten were to die, and public fear and revulsion had driven the Archbishop of Santiago to exact a promise from the Army commander that the remaining rebels, when captured, would be brought to trial and not summarily shot. Even then, Castro was fortunate that the patrol that found him in the mountains was commanded by an old school friend. By October 1953 he was a prisoner on the Isle of Pines and though held in solitary confinement for seven months, he was not maltreated and once allowed to associate with his fellow prisoners was able to set up classes for them in history and philosophy and to re-read the works, not of Karl Marx, but of José Martí, the hero of Cuban independence. Freed, he spent several months in Cuba before travelling to Mexico, where in December 1956 his expedition sailed from Tuxpam on the yacht *Granma* for Cuba. Delayed by bad weather, and awash with water so that they had to bail for their lives (it later turned out that a tap had been left running in the galley), it was late arriving and Batista's forces were waiting. Only a handful escaped with Castro to the Sierra Maestra, and so unprepared was its leader that neither he nor his companions had taken the precaution of obtaining maps or refreshing their memory of the area.

One of the few organized political movements allowed to survive under Batista, significantly, was the Communist Party, known in Cuba after 1944 as the Popular Socialist Party (PSP). PSP deputies sat legally in Congress – as long as they did so, Batista could always point to them as evidence both of his democratic credentials and his need for more aid from the United States. In view of what happened afterwards, Castro's support of the joint manifesto, the so-called Manifesto of the Sierra Maestra (July 1957) in favour of liberal democracy, free elections, freedom of the press and peasant ownership of land has been regarded in some quarters as cynical window dressing. Despite Castro's later actions, this view has no foundation in truth. Nor had Castro's attempt in 1958 to woo the communists, among others, any greater significance. Castro was a man of action rather than a thinker, and he really had no aim except to seize power. This proved unexpectedly easy. The Batista regime was so rotten that it began to collapse when a small local victory by the guerrilla forces coincided with spontaneous risings in Havana itself in November 1958. Batista and his henchmen packed their valuables and left on 1 January 1959, and Castro and his '26th of July Movement', named after the date of the Moncada rising, were free to do as they wished. The course of events shows that once again the victors had no very clear idea what to do, and it was some months before the vacuum was to be filled.

At first, Castro was above politics as leader of the revolution. The new Prime Minister was José Miró, co-ordinator of the opposition front, and the interim President was Manuel Urrutia Lleo, the judge who had allowed Castro a fair hearing at his own trial. At home there was a honeymoon period during which show trials were held of those soldiers and police of the Batista regime who had not escaped, and they were dispatched by firing squad to the cheers of rejoicing crowds. Beyond this, the new government lacked any clear policy, and law and order were breaking down. On 15 February Castro himself, impatient that nothing was happening, took over the post of Prime Minister. But government still lacked a programme, decisions were made ad hoc and justified afterwards, and the one clear trend in Castro's personal leadership was a strong reluctance to accept constitutional restraints on the revolutionary process. In the next few months, therefore, taxes were collected, the labour laws enforced and a land reform law decreed putting an upper limit on holdings, expropriating the large sugar estates and distributing them to the farm workers. The myth of the peasant leadership of the Cuban Revolution, perpetuated by Che Guevara, dies hard; there were, in fact, very few peasants in Cuba, only workers on the large estates who formed a rural working-class parallel to and having much in common with the urban workers. They were easily mobilized, therefore, and some left-wingers urged Castro to take the radical course of collectivizing agriculture instead, but he did not do so. In fact at this stage he was publicly critical of the proposals of the PSP in terms that he afterwards found difficult to explain and at the earliest opportunity sent his greatest potential rival, Guevara himself, out of the country on a mission, thus depriving him of the command of troops.

Meanwhile Castro had been preparing the abortive invasion of the

Dominican Republic on 14 June (see chapter 3). Shortly after he had assumed power he had personally visited the United States to ask for help, but from this point on relations with the United States rapidly deteriorated. Even in the first phase, during which Castro evoked some personal popularity in the United States and even appeared on the cover of *Time*, the Cubans had made such extravagant public demands on the US for economic aid that they were not taken seriously. They demanded the then colossal sum of $30 billion, a sum greater than the whole US aid bill. At the same time they sent a trade mission to Moscow to see if they could gain support in that quarter. This in turn alarmed opinion in the United States, and the provisional President, Manuel Urrutia, expressed concern felt by other Cubans.

Castro responded in a characteristically bold fashion. In one of his long, rambling speeches on nationwide television he denounced the provisional President as an enemy of the revolution. By resigning himself, he whipped up such a torrent of popular upheaval that Urrutia, his life in danger, immediately resigned. Replacing him by the complaisant Osvaldo Dorticós Torrado, a former communist who had long since dropped out of politics but was to serve as figurehead President from July 1959 to December 1976, when he was unceremoniously dumped, Castro took a sharp turn away from constitutionality, and towards confrontation with the United States. Soon afterwards, the only remaining independent revolutionary commander, Major Huber Matos of Camagüey, who had also dared publicly to criticize the regime, was arrested (October 1959). Later he was sentenced to 20 years imprisonment under trumped-up charges of plotting rebellion. Unlike Castro himself under the tyrant Batista, Matos was made to serve every day of his sentence.

It is hard to understand now why events then took the turn they did unless it is recalled that in October 1957, while Castro and his few followers had been establishing themselves in the wilds of the Sierra Maestra, the world had been astonished by the news that it was not the United States, but the Soviet Union, that had launched the world's first earth satellite. In Latin America, as elsewhere, a major shift was believed to have happened in the world balance of power. For the first time since before 1914 it was thought that there was a power that had the strength and the will to challenge the United States in its own sphere of influence. This belief was as yet wrong, but that was not known, and it explains what followed. From the beginning there were some members of the new Cuban government who, like Guevara, called for the extension of the revolution to the entire continent, though there were initially few who shared the view of the PSP that US imperialism was the uniting force behind the dictatorships of the region, and none, before mid-1960, who were communists or had any real knowledge of Marxism-Leninism.

With, it must be said, the full forms of diplomatic politeness, the United States government had asked for compensation for US nationals deprived of their property by the provisional government. Many of these had been engaged in corrupt activities and the provisional government was not conciliatory. However, though the US government did not take a stern view of the Dominican venture and the OAS merely agreed to 'study' the situation, it was only at this point that it became clear that the arms for which Castro had been asking would not be forthcoming. At this stage, therefore, an urgent invitation was extended to Moscow, which responded by sending a trade delegation to Havana and in February 1960 an agreement was signed by which the USSR agreed to buy 425 000 tons of sugar at once and a million tons a year for the following four years, in return for a trade credit of US $100 million.

The inevitable result of this deal was that Castro was denounced in the US as a communist. As diplomatic relations with the US deteriorated, the US Congress threatened to cut the Cuban sugar quota. At this point, on 3 March 1960 an explosion on board the French freighter *La Coubre*, as it unloaded a consignment of arms in Havana harbour, recalled the explosion of the USS *Maine* in 1898 and gave Castro the pretext and the enemy he had been looking for. Within weeks the U2 incident and the collapse of the superpower summit had left the Soviet Union free to respond, and diplomatic relations were formally renewed between the two countries in May 1960. Shortly afterwards the first consignment of Soviet oil arrived in Cuba. The US-owned refineries refused to refine it, and when they refused to do so were summarily confiscated. In retaliation Eisenhower himself ordered the cutting of the Cuban sugar quota. Three days later, when arms from Czechoslovakia were already available to the Cuban militia, the General Secretary of the Communist Party of the Soviet Union, Nikita Khrushchev, said in Moscow 'In a figurative sense, if necessary, the Soviet military can support the Cuban people with rocket weapons'. The fact that he simultaneously undertook to buy the 700 000 tons of sugar the US had foregone was striking enough to distract attention from the gloss Castro immediately put on his statement, claiming that the rockets were real and not merely figurative.

Castro had promised that if the quota was cut, the US mills would be nationalized, and on 6 July a decree to that effect was prepared. The seizures began a month later, but no condemnation came from the OAS leaders and when it appeared that no response would be forthcoming from the beleaguered US Administration, the measures were extended to other US properties. In September the cigar and cigarette factories were nationalized, followed by the US-owned banks. Castro's statements during this period show his strenuous efforts to secure real as opposed to figurative rockets to protect his regime, and immediately after his return from the UN in October Castro proclaimed the nationalization in addition of all Cuban-owned banks and 382 other Cuban-owned firms. It was then that he laid claim for the first time to the title of 'socialist'. State intervention was extended into every aspect of the national life. Printers were encouraged to take over newspapers, sugar cane workers their plantations; fishermen were urged to form co-operatives.

Khrushchev, like other Soviet leaders, was reluctant to recognize any route to socialism other than the Soviet one, but his rivalry with China laid him open to persuasion and by December 1960, when Eisenhower set the Cuban sugar quota for the first quarter of 1961 at zero, the Soviet Union, China and other countries of the socialist bloc between them had already agreed to purchase four million tons in the coming year. Economically the revolution was saved, though only for the time being. Its socialist credentials, however, had yet to be accepted.

THE BAY OF PIGS AND THE CUBAN MISSILE CRISIS

On 31 December 1960 Castro publicly accused the outgoing Eisenhower Administration of plotting to invade Cuba before its term expired on 20 January 1961. Its excuse, he said, would be that Cuba was allowing launching sites for rockets to be constructed on its territory. Two days later he demanded the reduction of US Embassy staff to 18, and two days after that the US responded by severing diplomatic relations.

It is hardly likely that the news that the CIA were training a force of Cuban exiles for an invasion of Cuba could have failed to reach the ears of the Cuban secret police, the G-2 (pronounced 'Ge-dos', so known to opponents of the regime as the 'Ge-dos-tapo'). The training was taking place on the Atlantic coast of Guatemala, on a *finca* (plantation) belonging to Vice-President Roberto Alejos Arzú himself, and despite US attempts to maintain security, the exiles' enthusiasm for breaking bounds in search of wine, women and song could not be checked. However, the exile force was not ready in time for the invasion to be launched by 20 January, and it was the new President of the United States, John F. Kennedy, who had the responsibility of deciding whether or not to let the plan go ahead.

The Presidential Seal of the United States shows an American eagle, one claw holding an olive branch, the other a sheaf of arrows, symbolizing peace and war respectively. Hitherto the eagle had looked towards the arrows; as a symbolic gesture Kennedy ordered that under his presidency it should look towards the olive branch. However, Kennedy had been informed by Allen Dulles of the existence of the exile force on 18 November, soon after his election, and with diplomatic relations already severed, Kennedy, once inaugurated, allowed the preparations to go ahead, though he reserved the right to cancel them if he thought fit. On 2 February he approved the plans for the invasion which was originally to have been at Trinidad on the south coast of Cuba; six weeks later the landing site was changed to Playa de Largos (the Bay of Pigs), and subsequently the date of the landing, originally fixed for 5 April, was twice postponed. Warned by air attacks two days before, on 17 April, the date on which the landing actually took place, the Cubans were fully alert and waiting for the exile force. Because the new site had not been reconnoitred properly, many of the invaders were killed trying to wade ashore, where, because of Kennedy's wish to maintain the 'cover' that the US had nothing to do with the landing, they were denied effective air cover against the attacks of the Cuban Air Force. The rest were easily killed or captured on land because the new site, unlike the old, offered them no chance of following Castro's own example and escaping to the mountains. It was on the wrong side of an inlet.

It was on 16 April, after the air attacks but before the landing, that Castro seized the strategic moment and formally proclaimed the revolution 'socialist'. Two days later, Khrushchev told Kennedy that he would give Cuba 'all the necessary assistance to repel aggression'. Still he hesitated officially to welcome Cuba as a full member of the socialist bloc, and over the next few months Kennedy recovered much of the ground the US had lost by accepting full responsibility for the disaster, rallying support in the OAS, and driving through Congress the legislation necessary to establish the Alliance for Progress, a multi-million dollar aid package designed to forestall the spread of communism by promoting economic development throughout the continent. On 1 December 1961 Castro forced his hand by announcing publicly: 'I am a Marxist-Leninist, and I shall continue to be one until the last day of my life.' The first part of his statement, unconvincingly buttressed by vague statements about having read communist writers at college, was certainly untrue; as to the second part, events were to show that in accepting Marxism-Leninism Castro had in no way renounced his freedom of action. In fact the Second Declaration of Havana, which was his response to the decision of the OAS on 31 January 1962 to suspend Cuba from that organization, was only superficially Marxist and conspicuously avoided most of the key phrases then crucial to orthodoxy.

By 1962 the magic of the revolution was waning as its economic difficulties multiplied. Some of these difficulties were the direct result of the US trade embargo, and many imported goods had to be rationed. Some, however, were not. The dislocation of agriculture was so great that there was a shortage of wheat, rice, potatoes, meat, chicken, milk and even black beans, the staple foodstuff of the poor. Meanwhile, the sugar crop, now as never before needed to pay for foreign exchange, was down to only 4.8 million tons, a million tons below target. At this critical juncture the Soviet Union, already in the process of agreeing belatedly to a new and expanded trade agreement, formally recognized Cuba as being engaged in 'the construction of socialism' (11 April). By 25 June at latest the USSR appears to have decided to go further. In order to safeguard its bridgehead in the new world, as the Cubans wanted, and to outflank the new Ballistic Missile Early Warning System (BMEWS) in Northern Canada and Greenland, it agreed to station intermediate-range ballistic missiles (IRBMs) in Cuba.

This was the first time that such missiles had been deployed by the Soviet Union outside its own territory, which perhaps accounts for its failure to camouflage the sites. On 29 August photographs taken over Cuba by the high-flying U2 reconnaissance aircraft showed that ground-to-air missiles had been emplaced, the pattern suggesting that they were to defend something even more important. Though the first IRBMs arrived in Cuba on 8 September, their launching sites were not at that point ready, and cloud cover was to delay positive identification of launching sites until 14 October. On 22 October Kennedy disclosed this information and proclaimed a 'quarantine' of shipping to Cuba; a few hours earlier Castro had on his own initiative placed his country on a war footing. The following day Castro asserted Cuba's right to have missiles. But it was the Soviet Union that alone could decide whether to continue the path of confrontation, and on 28 October it prudently decided to withdraw the missiles and end the risk of nuclear war. The Soviet Union was prepared to conclude a formal agreement with the United States, including measures for verification. Castro, who was not, it seems, consulted, refused to have anything to do with verification, and in consequence no formal agreement was ever concluded. Nevertheless, there was an agreement, which continued to govern US relations in the Western Hemisphere with the Soviet Union until its collapse in 1991. On the Soviet side, the missiles would be removed and no further 'offensive' missiles emplaced. On the United States side, there would be no further invasion of Cuba, which would be allowed to go its own way. Cuba would not, however, be allowed actively to support revolution in the Western Hemisphere, and the United States would continue to make use of its naval base at Guantánamo Bay. The Cubans did not like this, of course, but given their increasing dependence on Soviet support of all kinds they were not at that stage able to do much about it. Hence, though the powerful transmitters of Radio Havana continued to beam Cuban propaganda across the continent, there is no evidence from that time onward of active support for the existing guerrilla movements that had started in imitation of the Cuban example, and at Fort Gulick in the Canal Zone the United States set up the 'School of the Americas' to train Latin American military personnel in counter-insurgency techniques.

The problem with training armed forces in counter-insurgency, however, is that the training is equally useful as a preparation for insurgency. Even before the Cuban Missile crisis, the fear of communism among military officers had helped spur the fall of Frondizi in Argentina and of Prado in Peru. In 1963 the armed forces intervened in Guatemala, Ecuador, the Dominican Republic and Honduras, and the following year Brazil came under a new form of military government, one which did not intervene merely to replace a government or check an unpopular policy, but was determined to stay in power as long as might be necessary to carry out the modernization of the economy and society and make it strong in the face of the challenge of subversion. This fear, and the need for strong measures to combat it, was confirmed by the events of 1965 in the Dominican Republic.

INTERVENTION IN THE DOMINICAN REPUBLIC

Following the assassination of Trujillo in 1961, the Trujillista President, Joaquín Balaguer, who owed his titular position to the fact that he was a former secretary to Trujillo and a nephew of the dictator's second wife, immediately made the dictator's playboy son 'Ramfis', Commander-in-Chief of the armed forces. Ramfis had had long personal connections with the military, since in a dynastic style which had gone out of fashion in Europe at the French Revolution his father had made him a colonel when he was four years old and a general at six. Together Balaguer and Ramfis sought to increase US support and to remove the OAS sanctions imposed against the Dominican Republic after Trujillo's abortive attempt on the life of Betancourt. Some limited liberalization therefore occurred in the form of an Army purge and the return of exiles, among them opposition leader Juan Bosch who had by then been excluded from his homeland for 24 years. Bosch was a novelist of some distinction, a friend of both Betancourt and the President of Costa Rica, José Figueres and a democrat who opposed the leftward trend in neighbouring Cuba. Overtures were made to him as to the rest of the increasingly active political opposition, but Ramfis' unfortunate public utterances in favour of the military and against democracy precluded the formation of any broad coalition which included him. Violations of human rights continued, as did violent opposition to the Balaguer Administration. At the same time Ramfis came under pressure from his family not to continue allowing attacks on his late father's memory. Accusations of cowardice, especially from his mother, eventually led him to desperate measures; in murdering the surviving members of the group that had killed his father and hastening into exile. His uncles tried to return, but as US warships patrolled the coast on Kennedy's orders to show they were not welcome, they fled also, together with other members of the family and Trujillo supporters, in the dictator's private yacht, taking with them the dead body of their deceased leader and relative in the refrigerator which in happier times had sheltered only refreshments. Balaguer, with the chameleon's capacity to blend with his background, became an anti-Trujillista and resigned in favour of his Vice-President, whose loyalties remained firm.

Bosch won the December 1962 elections despite allegations that he was a communist and the opposition of the Church. Unfortunately, though he was not a communist, he proved not to be a very conciliatory leader. He adopted a political position that offended not only other powerful domestic interests, especially business and the armed forces, but also the United States. He was in favour of urban full employment, agrarian reform, the economic independence of the Republic from the US and Cuba's freedom to make its own political decisions. In consequence Bosch faced anti-communist demonstrations against his regime as well as a Haitian conspiracy, supported by exiled members of the Trujillo family, which culminated in his attempted assassination and the breaking off of diplomatic relations between the two neighbouring countries. He sought to constrain corruption, enhance civil liberties and legislate to break up the big estates, but his reforms were only just beginning to take effect when he was ousted in September 1963, briefly held prisoner in the presidential palace and then flown into exile again in Puerto Rico. The expectation of instantaneous change, which of course Bosch could not have achieved in the seven months for which he was president, may have contributed to the lack of popular opposition to the coup.

The anti-Bosch forces were led by Colonel Elías Wessin y Wessin, who remained as the 'strong man' behind the Triumvirate which took power. The Triumvirate promoted him to General and dissolved Congress, though its US-supported figurehead, Donald Reid Cabral, promised elections in due course. But Wessin had no desire to see Bosch re-elected, so these elections did not take place and popular antipathy to the regime increased. Conspiracy was rife in a military establishment bloated by the Trujillo years and without a tradition of defending the nation in foreign wars. It included constitutionalist officers who wanted a restoration of electoral politics, some officers who favoured a presidency under Balaguer and junior officers who wanted Bosch to resume power.

On 24 April 1965 constitutionalist troops began seizing strategic points in Santo Domingo. The Presidential palace was surrounded. Inside it Donald Reid Cabral resigned. A radio broadcast announcing that a counter-coup had occurred brought Bosch supporters onto the streets shouting '¡Viva la libertad!' A member of the PRD, José Rafael Molina Ureña, was appointed provisional President. But on 26 April Wessin's so-called 'loyalist' supporters in the Air Force began bombing the Presidential palace and so started what amounted to civil war. As the loyalists played for time, the Navy changed sides and bombarded the city, while the US took urgent measures to evacuate its nationals. On 27 April Molina resigned, but constitutionalist civilian bands, often led by military NCOs, attacked police stations, and, although virtually unarmed in keeping with the constitutionalist nature of their revolt, resisted loyalist tanks and machine guns as the loyalists tried to force their way into the capital. Military resistance began to crystallize behind the constitutionalist Secretary of the Interior, Colonel Francisco Alberto Caamaño Deñó. Bosch and the military leaders of the conspiracy had expected US hostility to their actions. What they had not foreseen was that President Lyndon B. Johnson would respond to the 'needs' of the military Right and send in the Marines on the evening of the 28th to suppress a supposed 'communist' threat. This was the first time since 1926 that the US had intervened openly in Latin America. Such a significant breach with the 'Good Neighbor Policy' established by Franklin D. Roosevelt was to have far reaching consequences throughout the continent, reviving hostility to the US for its association with the new wave of right-wing regimes that were coming to power after 1962.

As so often happens, it was easier to intervene than to withdraw. By 7 May the loyalists had formed a Government of National Reconstruction (GRN) which immediately handed over all its power to the loyalist General Antonio Imbert Barrera to suppress the revolt. By then the US had belatedly suggested the OAS endorse its actions by the creation of an Inter-American Peace Force (IAPF). Under this the soldiers of five dictatorships (Brazil, Honduras, Paraguay, Nicaragua and El Salvador) and 21 Costa Rican policemen joined the United States in restoring 'democracy' to the Dominican Republic by helping General Imbert's troops in their systematic massacre of constitutionalists holding out in the slums of the *barrios altos*. Finally, after the surrender of the last constitutionalists, the OAS was allowed to supervise the establishment of a provisional government which could prepare the way for elections the following year. The US nominee, Héctor García Godoy, was an able and pragmatic *político* of no very strong ideological persuasion. He had been an ambassador under Trujillo and Minister of Foreign Affairs under Bosch. He knew everyone. Above all he was a friend of the American Ambassador and of the United States. His Presidency (beginning 3 September) was accepted in the end by most of the leaders of both the formal political institutions and the parties for fear of further military action and an OAS withdrawal.

It is not clear how far the elections of 1966 were rigged – almost certainly to some extent, probably not enough to give the Presidency to Balaguer as opposed to Bosch. However, the climate in which the elections occurred could hardly have been more unfair. Whilst Balaguer, as candidate of the Right, was able to tour the country campaigning, Bosch's life was under threat and he was only able to leave his house briefly three times during the whole electoral campaign. Despite Balaguer's substantial victory, therefore, factional violence continued and the regime became increasingly authoritarian. In the 1970s the growing problem of urban terrorism led to widespread state repression and right-wing military and paramilitary violence. Opposition abstention made possible the re-election of Balaguer in 1970 and 1974. It was not until 1978 that international pressure from the Carter Administration, when a military revolt threatened to reverse the election of PRD candidate Antonio Guzmán, ensured that the electoral process was respected.

Guzmán, a rich landowner from Cibao, was a moderate within the PRD who had long been known as a friend of the United States. On the other hand he had been the first candidate of the constitutionalists for interim president in 1965 and had it appears been vetoed by Washington because of his closeness to Bosch. As President he displayed some of the personal faults traditionally associated with Dominican public figures, notably nepotism. At least 37 members of his family, including his daughter and son-in-law occupied important government posts. He did succeed in purging the armed forces and bringing them to some extent under civilian control. Guzmán was not able to deal, however, with his country's greatest problem and even today all major sectors of the Dominican economy are controlled by US interests.

CHE GUEVARA IN BOLIVIA

Ernesto Guevara de la Serna, to be known to history as Che Guevara, was born in Rosario in Argentina in 1928, the son of a well-to-do Argentine family of part-Irish extraction. From the age of two onwards he suffered severely from asthma, a fact which led him to be declared medically unfit for military service at the age of 18. Despite this, he was a keen sportsman and played scrum-half in his local rugby team. He does not seem to have taken an active part in either pro- or anti-Peronist activities, although his parents were deeply involved in the latter. At 19 he went to university to study medicine, and whilst a student travelled extensively both in his native Argentina and more widely in Latin America. This early experience of the rest of the continent helps explain his decision, when he qualified in 1953, to leave Argentina for Bolivia, intending to make his way to a Peruvian leper colony. Instead, then at the height of its radicalism he stayed to watch the Bolivian Revolution. Disappointed with what he saw as the slowness and conservatism of the Bolivian land distribution plans, he hitched a lift (on a United Fruit Company banana boat!) to Guatemala, which he saw as the alternative hope for the future.

Hardly had he arrived there in 1954, however, than the CIA-sponsored insurrection against the government began. The young Guevara took part in trying to organize resistance but, having failed, took refuge, in the time-honoured Latin American fashion, in the safety of the Argentine Embassy, where he stayed for two months before being allowed to leave the country.

It was therefore in Mexico City in 1955 that his future wife, Hilda Gadea, introduced him to a pair of Cuban exiles who were planning to overthrow the dictator Batista and were looking for a doctor for their expedition. The Cubans referred to him as 'el Che' ('the Argentine' – from the national tendency to use the term 'che' – literally 'mate' – in conversation as an endearment of sorts) and the nickname stuck. As we have already seen, their landing was opposed and only 12 survived to reach the mountains of the Sierra Maestra; in consequence all had to fight and Che Guevara, feeling that this was where his real skill lay, soon found himself in command of a column and subsequently second-in-command to Fidel Castro himself. With the collapse of the dictatorship and the emergence of the provisional government, therefore, he was a natural choice for a key ministerial post, and was given first the post of head of the National Bank (in which capacity his brief signature 'Che' appeared on the banknotes) and then the key job of managing the industrialization of his new country. His grateful colleagues also accorded him the unusual honour of decreeing him a Cuban citizen by birth.

Radicalized by his earlier experiences, Guevara, whose ministerial post took him to the Soviet Union in search of support, was chief among those who argued for the alliance with the Soviet Union that was consolidated by the Bay of Pigs fiasco. His many published statements do not, however, suggest that he was a communist in any sense before July 1960, or even that he had any profound understanding of communism at any time. He recorded his personal account of the struggle in the Sierra Maestra, later published in book form as *Reminiscences of the Cuban Revolutionary War*, but these show no ideological tint. Another series of articles, published in book form as *La guerra de guerrillas* (Guerrilla warfare), gave a practical guide to other revolutionaries. Conspicuously these articles do not recommend a reading of Marx, Lenin or Mao Tse-tung, rather the biographies of heroes of the past. Three fateful conclusions emerge in these works: that popular forces could defeat an army that it was not necessary to wait for the conditions to be right to start a revolution, the revolution could create its own conditions; that the countryside was the natural scene for fighting in Latin America. This theory, later called *foquismo* after its insistence on the paramount importance of the revolutionary group or 'focus' (*foco* in Spanish), helped sustain the wave of guerrilla movements that spread out in a great arc from Guatemala to northeast Brazil in the early 1960s.

But as Cuba was increasingly isolated, and his earlier enthusiasm for the task of industrialization was replaced by the dull routine of management, Guevara himself became impatient. Always a man of action, he was eager to play again a practical role in the revolutionary struggle. Like Castro himself, he hoped for nothing less than a tricontinental alliance of the emerging Third World against the capitalist countries. Even as a minister he had prepared the way by supporting the anti-colonial struggle against the former colonial powers, and, to the irritation of the Soviet government, denounced publicly Soviet policies of gradualism. He travelled to the former French Congo (then called Congo-Brazzaville to distinguish it from the former Belgian Congo, now Zaire), but failed to establish a satisfactory rapport with its Marxist rulers. Hence he returned to Cuba, and, after a period of reflection and preparation, formally renounced his Cuban citizenship, wrote a farewell letter to his parents asking them for their blessing, and, disguised as a Uruguayan businessman, beardless and with his distinctive hair shaved to simulate baldness, travelled by a roundabout route to Santa Cruz de la Sierra to set up a guerrilla focus in the Andes at a place called Ñancahuazú in the Department of Chuquisaca near Camiri in southern Bolivia. Within a few months his small group had been located and destroyed and Guevara himself, wounded and captured in a battle with Bolivian rangers at Quebrada del Yuro, was taken to the nearby town of Higueras and shot on 9 October 1967 on the orders of the Bolivian High Command.

Already a legend in his own lifetime, the brooding bearded figure of Guevara was displayed on posters and the slogan 'Che lives' scrawled on walls in Europe and North America as inspiration for the events of May 1968 in France and the student revolt in Berkeley, California. Even at the time, however, it was clear that the Bolivian expedition had been a fiasco. The expedition itself was badly planned and almost everything that could have gone wrong did. To begin with the choice of Bolivia for the scene of a peasant rising took no account of the fact that the Bolivian Revolution of 1952 had at least been partially successful. The Indian peasants did not have much land, but they did have some, and they were distrustful of promises; particularly so when they came from bearded strangers who were obviously foreign and to them represented not friends but the conquistadores who had taken their lands in the first place. The expedition had, it must be said, at least recognized the importance of learning the Indians' own language, and had studied Quechua; it was unfortunate, to say no more, that they then set up base in an area that spoke Guaraní. It was not the place that Guevara would have chosen, being of secondary strategic importance, and worse, it was short of animal life and fish that could have provided food.

From then on problems multiplied. The first attack was launched by an impatient subordinate before the group was properly ready, thus alerting the Bolivians to their presence. Attempts to link up with the Bolivian revolutionary elements foundered on Guevara's insistence that he, and not the leader of the Bolivian Communist Party (PCB), Luis Monje, must lead the uprising. Instead the group received a visit from the by-now world-famous figure of Régis Debray, popularizer of the *foco* theory in his *Revolution in the Revolution?* (published in Havana in 1967). Debray, referred to in the guerrillas' communications under the transparent incognito of 'Danton', fell into the hands of the Bolivians on the way home, creating a *cause célèbre* but more importantly, confirming that it was indeed Guevara himself that he had been to see. The guerrillas themselves were no more careful about security; they seem to have had an unprecedented enthusiasm for photographing one another and, when under pressure, buried the photographs together with other incriminating evidence under a large rock, where it was unearthed by the Bolivians. Among other figures whom they were able to identify was the ambiguous 'Tania la guerrillera', a double agent for both Cuba and her native East Germany, whose unwise habit of wearing a white shirt in the jungle made her a perfect target. Given this catalogue of absurdities, it was a fitting measure of the stupidity of Guevara's captors (among whom there is evidence there were agents of the CIA) to kill him and thus turn him into a martyr.

For the ultimate irony of Guevara's expedition was that it proved the unreliability of his basic propositions. Popular forces can win against a regular army, but only if that army is demoralized and unwilling to fight, and that seldom happens. The example of insurrection can create support, but publicity makes the insurgents vulnerable, and in an age of aircraft and radio insurgents can no longer count on mere remoteness for their safety. The countryside is not the natural arena for fighting in Latin America; most Latin Americans live in towns, and the key to political power remains the control of the national capital. Debray, in the article which brought him his initial fame, 'Castroism: the Long March of Latin America', had already demonstrated how with the occupation of the Bolivian tin mines in 1965 Barrientos had effectively blocked access to the traditional base of support that had made the 1952 revolution possible. But it seems that Guevara failed to understand the warning and compounded it by refusing to work with the PCB. Lastly, it appears that Castro's attitude towards the exercise was ambiguous; that he was glad to have his rival out of the way and was too cautious to compromise his own position by giving him effective help.

MEXICO: THE YEARS OF GROWTH

The one country that consistently maintained its position against the United States and refused to break off relations with Cuba was Mexico. In the post-war period Mexico had evolved into a state dominated by a single ruling party whose claim to have brought about a true social revolution was backed by the evidence of a fast growing economy. Between 1940 and 1975 it was Mexico's economic success and prosperity above all that made its government stable and confident.

This position had not come easily. As late as 1938 Cárdenas had been confronted by a military revolt in the north. The revolt was premature and the troops involved easily located by 'spotter' aircraft and dispersed. In 1940 the election of the official candidate, General Manuel Avila Camacho, was hotly disputed by the 'charismatic General Almazán, who had fascist support, and there was considerable violence. But as war approached, old enmities were overshadowed. In 1942 the sinking of a Mexican oil tanker, the *Potrero del Llano*, brought Mexico into the war as an ally of the United States; much to the surprise of many rural Mexicans, who expected to find themselves once again fighting the hated *gringos*. Mexico's new position as a bastion of democracy was confirmed at the war's end when in 1946 a civilian, Miguel Alemán Valdes, was chosen as the new President and the armed forces lost their special position within the ruling party, now renamed the Party of the Institutionalized Revolution (PRI).

Alemán represented the new industrial interests that were emerging in post-Revolutionary Mexico, and his six-year term (*sexenio*) was above all devoted to growth, leading under his successor to a reaction against corruption and waste. Growth, however, continued, and the debate about how it was to be used intensified. Whether by accident or design, in 1958 the Party turned to the left with the choice for the Presidency of Adolfo López Mateos, who as Secretary of Labour had won the confidence of the unions, and as President went on to distribute some 17 million hectares of land, more than any president except Cárdenas himself. The myth of the Revolution was boosted just when it might have otherwise been most vulnerable to the challenge from Cuba, and the 1964 election was another triumph for the Party, though the nominee, Gustavo Díaz Ordaz, the Secretary of Gobernación (Interior) was a colourless bureaucrat almost unknown to the public before his nomination.

The PRI, with its claim to represent the authentic revolutionary tradition, had thus far proved fairly immune to challenge from the Left. The fact, unique in Latin America, that the major opposition to it had since 1940 come from a pro-Catholic, right-wing party was an obvious advantage. But the arrest and imprisonment of the railway workers' leader, Demetrio Vallejo, in 1959, had already served as a reminder that the government was also prepared to use force to maintain its position, though hitherto in a rather cautious and subtle fashion. Faced in 1968 with major student demonstrations within weeks of the start of the Olympic Games, panic set in. Troops positioned on all sides fired upon a peaceful gathering of students outside the Politécnico in the Plaza de las Tres Culturas in the suburb of Tlatelolco and when the firing stopped, 217 lay dead and many more activists had been rounded up and arrested. Public opinion was stunned into acceptance, and when no further unrest occurred, the student leaders were released.

The crisis of the 1970s was economic rather than political, and it took the form it did at least partly because of the character of Luis Echeverría Alvarez (President, 1970–76). Like his predecessor, and three successors, he was chosen as candidate by the incumbent President, the 'Grand Elector', and like them he was a career bureaucrat who had worked all his life within the Party and never run previously for elective office. Early in his term of office, it began to be realized that at deep levels, under the existing oil fields of the Isthmus, there lay deposits much bigger and much richer than anything previously dreamt of. These discoveries coincided with the first oil shock of 1973–74, and the fatal decision was taken, in advance of the development of the oil fields, to embark on a vast programme of economic growth. Both Echeverría himself, and his successor Gustavo López Portillo (President, 1976–82) were to become very rich in consequence. But Echeverría had wider ambitions, and his defiance of the United States, though it won him three votes in the election for Secretary General of the United Nations, helped accelerate the economic crisis. In 1975 Mexico had to devalue the peso for the first time since 1954. Echeverría responded with a well-publicized expropriation of some large estates and the opposition failed to mount a credible challenge. In the euphoria López Portillo, an old childhood friend of the President, was elected virtually unopposed.

From then on, matters began to get thoroughly out of hand. Plans to develop the great southern gas fields depended on finding a market in the United States, but though President Carter was prepared to visit Mexico, his Administration was not prepared to pay the price the Mexicans were demanding. Mexican industry was not able to cope with the flood of new money, and much was wasted; as in the Alemán years, rumours began to circulate about huge projects for which money had been paid but of which no concrete evidence existed. In 1982, when the oil price fell sharply, the truth emerged. Mexico was bankrupt, owing nearly US $100 billion to its creditors.

Rising opposition in the 1982 election was overridden by the Party, and despite reports in the US press of corruption and ballot-stuffing in the north (where the opposition PAN surprisingly failed to win a single seat), the Finance Minister, Miguel de la Madrid Hurtado, was elected. His *sexenio* was a story of a series of desperate expedients to stave off complete financial collapse. With a population of over 80 millions (Mexico is now the largest Spanish-speaking country in the world) the threat of social unrest could no longer be ignored. As his Finance Minister put it, 'The trouble with asking Mexicans to tighten their belts is that so many of them have no belts to tighten'. When a devastating earthquake struck the capital in 1976 it demonstrated cruelly how the foundations of the regime had literally been undermined. While the remaining colonial buildings withstood the shock, modern hospitals collapsed like piles of playing cards because vital reinforcing members were missing and concrete was of substandard quality. Out of the mass demonstrations of the homeless there emerged from within the ruling party a new challenge, the Corriente Democrática (Democratic Current), calling for free, competitive elections and a new deal for the masses. In 1988, reformed as an official opposition party under the leadership of Cuauhtémoc Cárdenas, it presented a strong challenge, but official figures still showed a narrow majority for the ruling PRI and its candidate, the Harvard-trained economist Carlos Salinas de Gortari.

URBAN GUERRILLAS: THE TUPAMAROS IN URUGUAY

Uruguay for much of the twentieth century bore the reputation of a small haven of political tranquillity and democracy surrounded by the turmoil and dictatorship of its neighbours. It was 'the Switzerland of South America'. Much of this image rested on the dual legacy of Batlle, 'coparticipation' and extensive public welfare, as well it might since his reforms reflected the profound impression Switzerland had made on Batlle during his visit to that country. Nevertheless, these aspects of Uruguayan politics were never as unproblematic as they appeared to external observers and they have each contributed to the break-down of democracy in the long term.

The 1917 Pact of the Eight between the Colorado and Blanco parties was institutionalized in the 1918 Constitution which established a two-part executive. The Presidency remained, though with limited functions primarily concerned with foreign policy but also with internal order. Alongside the President, a National Council of government was created to perform most state functions. This body was to comprise nine members, six from the party winning the greater share of the popular vote, and three from the party that came second. Whilst this system was widely regarded as very progressive and democratic, it could, and perhaps should, also have been seen as a technical device for dividing the political spoils and limiting them to the traditional contenders for power. As such it reflects the Latin American corporatist tradition and the strong bureaucratic streak which characterizes the nations of the continent, not least Uruguay. As a constitutional spoils system, the dual executive might have been expected to reinforce clientelist politics – that is, the bringing of party supporters into paid government positions – and that is precisely what it did. During the 1920s the state bureaucracy increased by 50 per cent and by 1933 public employment consumed almost two-thirds of the national budget.

The Depression hit hard at Uruguayan prosperity, but the 1930s illustrate more clearly the problems of political democracy rather than, as yet, those of public welfare. In 1933, Colorado President Gabriel Terra dissolved Congress and assumed dictatorial powers. Ex-President Baltasar Brum, then serving as President of the National

Council was so despondent that he committed suicide. The following year Terra ensured that the 1918 Constitution was amended so that the collegial system continued to guarantee both main parties their share of ministerial posts, but only one faction from each of the parties could in future hold office at a time. As the 1938 elections approached, President Terra and the opposition (Blanco) leader, Dr Luis Alberto de Herrera, engineered the passage of legislation which prevented other factions of their parties forming an electoral coalition against them. Terra generously ensured that Colorado voters had a choice between two of his relatives as prospective Presidential candidates, and the elections were actually won by his brother-in-law, General Alfredo Baldomir.

It was, however, the protracted period of economic stagnation of the 1950s which caused not only disillusionment with political parties but also with the bureaucratic state itself. The high costs of Uruguayan public welfare, the untenable burden of the huge public sector (it is said that at one time the Uruguayan state airline, PLUNA, employed more than 1000 people and yet had only one aircraft in service) and the colossal number of old age pensioners, in particular, combined with low growth and negative trade balances to feed inflation. Uruguay remained a predominantly agricultural country dependent on beef exports for the bulk of its revenue, and after the prosperous years of the war the long decline was hard to accept. Falling urban living standards were taken as indicative of the state's failure to provide opportunities for mobility. Urban disillusionment coalesced with rural disaffection to enable the Blancos, now renamed the National Party, to win the 1958 elections after 93 years in opposition.

In 1951 by referendum Batlle's dream had been finally realized when the Presidency had been abolished altogether. The Nationalist victory, therefore, brought no dramatic change, the country's economic problems continued into the 1960s, and in 1966 the Nationalists were defeated. The *Colegiado* system was blamed for the national crisis. Another referendum restored the Presidency, which went to a General, Oscar Gestido, who, quite improbably in a Mediterranean-style country where there is no land higher than 2000 feet, had won his reputation as ski champion; a year later he died and was succeeded by his Vice-President, an ex-boxer called Jorge Pacheco Areco.

Meanwhile dissent had been growing outside formal political channels, most notably in the form of the urban guerrilla Movement for National Liberation. This movement, generally known as the

Tupamaros (from the name of Tupac Amaru, the Incan hero of eighteenth-century Peru), was first organized in 1962, but initially the leftist intellectuals who comprised the loose organization confined their activities to the organization of manual labourers. In 1965 they turned to violence, bombing the offices of North American companies in Montevideo. By the end of the 1960s they were a force to be reckoned with and in 1971 the government called in the Army to eliminate the guerrilla threat. The atmosphere of political violence that pervaded Montevideo, and the declining economic fortunes of the country, led to the emigration of thousands of middle-class families who had previously depended on the state for their liveiihood. Most went to Argentina though almost anywhere would do; there were long queues for passports at the Foreign Ministry and the graffiti at Carrasco Airport read: 'The last person to leave should turn off the light'. In this chaos, the apparently unthinkable happened. The Uruguayan Army, which had not intervened in politics during the twentieth century despite unconstitutional behaviour by civilians (in 1933, and again in 1942, when Baldomir postponed elections), took effective control of the government.

The Tupamaros contributed to the military intervention, not only by their illegal activities, but also by their parallel programme of seeking to discredit civilian politicians. It was not so much their publication of photographs of President Pacheco shaving while naked that caused him embarrassment, but rather the publication of his tax returns. Charges of corruption levelled at key public figures were further supported by evidence, and the military took up these accusations. In return, civilian politicians, particularly those of the less tarnished National Party, made similar charges against the military itself. The police were discredited by the way in which they had panicked and abused their powers, and one of the few casualties of the Tupamaro campaign was a US citizen, Dan Mitrione, whom the Tupamaros accused of having been sent to Uruguay to instruct the police in the techniques of torture they and the armed forces were soon using as a matter of course. Congress displayed a rare unity in opposing military attacks on the integrity of Uruguayan politicians in general, and thus the armed forces became locked into an intensive conflict over relative morality and status with civilians from the traditional political parties. Having been called into the political arena by President Pacheco in 1971 to deal with the Tupamaros, the military had found a political cause. They were doing battle with the Left in a much wider sense than simply responding to the emergency.

The Uruguayan Army at that time was large for the size of the national population: some 20 000 men. Like other Latin American military establishments it was essentially underemployed, with a top-heavy officer corps and a large number of relatively young retired officers who needed jobs and so were active in the political parties. During the 1960s pay and privileges had improved markedly, as substantial military aid flowed in from the United States, but privileges in particular were increasingly subject to criticism by civilian politicians. However, in 1972 President Juan María Bordaberry declared a state of siege in response to the guerrilla threat and during this military pay was doubled. Although by the end of the year the Tupamaros had been contained, factions within the armed forces favoured further political intervention; some along the nationalist and reformist lines exhibited in Peru, but the dominant tendency favoured the Brazilian model and received warm encouragement from the Brazilian military. What enabled these two factions to come together – and it took a full six months for preparations for their coup to come to fruition – lay outside the military institution in the bureaucratic, fragmented civilian power vacuum created by the traditional political parties.

The splintering of the two main political parties and an electoral system which gave the Presidency to the most popular faction of the most popular party, had in Bordaberry elevated a man much less popular than his Blanco rival. Jointly the Left and the National Party easily outnumbered Bordaberry's supporters in Congress. It was not even clear that Bordaberry had as much support in his own party as might be expected. Whilst the Colorados have traditionally represented the urban middle class, and the Blancos rural landowners, other conservative groups and the lower orders, Bordaberry, a Colorado, was from the conservative, landowning élite. The President therefore keenly felt his isolation, not only from the people and the legislature, but also from his own party. Nor was he a man whose democratic principles were so firm that they overcame his sense of personal vulnerability. He had been a fascist in his youth and a long-standing admirer of the Spanish dictator Franco.

Thus in a Presidential system with the President himself in effect promoting a coup against his own government, it was very difficult for any civilian group to resist the intervention of the armed forces. From June 1973 when Congress was closed by Bordaberry, though a civilian president nominally held office, Uruguay was effectively governed by a military junta.

The new society the military sought was to be vertically ordered and corporatist in character. Like the national security regimes in Brazil and, later, Argentina (see chapter 5), the military stressed security and set about eliminating every trace of 'leftist subversion', especially in the trade unions and the political parties. Soon Uruguay, once a haven of democracy, had more political prisoners per head of population than any other country in the world. Though relatively few 'disappeared', many were tortured. Society was to be depoliticized and traditional moral values restored. Like Brazil, whose influence became paramount, the country was thrown open to foreign capital, though without much success.

In 1976 Bordaberry was forced to resign. He had come to think that he was indispensable to the country, but the armed forces had other ideas. A new civilian figurehead was co-opted and the same style of government maintained until 1980, when the armed forces put to a referendum of the people a new constitution that would have enshrined the leading role of the armed forces permanently. To their surprise, the people voted it down. Hence in September 1981 Lieutenant General Gregorio Alvarez Armellino was chosen as president by the junta. Already increasing economic problems signalled, as they did elsewhere in the region, that the armed forces had not achieved the economic development they had promised. Hence, when in 1982 some political party activity was again permitted as a prelude to elections in 1984, opposition rapidly mounted and the regime again clamped down in 1983. The Blanco leader Wilson Ferreira Aldunate was arrested as he returned from exile, and with him in custody the armed forces were able to achieve both a dignified retreat to barracks and a controlled hand-over of power through a pact with political 'moderates'. Under this, civilian politics were restored and Julio María Sanguinetti of the Colorado Party was elected and took office as President in 1984, though with less than third of the popular vote.

Uruguay is a unique case of a country in which armed insurgency was able to result in the fall of an old and well-established political democracy, but where the determination of the people not to accept the domination of the armed forces was ultimately successful in obtaining the restoration of democratic government under the civilian leadership of a Blanco, Luis Alberto Lacalle. Although the 1989 plebiscite on the military amnesty shows that the Uruguayans do not have sufficient confidence in their new democracy to test it by putting the armed forces on trial, in the cases to be discussed in the next chapter, democracy was much less secure and the restoration of civilian rule much more problematic.

1a. Bolivian tin miners at Potosi – most die before the age of 30 (*Tony Morrison, Camera Press*).

1b. Easter fair at Ayacucho, Peru (*Patrick Knight, Camera Press*).

Emiliano Zapata, Mexican revolutionary leader, 1913 (*Reuter*).

2b. Getúlio Vargas, President of Brazil, 193 45 and 1950–54 (*Camera Press*).

2c. General Alfredo Stroessner, President of Paraguay, 1954–89 (*Diego Goldberg, Camera Press*).

3. President Juan D. Perón of Argentina and his second wife, 'Evita', 1948 (*Popperfoto*).

4a. Members of 'Papa Doc' Duvalier's notorious 'Tontons Macoutes' with their chief, Mme. Adolphe, wife of the Minister of Health (*Guido Mangold, Camera Press*).

4b. Pentagon reconnaissance photograph of ballistic missile site in Cuba, October 1962 (*Popperfoto*).

5. Brazilian Indians with armadillo (*Popperfoto*).

6. Young Sandinista soldier (*Pier Cavendish, Camera Press*).

7a. Two Nicaraguan poets: President Daniel Ortega with Minister of Culture, Fr. Ernesto Cardenal, 1986 (*Louis Dematteis, Reuter*).

7b. Education has become a priority in Sandinista Nicaragua (*ADN-Zentralbild Berlin/GDR*).

8. Chilean Army Chaplain celebrates Mass for the Junta at Bernardo O'Higgins Military Academy, Santiago, 1974 (*Diego Goldberg, Camera Press*).

5 The Military and Development

THE SPREAD OF DICTATORIAL GOVERNMENT

The attempted kidnapping and killing of US Ambassador Gordon Mein in Guatemala in 1967 heralded an outbreak of urban violence which took many forms: bombings, political assassination, hijacking of aircraft and kidnappings. The choice of diplomats and executives of transnational corporations for kidnapping and ransom demands was no accident; the Left saw the political systems of Latin American countries as integrated with and hence sustained by the world capitalist system, led by the United States. This rise of urban terrorism in Latin America, coupled with the emergence of left-wing governments in Peru, Bolivia and Chile, formed the pretext for changes that in the 1970s led to the emergence of a new wave of military governments in Latin America.

There was, however, a substantial difference between these governments and the traditional rule by generals. First of all, military rule was not seen as temporary. The purpose of military rule was, its proponents believed, to stay in power as long as might be necessary to obtain its objectives. Secondly, the objectives were themselves different. The aim was not simply to put right the 'incorrect' results of an election, or to reverse a previous military coup, but to eradicate as far as possible the entire basis for left-wing power, and it was based on a set of ideas commonly called 'national security ideology' – the belief, strengthened in military circles by the effect of contact with US military personnel, that national security was threatened by the spread of revolutionary ideas that ran contrary to the values of Western Christian civilization, and that any means were justified in countering the threat. The governments themselves differed substantially according to the circumstances in which they came to power and the way in which they operated, but they had one common factor: the realization that economic development was the key to power.

This pattern of economic development led by the armed forces the Argentine writer Guillermo O'Donnell has termed 'bureaucratic authoritarianism'. Insofar as the armed forces, being salaried state employees, are 'armed bureaucrats' this term is an attractive one, but it fails in itself to emphasize sufficiently the distinctive characteristic of the phenomenon, its belief in authoritarian government as a necessary condition for economic development. For that reason the term 'military developmentalism' is preferred here; an ugly phrase for an ugly thing.

ARGENTINA AFTER PERON

The ousting of Perón in September 1955, known by anti-Peronistas as the 'Liberating Revolution', was followed by a brief period of Catholic Nationalist military government, which sought to re-integrate Peronism into Argentine politics. The replacement soon afterwards of General Lonardi by General Aramburu as president, however, expressed the underlying dominance of hard-line anti-Peronists. They sought to demobilize labour and to keep it demobilized. Peronist resistance (*la resistencia*) to incursions into areas in which labour had gained under Perón was impressive, but behind it the nature of industrialization itself was changing from the mid-1950s in a manner that would in itself reduce the influence of organized labour. Foreign involvement in the economy encouraged by the internationalist orientation of the Aramburu government further enhanced the power of capital as against labour, as medium-sized manufacturing enterprises increasingly yielded to big business.

This process continued under the Radical government of Arturo Frondizi, who, despite making overtures to Peronism, presided over the acceleration of the demobilization of rank-and-file labour and the growth of union bureaucracy; features which were to last until the end of the 1960s and would be supportive of the institution of direct military rule in 1966. The three civilian governments of the later 1950s and early 1960s were marked by political and economic crises, and survived at the discretion of the military, which itself experienced political in-fighting which probably delayed the return to military rule. A stagnating economy with relatively slow growth, compared to the great economic successes temporarily being registered elsewhere in Latin America, massive budget deficits and economic drift based on an absence of purpose, reflected Argentina's lack of a clear identity. Inflation, unemployment and flight of capital, all co-existed with political problems primarily associated with the persistence of Peronism. Yet they also expressed the underlying disunity of the fragmented party system. By June 1966, with organized labour divided, pressures from business interests rising, and compromise between competing military factions temporarily achieved, General Juan Carlos Onganía assumed power in a bloodless coup against the ineffectual civilian government of the Radical, Dr Arturo Illia; a coup which supporters termed 'the Argentine Revolution'. Onganía dissolved Congress and the provincial legislatures. The Supreme Court ceased to operate. All political parties were suspended. Police powers as well as military ones were enhanced in the political sphere and political arrests occurred as individual rights were disregarded. State violence increased, especially in the purging of the universities to eliminate the student base of Peronism. Manifestations of youthful 'decadence' were given military treatment; soldiers patrolled the streets administering compulsory haircuts to young men whose hair, in the generally prevailing fashion, was deemed too long. In the economic sphere, on the other hand, the watchword was 'rationalisation', resulting in the further opening of Argentina to foreign capital penetration. Measures taken under this head included reductions in overmanning of public utilities, removal of rent and price controls but control of wages and salaries, and a credit squeeze which hit nationally-owned, small to medium-sized enterprises particularly hard. Thus the Onganí regime succeeded in alienating many members of the middle class, whether salaried or self-employed, and not just organized labour. Labour resistance became more apparent towards the end of the decade. More seriously, so did the activities of guerrilla groups, and not only Onganía, but the continuance of military rule itself was challenged by an increasing number of assassinations of union leaders and of military officers by the Montoneros (Peronist guerrillas). The beginning of the end of military rule, however, was marked explicitly by a popular rising in Córdoba in 1969. Although the origins of the rebellion seem minor now, a rise in student refectory prices bringing the student population of the city onto the streets and a change in Saturday working (the abolition of the full day's pay for a half day's work termed the 'English Saturday' in Argentina) having the same effect among car workers, the city was beyond the control of the military authorities for some hours. Known as the Cordobazo (the blow of Córdoba), the rising was suppressed by force but key elements in the Army took note and sought to control the forces of change.

Hence Onganía was replaced in 1970 by General Levingston, a man so unknown to the general public that his photograph had to be displayed to show them what he looked like. He was a front for the senior General Lanusse, who assumed power in his own right the following year. He did so to oversee what he had come to realize was inevitable, the restoration of civilian government and the eventual return of Perón from almost two decades of exile in Madrid. Perón himself being prevented by residence qualifications from standing as a candidate, in March 1973 a left-wing Peronist, Dr Héctor Cámpora, won the Presidential elections. Within months, with Lanusse safely out of the way after a curious apology to the people of Argentina for his unconstitutional behaviour, Cámpora in turn (reluctantly, it is said) stood down in favour of his leader. Perón returned by air on 20 June, but the triumph his supporters had planned turned to disaster as rival factions fired on one another and there were many deaths, the road from Ezeiza International Airport being strewn with their bodies. The plane carrying Perón had been diverted elsewhere. Though in September of that year Perón was elected with some 61 per cent of the popular vote, it was already ominously clear that the violence unleashed was going to be too much for him to control.

Guerrilla action was escalating when Perón's death on 1 July 1974 removed the last vestiges of control. His successor was his Vice-President and third wife, María Estela Martínez de Perón, known as 'Isabel', whom he had met when she was a dancer in Panama and had hired to type his political testament, *Force is the Reason of Beasts*. Inexperienced as she was in practical politics, Isabel, as her husband had done some years before, soon fell under the influence of an *éminence grise*, José López Rega, a mystic and it was said a sorcerer (as witness his nickname 'el Brujo'), who moved the administration sharply to the right. From his Ministry of Social Welfare, López Rega controlled a paramilitary organization, the right-wing Argentine Anti-Communist Alliance (AAA), which provided 'death squads' for the elimination of 'terrorists' and was to provide the infrastructure and the ideological justification for the military to do the same in due course.

By March 1976 the economic incompetence of the Peronist government, especially its half-hearted attempts to appease in turn various sectoral demands, had led to hyperinflation. Worse still from a purely economic point of view, increasing alienation accelerated the use of bombings, kidnappings and murders against businessmen and business targets, especially foreign-owned companies. Terrorist attacks and paramilitary shootings became generalized and added to the chaos and disorder. Arguments continue about which came first: leftist subversion or rightist violence. It does not really matter since the overall effect was the same. Economic chaos and political disorder therefore formed both the cause and the justification for the seizure and detention of Mrs Perón and the installation of a new military government under the austere Commander-in-Chief of the Army General Jorge Videla.

Isabel Perón was seized as she left the Casa Rosada (the Presidential office building at the northern end of the Plaza de Mayo in Buenos Aires) to return to the Presidential residence in the pleasant suburb of Olivos. Initially she was imprisoned in the south of the country before being returned under house arrest to the *quinta* she had shared with her late husband in the southern suburb of San Vicente. There she remained until her release in 1981, when she went into exile in Madrid. During her exile and through the early period of democratic government under the Radicals she remained titular head of the Peronist movement. The realization that her occasional presence in Argentina cost the Peronists thousands of potential supporters in reminding the electorate of the chaos over which her government had presided, belatedly led in 1986 to her being replaced as leader of the movement.

The 1976 regime, like the 1966–73 one, but unlike previous Argentine military governments, saw itself as holding power for the foreseeable future. It was not to be a transitional arrangement which would presage the election of a new, more acceptable civilian government, but a permanent one, which would stay in place to preside over nothing less than the total reorganization of civil society to expunge communism and other features deemed contrary to the Western way of life. This Process of National Reorganization (usually known simply as 'the Process') was to penetrate all aspects of Argentine society, beginning in the schools and universities. Teachers were once more purged, subversive (and not-so-subversive) books were burnt, artists were proscribed and driven into exile, formal political channels were closed down and, most notoriously, a wholesale counter-terror was unleashed on all suspected of being left-wing or having left-wing sympathies. Estimates of the number who perished in the first two years of what became known as 'the Dirty War' (la guerra sucia) fluctuated wildly at the time, but it is now known that some 9000 were killed and it is all but certain that the real figure was over 15 000. Many of those who were rounded up, tortured and 'disappeared', it is certain, had no left-wing credentials. Friends and relations, seized on suspicion, also died, some children on the argument that since their elder brothers and sisters were suspects, they too in time would grow up into 'subversives'. Women were seized, raped and tortured only because they were attractive, and the babies of some of the 'disappeared' were taken from their mothers at birth and given to military families.

The justification of this horror was that it would end subversion and make Argentina economically strong. However, the economic policies of the regime were disastrous and led to corruption on a scale even greater than anything that had gone before. Corruption was not confined to the looting of the property of 'subversives' and their families, nor to the labelling as 'subversive' of individuals whose property was desired, but it permeated all the economic dealings of the regime. As the economy was opened up to foreign capital, loans were sought for grandiose developmental schemes, and a substantial proportion of these funds disappeared into the pockets of both civilian contractors and their military contacts. The peso was deliberately allowed to become overvalued. This made the foreign loans seem cheap in the short term, but it also encouraged consumer imports and a frantic spending spree. At the first sign of trouble, then, domestic capital took fright and fled abroad to more secure financial markets.

By 1980 the 'Dirty War' had been 'won', but the economic crisis deepened and began to lead to bankruptcies. Videla, as promised, handed over power at the end of a five-year term to General Viola (1981), who was regarded as more moderate. But within months he in turn was displaced in a putsch by the hard-liner General Galtieri, who once in control of the junta engineered his own succession to the Presidency in December 1981 without, however, relinquishing command of the Army. Continuing economic problems at home, the reassertion of the influence of organized labour in large public demonstrations, and divisions in the officer corps now that any threat of subversion appeared to have been ended, had given Galtieri the opportunity to ally himself with fiercely nationalist elements in the Navy and Air Force. The invasion of the Falkland Islands (Islas Malvinas) in April 1982, and the subsequent defeat of Argentina by the British Task Force, brought about a more clear-cut abdication of power by the Argentine armed forces than was experienced in other Latin American countries. A period of transition during which the military destroyed evidence of their crimes and sought guarantees of their personal safety and that of the military institution, preceded an open, honest and relatively peaceful election which returned the Radicals to power and Dr Raúl Alfonsín to the Presidency.

MILITARY RULE IN BOLIVIA

For Bolivia, 1964 marked the reassertion of direct military rule after the protracted period of MNR government. An attempt at the assassination of General René Barrientos Ortuño, who had fought with Air Force elements on the side of the MNR rebels in 1952, encouraged the popular acclaim of this earthy, charismatic figure and led President Paz Estenssoro reluctantly to field him as his Vice-Presidential candidate for the 1964 elections. Paz retained power because the opposition parties boycotted these elections, but in November fell prey instead to the personal ambitions of his Vice-President, who led the coup against the MNR regime. For two years Barrientos ruled as joint President with a colleague, General Alfredo Ovando Candía; in 1966 he was elected in his own right.

Barrientos' popularity stemmed at least in part from the fact that he was the first President of Bolivia to speak Quechua, the mother tongue of many of its inhabitants. He also inherited the clientelist network established by the MNR and made many tours of the country distributing largesse in the forms of footballs, bicycles and other material goods. His regime was personalist, corrupt and chaotic, exhibiting the style associated with the traditional caudillo. His was not a tight institutional dictatorship of the kind set up in Brazil in 1964 and two years later in Argentina. The Barrientos regime was in foreign affairs pro-US, pro-foreign capital and anti-communist, but it did not develop the ideology of the national security state. The armed forces were expanded and their political role greatly enhanced, but collectively they never achieved even the level of unity associated with military interventions of the 1960s and 1970s elsewhere in Latin America. Repression was unsophisticated and arbitrary. Factionalism within the military institution was contained in the short-term by co-opting key factional leaders into government. Barrientos succeeded in retaining peasant support, though fewer people benefited from the redistribution of land then under the previous regime. His government was most criticized abroad because it was, as might have been expected, hostile to organized labour and to the political left. As early as 1965 Barrientos imposed a state of seige and used troops to dismantle the miners' militias, and to occupy the mines. Escalating state violence was also the order of the day against the increasing activity of guerrilla groups, notably that led in person by Che Guevara.

The death of Barrientos in 1969, when the helicopter he was piloting flew into power lines, led to a brief Vice-Presidential succession followed by a disparate series of corrupt and unstable military governments interspersed with brief civilian interludes. Despite the common institutional base of the military governments, they covered a wide spectrum of ideological positions. General Ovando, who served on his own briefly as President (1969–70) was a moderate reformist in the tradition established by the MNR. He was succeeded after a violent contest for power between rival military factions by General Juan José Torres González, whose radical ideology led him to seek Soviet aid, attack the US and mobilize organized labour. In so doing he stirred up centrist as well as right-wing civilian opposition and alienated many of his brother officers, preparing the way for the bloody coup that brought Colonel Hugo Banzer Suárez to power.

Banzer's own attempted coup earlier in the year had failed and its leader was imprisoned. The collapse of the Torres government in August 1971, however, led to his release. He proclaimed himself President and embarked on a further wave of violence against the political Left, especially students, who at that time were particularly suspect. Whilst civilian opposition was suppressed, opposition within the military was contained. Banzer had the support of Brazil, and, behind it, of the United States, following the Nixon-Kissinger policy of so-called 'benign neglect'. Further, some domestic civilian elements were behind him, most importantly among the agro-industrial sector, and some political factions, notably that of Paz himself. MNR supporters were given seats in Banzer's Cabinet in coalition with the right-wing Falange Socialista Boliviana (FSB).

Banzer had in fact been rapidly promoted under the MNR regime, becoming a full colonel at the age of 35. He was still only 44 when he became President. His relative youth and his US military training were reflected in the ideological character of his government, which had much more in common with the 'bureaucratic-authoritarian' regimes of Brazil and Argentina than the regime of his predecessor Barrientos, though this was because of the heavy and growing influence of Brazil, and Bolivia moved away from previously close relations with Argentina. Military rule was seen as a long-term necessity to be accompanied by depoliticization of the masses and modernization of the economy, especially by the expansion of education and the construction of roads. Although Soviet aid was retained, Banzer sought and obtained increased US financial assistance and opened up the Bolivian economy further to foreign capitalist penetration.

Massive devaluations of the peso in accordance with IMF requirements and removal of subsidies on basic goods and services led to high inflation and huge increases in the cost of living. Demonstrations were repressed and ugly stories of peasant massacres began to circulate. In November 1974 civilian elements were dismissed from the government and Paz was exiled. Economic problems were increasing; repression accelerated the development of internal opposition including that of the Church. National strikes in 1976 led the government to close the universities and made it clear that the successful repression of labour was no longer possible. President Carter's election in the United States added pressure on the question of human rights. In 1978, after the longest period in office of any Bolivian leader since Independence, Banzer held elections and so lost the power which on three occasions he has tried to regain by election. The elections were won by a civilian coalition called Democratic and Popular Unity (UDP), which again included Paz' breakaway faction of the MNR. General Juan Pereda Asbún, whom Banzer had placed in charge of the repressive Department of Political Order, annulled the elections and assumed office himself. Immediately he faced internal unrest and US pressure which increased until a left-wing coup of junior officers displaced him. The Army commander, General David Padilla Arancibia, became President, supported by the Left, with the stated intention of returning power to the civilians and allowing the military to return to the barracks. Bolivia's was the first of the military developmentalist regimes to decide to do so, but unfortunately it was not immediately to be successful.

Indecisive elections in July 1979 resulted in almost equal votes for the two old rivals of the MNR: Dr Siles Zuazo and Dr Paz Estenssoro. Congress too was divided and established instead an interim government under the President of the Senate, Walter Guevara Arze. Deeply suspect because of the role he was believed to have played in conveying the text of his namesake, Che Guevara's diaries to Havana, Guevara lacked support both in Congress and among the Army, and presided over a deepening political and economic crisis. Public unrest again met fierce military repression. Another coup led to the two-week Presidency of Colonel Alberto Natusch Busch, under whom soldiers ran amok in La Paz and as many Bolivians died in this brief military interregnum as in the whole seven years of General Banzer. In face of popular resistance, military commanders again allowed Congress to restore civilian government under interim rule of the MNR President of the Chamber of Deputies, Dr Lidia Gueiler Tejada.

Dr Gueiler, the second woman in the world (after Isabel Perón) to be chosen as an executive president, was an able leader who in happier times might have done very well. Instead she was faced with the same problem as her predecessors, a corrupt army deeply enmeshed in politics and unwilling to surrender its valuable personal and institutional privileges. In April 1980 she tried to break out of this constraint when she replaced the Army commander with her cousin, General

Luís García Meza. The following month the UDP again led in indecisive elections and Hernán Siles Zuazo was chosen as prospective President after tough congressional bargaining. But he was not to assume the office just yet. In June, Dr Gueiler survived a crude abortive coup through her prudence in locking her bedroom door and thus delaying the military conspirators for long enough to allow her to telephone for help. The following month, García Meza intervened, with the advice and encouragement of the Argentine Army, to prevent the succession of Siles. Political arrests and the exile of Siles were only the preludes to a regime even more repressive and economically disastrous than its predecessors, if fortunately short-lived. Those lucky enough to be released after being interrogated as suspected subversives by the García Meza regime reported to human rights organizations their identification of many of the officers involved in the repressive process as Argentines. Again the characteristic use of 'che' gave their national origins away. Labour leaders were tortured and killed, but passive resistance among workers was strong and divisions among the Bolivian officer corps were widened. With military encouragement, the growing of coca and the smuggling of cocaine was transformed into an illegal industry so widespread that it was impossible to eradicate and so vast that its turnover was believed to exceed that of the legal economy. Hence, the United States and other countries refused to recognize it, US opposition to the regime being based more, it seemed, on its opposition to narcotics than its desire to promote human rights.

A military junta under General Celso Torrelio Villa displaced García Meza in August 1981, but in turn yielded power to the Army Chief of Staff, who proved no more competent to deal with gathering economic catastrophe. Finally, the discrediting of military government in Argentina helped precipitate the move back to civilian government and in near desperation elections were brought forward and Siles inaugurated in October 1982. At last he was again to have the chance to show what he could do to put matters right. The problem was that for many years it had been too late, and in the meanwhile he had changed. In 1986, wholly discredited by economic failure, he was replaced in a free election by Dr Paz.

THE BRAZILIAN REVOLUTION

Following Vargas's suicide a series of brief constitutional, but non-elected presidents flitted across the stage before new elections took place. At one point, the situation became so chaotic that two separate military factions dispatched tanks to the Presidential palace. One of the factions was held back by the traffic. When they found their rivals already in possession, as John Gunther recalls in his *Inside South America*, 'the enemy crews then proceeded to play football together, using their tanks to mark the goals'.

In 1956, Dr Juscelino de Oliveira Kubitschek, who had won the elections rather unconvincingly on behalf of a coalition comprising the Labour Party and the Social Democratic Party, assumed the Presidency with João Goulart ('Jango') as his Vice-President despite military opposition to Goulart, whom they regarded as a dangerous left-winger. Kubitschek, born of Czech stock in Minas Gerais, and a medical doctor by training, was an unusual combination of dreamer and practical man. His most notable achievement in office was to fulfil a century-old dream and transfer the capital four hundred miles inland to a new city, Brasília, planned and built on a virgin site in the state of Goias. The new city, designed by architects Lúcio Costa and Oscar Niemeyer, in the shape of an arrow pointing towards the Brazilian interior, symbolizes the opening up of the heartland of the nation. Characteristically they did not design the houses of the people who were to live there; that was left to private enterprise. Kubitschek also built up the national car industry, but this further advance on the economic front was overshadowed by the high spending and corruption for which he was formally charged in 1964. It has been said of Kubitschek that he promised '50 years' progress in five' but delivered 40 years' inflation in four.

The 1960 elections returned to the Presidency another extraordinary character, the dynamic reforming governor of São Paulo, Jânio Quadros, his emblem a broom with which he would clean up government. João Goulart was again returned to the Vice-Presidency as representative of the Labour Party, on a separate ticket from the coalition of social democrats backing Quadros. Hence when after less than a year in office Quadros unexpectedly resigned in a fit of pique, he plunged the country into crisis. The Army resisted the succession of Goulart, and the President of the Chamber of Deputies became interim President while a formula was worked out allowing Goulart to take the Presidency only after the Constitution had been amended to create a new office of prime minister and so reduce Presidential powers. At a time of ideological polarization within Brazil, and following the Cuban Revolution, Goulart was associated more clearly with the political Left than perhaps his actions warranted. Like his brother-in-law, Leonel Brizola, then Governor of Rio Grande do Sul, Goulart was a nationalist and opposed US intervention in Brazil. He made promises of reforms, including agrarian reform, but was constrained in what he could do by the economic circumstances in which he had to operate. Brazil's development problems in the early 1960s remained much the same despite Kubitschek's expenditure on grand schemes. The interior was still underdeveloped; the nation lacked the essential infrastructure of roads and railways. Only some 5 per cent of potential arable land was under cultivation. Thus despite its massive economic potential, especially in terms of hydroelectric power, mineral and agricultural production, Brazilian GNP per head of population was low. Likewise, in human terms, social problems were immense. More than half of the population was under the age of 16, about half were illiterate, housing conditions in the *favelas* (shanty towns) around the major cities were appalling and the infant mortality rate remained colossal; this last reflecting the inadequacy of health services and the poor standard of public sanitation and water supply as well as the poverty of the population. Goulart's Presidency came at a time when increasing political and economic demands in consequence of the rapidly growing population coincided with a short recession. Between 1956 and 1963 the economy had grown at an annual rate of between 7 and 9 per cent, at the cost of accelerating inflation. When the recession came, inflation continued to rise, touching 1200 per cent per annum.

Declining support for the civilian regime was a natural consequence of falling income and the accompanying industrial unrest. Respect for political leaders was already low – as a gesture of contempt for the government in the local elections of 1962 many *Paulistas* (inhabitants of São Paulo) cast their votes for Cacareco, a favourite hippopotamus in the local zoo. Nevertheless, the following year Goulart was able to muster enough votes in a plebiscite to throw off the shackles the armed forces had fastened on him and to recover the Presidential powers lost in 1961. But Goulart's incompetence contributed to the worsening economic situation, not to say crisis, of 1963–64. The cost of living continued to spiral, the government deficit to widen. As capital left the country, US aid to Brazil was cut. The economic crisis was paralleled in the instability of government personnel and in Goulart's increasing inability to get Congress to agree to his proposals.

In September 1963 there took place in the new capital, Brasília, a revolt by several hundred NCOs and enlisted men in all three services. The President of the Chamber of Deputies was among the hostages taken by the rebels. Though the revolt was quickly suppressed, considerable fear was generated among right-wing politicians recognizing their own vulnerability and senior officers concerned to maintain military discipline. Goulart did not condemn the revolt and thus fed rightist fears that he would use the military for his own purposes at some future date. When in October Goulart asked Congress to approve the imposition of a state of siege to contain the wave of industrial unrest and political violence sweeping the nation, Congress refused and Goulart withdrew the request. The violence continued and many senior military officers began to believe that not only was military discipline threatened, but public order had actually broken down. In March 1964 Goulart brought matters to a head with a mass rally at which he decreed the nationalization of some private oil refineries, the expropriation of some underutilized land as well as the enfranchisement of illiterates. Brizola, then still a relatively youthful firebrand, also made a rousing speech in which he threatened the dissolution of Congress if it did not ratify these decrees. This was the signal the armed forces had been waiting for. Public opposition, already high, increased further with women marching in protest against Goulart's policies which they claimed were an attack on God and on the family. Senior officers, noting the President's clumsy attempt to win support among the Navy by giving them an aircraft carrier, were confirmed in their view that he and his brother-in-law were stirring up insubordination in the ranks. Matters came to a head in 1964 when a military revolt broke out in Minas Gerais in protest at the presence of what were vaguely referred to as 'communists' in the government. The governor of the state supported the revolt and Goulart ordered troops to put it down. In the confusion that followed it soon became clear that Goulart had in fact lost control of the Army and that key elements of it had moved over to support the rebels.

The coup that followed, subsequently termed 'the Brazilian Revolution', brought the Army Chief of Staff, General (later Marshal) Humberto Castello Branco, to the Presidency. An honest man, a hero of the wartime Expeditionary Force, and, within limits, a constitutionalist, he allowed Congress to 'elect' him initially to finish Goulart's term, and later to extend that term to 1967. The new government received the immediate good wishes of the Johnson Administration in the United States and in due course the restoration of US aid. The independent foreign policy of the early 1960s gave way to an unashamedly and uncritically pro-Western stance which would lead Brazil the following year to support US intervention in the Dominican

Republic. But the purpose of the high ranking military officers of the Higher War School (Escola Superior de Guerra – ESG) who had planned for such a takeover was not simply to depose a president, but to reconstruct Brazilian society, and the stresses soon showed. Though Congress continued to meet, the constitutionalism of the new regime was only formal and was ignored whenever it happened to be convenient. Most left-wing politicians were deprived of their political rights for a long period of years, and the number of political prisoners and exiles continued to mount as a series of purges occurred throughout the first year. Most ominously, within three months of the military coming to power, a new and formidable secret police organization was created. Responsible only to the President, the new organization, euphemistically termed the Servicio Nacional de Informações (SNI) was given a free hand in all matters of national security both internal and external. Not surprisingly it soon grew out of the control of the hard-liners of the ESG who had set it up. In the meanwhile, the military attempt to restore order inevitably meant a further concentration of power in the hands of the federal government and from the outset the states lost much of their autonomy. Then after the Social Democratic/Labour Party alliance did well in the elections of 1965, pressure from hard-liners within the government mounted and Castello Branco, despite his constitutional inclinations, became increasingly authoritarian. Existing political parties were abolished, elections were to be indirect only and Presidential authority was enhanced to include such powers as the power to annul elections. Realizing that the complete suppression of opinion could be danger-ous, however, in 1966 two new parties were brought into existence: the pro-government Aliança Renovadora Nacional or ARENA, and a small legal opposition party, the Brazilian Democratic Movement (MDB).

The new regime's economic policy was stabilizing in the short term and inflation was reduced. But the new regime had taken power with the intention of holding on to it for long enough to make Brazil economically strong and able to hold its own in the outside world, and inevitably this had other important economic effects. Taxation was reformed and public expenditure cut in most areas. Where state spending was increased, as, for example, in education, it was done in a fashion that increased rather than decreased inequality, since the additional funds were devoted mainly to the expansion of secondary and higher education in accord with the national plan to produce more skilled managers. The unequal distribution of income that characterized the period after 1964, moreover, had the conscious purpose of creating the kind of domestic market needed to encourage further economic growth in manufactured goods such as consumer durables. However, by 1967 little had been achieved. Brazil still had the largest foreign debt in the world. Nine-tenths of its foreign exchange earnings were still derived from agriculture, but since Goulart's measures had been revoked, land utilization was as inefficient as ever and food was still being imported. Industrial development was down and unemployment up.

The choice of General Artur Costa e Silva to succeed Castello Branco in 1967 represented a further victory for the hard-liners. Costa e Silva had played a leading part in the coup of 1964. Under the combined influence of the unrest of 1968 and the outbreak of urban terrorism in South America, the regime took a sharp turn to the right. In November 1968 what Brazilians term an 'internal coup' took place as the government assumed total control. The Fifth Institutional Act swept away the remaining vestiges of constitutional government and installed a frankly authoritarian regime, under which the SNI, the military intelligence organization which it had superseded, and other competing intelligence agencies sought out, tortured and occasionally assassinated real or suspected terrorists. When Costa e Silva died suddenly in 1969 his figurehead civilian Vice-President was not allowed to succeed him and his policies were continued by General Emilio Garrastasú Médici, the former head of the SNI, who served as President for a five-year term from 1969 to 1974.

When Médici left office the urban guerrilla threat, which had never been very serious, had been eliminated and repression had eased off. Meanwhile, between 1967 and 1974 Brazil had experienced its 'economic miracle', achieving average growth rates of between 11 and 13 per cent per annum. The miracle was, however, more apparent than real, for three reasons. The rates of growth were not really much greater than those achieved under the despised civilian regimes before 1964, yet they had been achieved at a much higher social cost in terms of deprivation and inequality. Brazil was still exporting only 5 per cent of its manufacturing output and by 1974, in response to the 'first oil shock', the slowdown had begun. Worst of all, as oil prices tripled overnight, Brazil was in the almost uniquely uncomfortable position of having no sources of oil of its own.

For the rest of the decade, therefore, successive military regimes tried to grapple with these unpalatable facts while using the declining threat from the revolutionary Left as an excuse for a very gradual process of 'decompression' (*distensão*). From a position of strength, the armed forces would slowly retreat to barracks over a period of many years, whilst retaining their ability to control the people and institutions they left behind, a process of liberalization but not of democratization. In practice the process proved much harder to control than they had imagined, as they had not reckoned with the irrepressible Brazilian urge for change. Both General Ernesto Geisel (1974–79) and his successor General João Baptista Figueiredo (1979–84) found themselves caught between civilians pressing for faster liberalization and hard-line military factions who did not want any opening (*abertura*) at all.

General Geisel, a Lutheran, tried to rule the world's largest Catholic country single-handed. Under his rule censorship was softened and political parties restored to legality. But even by the end of the 1970s, before the full effects of the 1979 oil shock had been felt, the 'miracle' had gone sour, and in face of increasing unrest repression was again tightened. General Figueiredo, a cavalry officer, tried to appear a man of the people, but the effect of a well-publicized walkabout in a supermarket was rather spoilt by his reported comment afterwards that he much preferred the smell of horses to the smell of people. He proved none too impressive at managing the economy either. The debt situation was already out of control, and the discovery of petroleum on the continental shelf some 100 km off Brazil's northeast coast came too late to help. In fact by the time either it or the military project to replace it altogether by distilling fuel alcohol from sugar cane was able to contribute significantly, the price of oil had again fallen. By 1982, therefore inflation was again over 100 per cent and labour unrest rising. Pressures for *abertura* led to the reintroduction of direct elections for governors of states in November 1982; the opposition won all the major governorships. In the following year, Brazil experienced the most serious riots and demonstrations since 1964, most notably in São Paulo, over the cost of living and rising unemployment, and the final decision was taken to engineer an early transfer of power to an elected civilian president.

The sheer size of the Brazilian economy meant that even with such problems it was still relatively strong. In addition, although the rapid development sought by the military did not occur in the way that they had envisaged, Brazil, among Latin American countries, is still seen as having a tradition of firm economic management. On the political side, the military may have withdrawn from direct participation in government, but it is by no means clear yet that real civilian democracy is on the cards. Despite the expanding electoral participation of 1945–64, there was still a high degree of military intervention in the political process then and there is little evidence that intervention will cease in the future. The armed forces cleared the way for the election of Tancredo Neves, the leading opposition candidate, in 1984. On the day of his inauguration, however, Neves, who had disregarded the preliminary warnings of pain for fear that the military would have second thoughts, was rushed to hospital with a burst appendix and peritonitis and, despite heroic efforts to save him, died a few weeks later. In this way his Vice-President, José Sarney, became first Acting President and then President in his own right. Sarney, however, who owed his position to the fact that at the last moment he had led his faction of the PDS (a faction of the former pro-military ARENA) into the Neves camp, lacked his running-mate's credibility and charm, and was soon deep in trouble with a Congress which he could not control and a Constituent Assembly which tried but failed to cut short his Presidency. With direct elections restored for the first time in eighteen years and inflation running at over 1700%, Brazilians in 1989 rejected two strong left-wing candidates in favour of the candidate of the centre-right, the telegenic Fernando Collor de Mello, who at his inauguration in March 1990 promised drastic economies and a major campaign against corruption but by August 1992 was himself facing impeachment.

CONTROLLED REVOLUTION IN PERU

Peru followed a distinctive course. The Peruvian Army shared the concerns of its fellows in Argentina and Brazil. However, the ideas taught in its school for senior staff officers, the Centro de Altos Estudios Militares (CAEM), were different. The armed forces, it was said, should not simply seek to resist the pressures building up for change; instead they should carry out a controlled social revolution which would pre-empt such pressures.

The military government which held office between 1962 and 1963 saw its role as the traditional one; to remove an unsatisfactory president, and 'hold the ring' while fresh elections resulted in the choice of a more suitable candidate. But urged on by the junior officers who had helped make the coup, the interim government proclaimed a 'Year of Literacy' on the Cuban model. The elections of 1963 gave victory to a very traditional candidate, Fernando Belaúnde Terry, a moderate Catholic, well connected and an architect by profession, and the Army turned to political action programmes in the countryside that were to bring many of them face-to-face for the first time with the real problems their country faced.

By 1967 the uneasy compromise was beginning to break down. The government's economic programme was in trouble. Demand for copper had been slack and the sol had to be devalued. In military circles there was growing suspicion that the United States was not going to keep its old promises of aid, and when in 1968 Belaúnde proposed compromise in the long-running dispute between the Peruvian government and the International Petroleum Corporation, whom, the government alleged, had been illegally exploiting important oil resources in the La Brea-Pariñas region, the Army acted. In the small hours of 3 October 1968, Belaúnde was carried out of the Presidential palace, kicking and shouting 'These are traitors! scoundrels!' It did no good – they removed his shoes and placed him on a plane to Panama.

The military government which took power did so under a secret plan, the existence of which was not publicly known till 1974. It was called, not wholly imaginatively, 'Plan Inca'. In accordance with it, the new government headed by General Juan Velasco Alvarado immediately expropriated the disputed IPC holdings and proclaimed its independence of all outside influences. To cancel dependency was to be the fundamental objective of Peru's nationalist revolution. As Velasco said, however, the revolution he had in mind was neither capitalist nor communist, since 'capitalism had failed and communism would not work'. As for support for its ideas, the new government consulted mainly with its principal constituency, the armed forces, but the changes themselves were widely accepted and until 1976 the government, though without a popular mandate, had little need of coercion. The effect was to break the economic base of the coastal oligarchy that had dominated Peru, but to set in their place a military corporatist regime directed, like its predecessors, from above.

In 1970 the government inaugurated a major land reform by Decree Law 17 776, enforcing the expropriation of the great coastal estates which were re-organized in workers' co-operatives. Already legislation had begun the systematic development of the manufacturing sector by nationalization of the principal industries and within four years the government achieved its objective of central control of the primary and most of the secondary manufacturing industries. Workers were given representation on state boards, and an even greater role in determining policy under the provision made for what was termed 'social ownership' of many other enterprises. The government's intent to organize workers under its own leadership, and to undercut the popular support Aprismo had held since the 1930s, was co-ordinated by an organization called the National System of Aid to Social Mobilization (SINAMOS), which was to promote community organization and so social mobilization in support of the government's plan throughout the sparsely populated regions of the *sierra* and in the remote regions of the Amazon basin. The plan was from the beginning beset by both natural and manmade crises. Over 50 000 died in an earthquake in 1970 which by especially ill luck caught many people in their homes watching the national team playing in the World Cup. The fishing industry was disrupted by the appearance of the warm *niño* current driving the anchovy away from the coast, as well as by overfishing. The price of copper fell on the world market by two-thirds between 1974 and 1976 as the Vietnam War tailed to its end. And the government was caught unexpectedly in a storm of controversy when it tried in 1973 to muzzle the press by placing it under workers' control, in a way very similar to that followed in Cuba. The President suffered from circulatory problems leading to an aneurysm of the abdominal artery. He was rushed to hospital but had to have a leg amputated. As a semi-invalid he welcomed the delegates to the Non-Aligned Summit in Lima in 1975; then while they conferred he was displaced in a bloodless coup by his Prime Minister, General Francisco Morales Bermúdez, who said good-bye to them at the end of the meeting. Discreetly the delegates made no comment. A year later Morales conceded to US pressures, ending subsidies, denationalized the fisheries, ended agrarian reform before it had reached the *sierra* and proclaimed a state of emergency. The Peruvian revolution was over – at least for the time being. Failing to find any other way out, elections for a Constituent Assembly were held and in 1980, under a new Constitution, Belaúnde returned to the Presidential palace he had left involuntarily in 1968.

In his second term Belaúnde's one goal seemed to be to finish his term. In this he succeeded, becoming the first Peruvian civilian to do so for 40 years. But as the country drifted, weighed down by the debt incurred in the military years, a new threat arose, a Maoist revolutionary movement termed, with reference to the phrase of Mariátegui, 'Sendero Luminoso' or 'The Shining Path'. To combat it, civil rights were suspended, martial law proclaimed and virtually all the Departments of Ayacucho and Huancavelica given over to military government, but the movement survived, discrediting the government by a series of simple but effective demonstrations, a favourite being to dynamite the electricity pylons that carried current into the capital and plunge it into darkness while their own slogan was illuminated on the hills above. In 1985, Alan García became the first APRA candidate allowed by the armed forces to take office.

Though the Apristas held office, the Army has retained significant power, and García's challenge, that Peru would and could afford to pay no more than 10 per cent on its debt, though wildly popular with other Third World spokespersons, has left Peru boycotted by the IMF and so cut off from new private investment which it desperately needs. It will be the greatest of ironies if in this way the guardians of capitalist orthodoxy succeed in establishing in Peru a revolutionary movement which promises to rival the Khmer Rouge of Cambodia in bloodiness if it should ever come to power. In 1990, with APRA's popularity down to a derisory 3%, Peruvians rejected the famous novelist Mario Vargas Llosa for an unknown businessman of Japanese descent, Alberto Keinya Fujimori Fujimori.

FROM DEMOCRACY TO DICTATORSHIP IN CHILE

In the 1950s, with Jorge Alessandri, son of Arturo, in the Moneda, the Presidential palace in the grey downtown heart of Santiago, Chile took on that appearance of a stable democracy which was to prove so deceptive. Both Left and Right in the period after 1946 remained committed to the ideal of electoral democracy. But the communists could not avoid the temptation of fomenting strikes against the government of which they notionally formed part, and so played into the hands of their enemies, and with the formal banning of the Communist Party in 1948 its support simply passed to the rival Socialist Party, also a Marxist party and in some respects more radical. Marxism was widely popular, enjoyed substantial working-class support, union and political organization, and it was natural to believe that its time would come. It very nearly did in 1964 when the candidate of the Socialist Party, a country doctor called Salvador Allende, came a very close second to the Christian Democratic candidate, Eduardo Frei, despite the frenetic efforts of the Church hierarchy to denounce Allende as a communist. It came instead in 1970. The more radical elements amongst the Christian Democrats pressed successfully for the nomination of a more radical candidate than Frei, who was debarred from succeeding himself. They nominated their most able spokesman, Radomiro

Tomic, son of Yugoslav immigrants. But their more conservative
support, some of which was inherited from the party's unsavoury
predecessor, the pro-fascist Falange, deserted them, and voted instead
for Jorge Alessandri, seeking a second term; the non-socialist vote was
split, and Salvador Allende was elected.

US firms were aghast and some of them asked their government to
intervene to prevent Allende taking power. No effective action seems
to have followed. The military commander, who supported the
constitutional order, was assassinated, but no revolt occurred. The
Christian Democratic majority in Congress, who had to ratify the
election, demanded certain guarantees, but these were given and they
ratified it. Allende was sworn in and his coalition government, Popular
Unity (UP), immediately embarked on a large-scale programme of
nationalization and radical reform, which was sufficiently popular to
give the UP a narrow majority in the congressional elections of 1972. It
was already too late. However sincere in his constitutional beliefs,
Allende had failed to realize the dilemma inherent in carrying out such
a radical programme within the limits of constitutional legality. As a
Marxist, he might have called for all-out revolution, formed a Red
Guard and fought for dominance in the streets. As a constitutionalist
he might have postponed the more radical elements of his programme
to capture the Christian Democrats. Instead he unwisely lost no
opportunity of assuring the Army of his devotion to the Constitution,
while in the countryside his government either connived at or failed to
stop unofficial land occupations and a series of violent acts carried out
by the militant Movement of the Revolutionary Left (MIR). The
Chilean middle class, and especially the self-employed, began to resist
the implementation of government policies. Middle-class housewives
stood at the doors of their houses in the evening and beat on the
bottoms of empty pots as if to suggest there was never anything in
them, while a national truckers' strike disrupted Chile's spinal pattern
of production and distribution and brought the economy to crisis
point. When the coup that toppled Allende finally came, in September
1973, it was in no way a normal Latin American coup, but with both
sides already armed, it was rather a very short-lived but extremely
vicious civil war.

The Army, led by its commander, General Augusto Pinochet
Ugarte, seem to have been well prepared, apparently with the help of
the CIA, whose agents were active in fomenting resistance to the
government. But troops moved into action only when the possibility of
a naval revolt forced their hand. Tanks took up position and shelled

the Moneda. Allende died as it burned, allegedly by suicide. Troops rounded up large numbers of suspects and incarcerated thousands in the National Stadium. Like many more thousands in the countryside, some were shot out of hand, others tortured with the most revolting cruelty, with beatings, immersion, electric shock and repeated rape. The nature of these tortures, so consistent with those reported by hundreds of witnesses and victims not only from Chile, but also from Argentina, Uruguay, Brazil and Central America, was evidently not in any sense capable of being regarded as rational; rather it was deliberately intended to humiliate and degrade, especially in its sexual features. Worse still (if that is possible), it was not directed systematically; rather the discretion left to local commanders and the freedom with which they used it to round up people just because they were young, students, suspects or even just relatives of suspects shows that the use of torture had the wider purpose of frightening people into conformity with the policies, however evil or absurd, of the dictatorship that was to follow.

From 1973 to 1990 Chile was under the rule of General Pinochet. In the first phase, the country was subdued. To their shame, the Christian Democrats, who had obviously believed that if a coup came they would be allowed to return to power, accepted the coup and made little or no effort to prevent the atrocities. Censorship was established, representative institutions dissolved and a junta formed of the four service commanders (in Chile the police or Carabineros are regarded as a military service). In the second phase, the unconstitutional rule continued, while the new regime by decree reversed the nationalization measures of the Allende years and made a determined effort to establish an unrestrained free-market economy on the Chicago model. The sale of public enterprises and the inflow of foreign investment, drawn by the honeypot of a dictatorial regime allowing unlimited profit, brought great prosperity to the middle classes, who closed their ears to the suffering around them. In the third phase, after a pseudo-constitutional regime was established, General Pinochet formally retired from the Army and was appointed President and confirmed as such in a plebiscite, but no Congress existed and the junta remained as the ultimate guarantee of military supremacy. In the early 1980s the boom ended and the bankruptcies began, though as the prosperity ebbed the middle classes were still able to retain their share as the poor grew poorer. In 1988, to the great surprise of General Pinochet, the Chilean people showed they had not lost the habit of democracy after all. They took the only opportunity they had been given to vote against the unconditional prolongation of his term by plebiscite. Elections were called and the Christian Democratic leader, Patricio Aylwin elected, but by the time he took office in March 1990 General Pinochet had already ensured that both enormous power and resources would be retained for himself and the Army he continued to command.

ECUADOR'S OIL BOOM

Ecuador has, for most of the twentieth century, exhibited rather an odd form of political struggle, which has broadly amounted to a tradition of conflict between two élites. Poor communications and the severe limits on the extent and power of national institutions, including the military, have contributed to regionalism. Regional issues have influenced the achievement of power and also policies once power has been achieved. Regionalism has remained such a powerful force in Ecuadorean politics that it has kept government in the hands of the élites and has limited reforms that might otherwise have been expected.

The economic crisis of the early 1930s in Ecuador hit one of the two rival regional élites, the coastal landowners and traders, particularly hard, and their representatives, the ruling Liberals, found themselves in a political crisis too. The political recovery of the Conservatives, who had dominated the early history of the country and represented the other important regional élite, the Sierra landowners, seemed to be on the cards. Nevertheless, the Liberals, who succeeded in using constitutional procedures against the elected Conservatives, moved the political tussle into the military arena where each party found some factional support. After a four-day civil war in August 1932, the Conservative forces were defeated and the Liberals established a new government. Despite the support of some middle-class elements, this government could only achieve power through electoral fraud and faced a growing opposition supported by the Left.

José María Velasco Ibarra, the lawyer from Quito who was to dominate Ecuadorean politics for a generation, had been born in 1893 and studied at the Central University. A brilliant orator, he needed, as he once said only 'a balcony' to rouse masses and to achieve power. But his self-proclaimed 'socialism' was subordinated to his drive for personal power and his distrust of organized political parties stemmed from the populist desire to create a vast amorphous 'movement' that would raise him to power without the inconvenience of detailed programmes or policies. Mobilization of the urban working class by the populist Velasco made further fraud impossible and he was fairly elected, assuming the Presidency for the first time in 1934. But once in power he immediately began to exhibit the pattern of behaviour he would display for the rest of his long political career. He set about antagonizing the opposition, beginning with the Right, and, when he was challenged, tried to institute a dictatorship. This led to his deposition in August 1935 and his first period of exile in Colombia.

The political chaos which followed Velasco's departure was met by a period of authoritarian rule by two civilian presidents co-opted by the armed forces. The Central University was closed and political opponents imprisoned or sent into exile on the Galápagos Islands. Direct military rule under General Alberto Enríquez was less repressive and formed a transitional period until the military handed power back to the coastal middle class. Despite growing middle-class and leftist disaffection with the continuing domination of the internationally-oriented élite and its policies, Dr Carlos Arroyo del Río 'won' the 1939 elections as the candidate of the oligarchy against Velasco. The scale of the fraud was so massive that nobody could doubt that it had occurred. Velasco's indignation was supported by a brief military uprising, but this was soon quelled and Velasco himself shipped off to exile in Colombia again.

The weakness of Arroyo's fraudulent government was to cost Ecuador dear. So many troops were needed to support his regime that the country was unable to withstand the 1941 Peruvian invasion of the Marañón River basin and the capture by Peru of half of Ecuador's national territory, which it was then forced to sign away in 1942 under the Protocol of Rio de Janeiro. By 1944 Arroyo was so unpopular that nothing could sustain him in power and he resigned. A coalition of opposition groups was formed and called on Velasco again to assume the Presidency, but, in a manner quite characteristic of Ecuadorean politics, this coalition began to fragment as soon as it had achieved its primary purpose. Economic problems, and in particular the rising cost of living, led to public disorder. Hunger marches were, however, forcibly dispersed and in 1946 Velasco again declared his regime a dictatorship, thus consolidating the opposition which led in 1947 to his arrest and exile.

Paradoxically, a brief interim Presidency was to usher in Ecuador's longest period of stable civilian politics to date. Three full Presidential terms punctuated by relatively peaceful elections brought to power in turn a liberal-leaning independent, Galo Plaza Lasso (son of former

President Leónidas Plaza, later Secretary General of the OAS); the populist Velasco, for the only one of his five Presidencies which went its full term and ended peacefully; and a Conservative, Camilo Ponce. The economic boom Ecuador enjoyed through production of coffee, cocoa and bananas certainly contributed to its stability during the 1950s. But at the same time a destabilizing demographic shift to the coast occurred and the move of workers into urban areas was paralleled by a growth in the middle class. By the end of the decade, commodity prices were already falling, and growing labour unrest was met with government repression. The crisis again assured Velasco of a massive majority in the 1960 elections.

Popular belief that Velasco could and would resolve the crisis was, however, misplaced. Demonstrations against the President in 1961 brought out his authoritarian streak and led to the proclamation of a state of emergency. Again the armed forces stepped in to remove him from power. He was succeeded by his Vice-President, Carlos Julio Arosemena. It was not Arosemena's rather inappropriate personal habits that encouraged the military, the Church and the élites to unite against him – even though they included being drunk at public functions, insulting foreign diplomats and shooting at waiters in bars to make them move faster. It was his moderately left-wing nationalism that alarmed the armed forces and the orchestrated campaign against him simply gave them the excuse they needed. In 1963 he was supplanted by a military junta, authoritarian in style, but aware of the need to advocate reformist policies. However, as the fear of 'communism' declined, these policies increasingly drew the opposition and resistance of the economic élites. The military abdicated in 1966 in favour of the liberal bourgeoisie who initially had the support of the Left in their opposition to the armed forces, but who faced a growing economic crisis as international demand fell for Ecuador's commodity exports, and for bananas in particular.

With the economy in crisis, Velasco again won in 1968 though with a narrow majority. Within a year, with the crisis deepening, he again resorted to repression in face of popular unrest, and in June 1970 again declared his regime a dictatorship. With age, Velasco appeared to have turned to the right, and the coastal élite, fearing that a military takeover might bring a left-wing, reforming military government like that in neighbouring Peru did not oppose him at this stage. When the coup did come, in February 1972, it was to forestall elections in which the victor was expected to be a new type of left-wing populist leader, Assad Bucaram. Velasco again found himself heading for exile, this time in Buenos Aires. It had been his last experience of power, as he died in 1979.

Bucaram was a populist in the Velasco mould, though the two men were bitter political opponents. His strongest support was amongst the urban poor of the port-city of Guayaquil, but he alienated the middle classes by his Lebanese parentage, his violent and often uncontrolled oratory, and his *macho* style, which involved occasional public fist-fights and, once, waving a pistol on the floor of Congress. It was bad luck for him that his candidacy for the Presidency at the head of the Concentration of Popular Forces (CFP) came at a time when the non-military role of the armed forces, in the spheres of agriculture, industry and trade, as well as politics, had been greatly expanded. The military remained factionalized, with the rival Peruvian and Brazilian examples influencing different cliques within it. But all factions realized the significance of the discovery of oil in Oriente Province in 1967. They wanted the military as an institution to benefit from the wealth that began to flow by pipeline across the Andes in 1972, and they certainly did not want it frittered away by another populist leader with the masses to satisfy.

General Rodríguez Lara, a highland landowner from Cotopaxi, had been trained in the School of the Americas in Panama and in the United States and was expected when he took power to take a pro-US, internationalist position. To the surprise not only of the US, but also of the domestic élite that had supported the military against Bucaram and the CFP, Rodríguez showed himself to be something of a reformist and conflicting pressures within the armed forces and the junta of which he was chairman, pushed him in the direction of a strident nationalism. Legislation to control the activities of foreign oil companies was introduced, and after Ecuador's admission to OPEC (of which it became a full member in 1973), the government followed OPEC policy with regard to pricing and took steps to assume first a shareholding and then a dominant share in the industry, despite its lack of experience of managing anything like it. The assumption was that the huge revenues which were confidently expected would be ploughed into development, but the Rodríguez government's developmentalism was both capital-intensive and regionally concentrated, leading to unemployment and internal migration. Thus the marginal sectors of urban areas, especially Guayaquil, burgeoned, and shanty-towns spread whilst middle-class wealth went on debt-enhancing luxury imports. Although development of the infrastructure did bring in increased foreign investment at first, increasing controls on both foreign and domestic capital alienated investors along with the élite elements who had helped bring the military to power and now urged them to return to barracks. By 1975 oil demand had dropped. Oil companies might have boycotted Ecuador in protest at what they saw as the government's nationalist policies, but they had no need to do so; with Alaska and the North Sea coming on stream Ecuador's production was too small and too expensive to attract their interest. A massive decline in government revenue followed and was compensated for by unwise borrowing. The end of 1975 saw an unsuccessful coup; on 11 January 1976 the three service chiefs stepped in and established a new junta under the chairmanship of Rear Admiral Alfredo Poveda, who had previously held the post of Minister of the Interior under Rodríguez. The new government, then, represented only a modest shift away from nationalism towards the influence of more conservative economic interests. In addition, it came at a time when increasing labour strength and mobilization were expressing themselves in widespread strikes. The new government cracked down hard against labour, but worsening food shortages and other economic problems caused by the government budget deficit and soaring debt charges reduced their capacity to control the political process, and in 1979 Ecuador became the second South American country to revert to civilian rule.

Before this happened, the armed forces were able to secure at least one objective – the amended Constitution, by requiring the President's parents to be Ecuadoreans by birth, excluded Bucaram, who in any case died in 1981. But despite fiddling with both electoral procedures and results, they could not prevent Bucaram's son-in-law, Jaime Roldós, from being elected President with 68.5 per cent of the popular vote. At 38, Roldós was Latin America's youngest-ever democratically elected President, but the bright hopes his election raised were soon to prove ill-founded. Bucaram soon fell out with his son-in-law and began to oppose his policies. In so doing he removed most of the President's support in Congress, and Roldós had to establish a new, unstable coalition there. He had just done so when, at the end of 1980, he, his wife and his Minister of Defence were all killed in an air crash. Vice-President Osvaldo Hurtaldo assumed power and so had the bad luck to be in post to preside over the acute economic crisis of the early 1980s. Initially opposition to government economic policies came primarily from élite groups, but then austerity measures as part of an IMF stabilization package led to increased popular opposition.

The declining popularity of the Hurtado government was, however, only one of several factors that contributed to the electoral success of the political Right in 1984. The greater organization and unity of the Right, which enabled them to field one candidate, helped, as did the regionalism and personalism that have characterized Ecuadorean politics. The right-wing candidate, León Febres Cordero, a business-man, was able to pick up the massive coastal vote in the second round of the election, despite having lost the first ballot. He also used personalist appeals by refusing to debate policies and emphasizing personality differences. He invoked Ecuadorean machismo by arriv-ing at political meetings on horseback. As a US-trained engineer, millionaire and President of the Guayaquil Chamber of Industry, it came as no surprise that Febres Cordero advocated policies represen-tative of the interests of the coastal oligarchy. He combined an authoritarian style with the economic liberalism of the free marketeer. In fact in his zeal for monetarism he went far beyond anything that had been seen in Latin America in recent years, cutting protective tariffs and encouraging agricultural exports in accordance with the idea of comparative advantage.

Being in power in Ecuador, however, seems to be the sure way of ensuring that one loses the next round of the succession struggle. From the outset the Febres Cordero government faced opposition. But its policies soon brought growing challenges and decreased electoral support. Terrorist attacks, previously almost unknown in Ecuador, began and led to severe repression accompanied by violations of human rights. Not only did congressional opposition flourish in such circumstances, but so, as on previous occasions, did unrest among the armed forces, a group of whom kidnapped the President. Despite his macho image, he immediately capitulated to their demands. By the 1988 elections his popularity had declined so far that his party's candidate came third with only 13 per cent of the vote. The victor in a second-round ballot was Dr Rodrigo Borja Cevallos, of the opposition Democratic Left (ID), who secured victory by 1 762 417 votes (46 per cent) to 1 572 651 (41 per cent) for Sr Abdalá Bucaram Ortiz, son of the former populist leader. At the inauguration ceremony, the outgoing President characteristically refused to hand the sash of office to his successor, who within hours had announced an emergency economic package, devaluing the sucre, placing sharp constraints on non-essential imports and doubling the price of petrol to the equiva-lent of US$0.50 a gallon.

MILITARY GOVERNMENT IN CENTRAL AMERICA

In Central America, military intervention also took place, but in these smaller and less sophisticated societies it took a much cruder form. Only in Guatemala does the characteristic pattern of 'military developmentalism' appear, though a decade earlier in El Salvador a series of military led governments did succeed in bringing about some economic development, but at the cost of creating pressures for further change, which they proved unable to handle even by the most severe repression.

In Guatemala the forces of traditionalism had re-asserted themselves in 1963 when the Commander of the Army deposed President Ydígoras and assumed power in his own right. Ydígoras, with his sympathy for the United States, had gone too far in accepting US aid to counter the guerrilla movements that had appeared in 1960. The final straw that alienated the Army, however, was his move to allow ex-President Arévalo to return to the country to stand for election. Ydígoras' successor, General Enrique Peralta Azurdia, rejected US assistance in combating the insurgency that earlier US intervention had helped increase. The victory of a civilian in the 1966 elections, and the fact that he was allowed to take office, were the results of tragic circumstances; the candidate of the democratic Left was shot shortly after his nomination, and his brother, nominated in his place, proved too strong to resist. Nevertheless, Julio César Méndez Montenegro (President, 1966–70) was only allowed to hold office after he had agreed to the Army being given a free hand in the devastating campaign planned and led by his military commander, General Arana.

In the next four years terror, countering a wave of kidnappings and assassinations, brought a measure of relative peace, though at the cost of serious losses among the ruling élite. Key figures were killed by guerrillas, rural and urban. In return the death squads killed civilian politicians, trade union leaders and anyone whose education or social standing made them suspect of left-wing sympathies. General Arana's election to the Presidency in 1970 then ushered in 16 years of military rule under five presidents. During the government of Arana and that of his successor, a descendant of Swedish immigrants with the unpronounceable name of Eugenio Kjell Laugerud, the regime, though authoritarian, was relatively liberal. Guerrilla activity continued, but the groups, split by their adherence to rival versions of Marxism, did not pose a great threat and measures to carry out some limited co-operative development in Indian districts, though denounced as communistic by the hard Right, seemed initially successful.

In 1976 a serious earthquake struck the central uplands, devastating the capital, making hundreds of thousands homeless and severing the very inadequate road and rail communications. But reconstruction still lagged when in 1978 at Panzós in the Department of Alta Verapaz soldiers brought in by local landowners fired on a gathering of more than 700 Kekchi Indians who were demonstrating peacefully in support of their land rights. Some 140 were killed and over 300 wounded.

This incident, bad enough in itself, was the catalyst for an horrific onslaught by the armed forces on the Indians who made up the majority of Guatemala's population. The Conquest had driven the Indians up onto the higher and less desirable lands, while the introduction of coffee in the 1880s had reduced their proportion of the available land still further. Then as health and hygiene facilities were improved, the population increased rapidly, intensifying pressure on the usable land to breaking point and making an ever larger number of Indians dependent on seasonal work on the banana and cotton plantations of the lowlands in order to earn enough to stay alive. The last straw was the decision by the military government to create a development zone across the north of the country, in the area in which as it soon turned out, oil was to be found. Led by General Romeo Lucas Garcia (President, 1978–82), who was himself a large landowner in Alta Verapaz, the armed forces, officered by *ladinos* (Guatemalans of predominantly European extraction), fought as if every Indian was a rebel and the conflict took on an overtly racialist character. Whole villages were massacred and large areas of the country turned into 'free-fire' zones. Guatemala was in effect in a state of civil war.

Eventually resistance within the Army led to the deposition of Lucas Garcia by General Efraín Rios Montt. Although the brother of the Bishop of Escuintla, Rios Montt had been converted to one of the charismatic Protestant sects which had spread widely in the country in the previous 20 years, supported by money and missionaries from the United States. Their strongly anti-communist beliefs made them and their ideas acceptable to the military élite, who in any case saw the Catholic Church as weak and riddled with Marxist ideas. Rios Montt promised 'rifles and beans' (*fusiles y frijoles*) to those who supported him; death to those who did not. But the situation did not change, and a year later he too fell to a military coup by his Commander of the Army. With the situation still highly volatile, it was this last who finally took the decision to allow both elections and the choice of a civilian as his successor.

Though the armed forces have traditionally wielded power in both

El Salvador and Honduras, in neither case have they taken the lead in promoting development. In Honduras constitutional government has had a fitful existence since the retirement of Carias in 1948. Military coups in 1956 and 1957 gave way to civilian government under Ramón Villeda Morales, but he was overthrown in 1963 for fear of a more liberal successor. The military junta that succeeded him then rewrote the Constitution to secure the choice in 1966 of a military president, the corrupt and authoritarian General Osvaldo López Arellano. It was he who made the fateful decision in 1969 to launch the 'Football War' on El Salvador. The root cause of this savage conflict which, despite its apparently trivial pretext (a disputed decision in the third qualifying round for the 1970 World Cup) lasted for 13 days, killed 2000 people and resulted in serious industrial damage, was the fact that El Salvador, the most overcrowded state on the American mainland, had been receiving a continuous stream of workers from less developed Honduras in search of jobs. The war itself was brought to an end by the mediation of the OAS. But in consequence of it Honduras withdrew from the Central American Common Market (CACM), thus effectively bringing its development to a halt, while many Hondurans who had been working in El Salvador had to return home.

In 1975 the suicide of Eli Black, head of United Brands (which in a mere six years had grown from a small metal box company until it had taken over the once mighty United Fruit Company), led to the disclosure that López Arellano had been paid half a million dollars to break ranks with the leaders of other banana producing countries and stop the price increase for which they had been fighting. Within a week he had been deposed by General Juan Alberto Melgar Castro (President, 1975–80). In 1980 Honduras was still the least developed country in Central America and one of the poorest on the continent.

In El Salvador the situation was rather different. El Salvador, down to the outbreak of civil war in 1980, was dominated by the same tight oligarchy of leading families, the so-called 'Forty Families', who had ruled in the early years of the century. But panicked by agrarian unrest in 1932 into support for the bizarre Theosophist dictator, Maximiliano Hernández Martínez (President, 1930–44), they accepted military rule after his fall for fear that new elements might succeed in breaking into the charmed circle of the élite. In 1948 a coup by junior officers installed a modernizing military regime. Regularized by elections in 1950 the new constitutional order lasted for a decade, until Colonel José María Lemus tried to arrange for his own re-election. He was speedily deposed in 1960 by a fresh revolt of junior officers, while students demonstrated against the government in favour of Cuba. Fearful that even the mildest reform might lead to a communist takeover, a new civil-military coalition was quickly formed behind a rival junta, who established a new official party, ironically termed the Party of National Conciliation (PCN).

Under Colonel Julio Adalberto Rivera (1962–67) and his successor Colonel Fidel Sánchez Hernández (1967–72) the PCN, with the support of the US through the Alliance for Progress, became the main beneficiary of the CACM, though at the cost of the social strains that were to lead to the outbreak of the Football War. The leader of the new Christian Democratic Party, José Napoleón Duarte, who had been elected Mayor of San Salvador in a landslide in 1964, now emerged as a dynamic rival to the official candidate in 1972. Development had had the effect of mobilizing public opinion in favour of a greater liberalization of politics and more economic equality, and Duarte offered a constitutional alternative. Sadly, however, the armed forces denied him his victory, with disastrous results. On the surface nothing appeared to have changed. The official candidate took office and in 1977 was able to hold fraudulent elections and impose his military successor, General Carlos Humberto Romero. For two more years, till the success of the Nicaraguan Revolution, he was able to maintain order at the cost of a sharp escalation in the use of force. But below the surface it required only a spark to release the explosive potential of frustrated change locked up in nearly four decades.

Lastly in Panama there emerged in the 1970s a military-led revolutionary regime which somewhat resembled that of Peru under Velasco Alvarado. For most of the period since the Second World War, starting with a coup that deposed Arnulfo Arias in 1941, Panama had been firmly in alliance with the US. Its small élite benefited out of all proportion. After the war, the spread of 'flags of convenience' left Panama on paper one of the largest maritime nations in the world. Fortunately, perhaps, it was never called upon to back up its pretensions by providing military escorts for any of its vessels, since this would have been quite beyond the capabilities of its small police force. Yet, as we have seen, the police took over the role in internal politics which in other Latin American countries was performed by the armed forces, and in 1949, when the Presidential succession was disputed, a police coup decided the matter and Arias took office for the second time. In 1952 he was again deposed and power seized by the Commander of the Police, José Antonio Remón, who in 1953 renamed the police the National Guard, which more accurately reflected what they really were. Remón gave the country three years of reasonably stable government before he was gunned down in his car as he was leaving the racecourse.

Under his civilian successors, in the postwar climate of decolonization, the emotive issue of the US presence in the Canal Zone aroused considerable unrest among students. The Eisenhower Administration agreed to a review of the 1936 Treaty which increased the annuity paid for the use of the Canal and gave Panama a greater share of the revenues raised in the Zone. But economic growth left the majority of the population in relative poverty, while unrest continued among students angered at their feeling of inferiority in their own country. Sensitive to the potential dangers, President Kennedy made the further important, though symbolic concession, that in future the Panamanian flag would fly alongside that of the United States in the Zone. In 1964, however, US Marines fired on students who, to shame their elders into action, marched unarmed into the Zone and demanded its liberation. Twenty-one students were killed and more than 400 wounded, but the Canal Zone was at last recognized as Panamanian territory, since by this time even the US Joint Chiefs of Staff had realized that the important thing was whether they could use the Canal, not who owned it.

Meanwhile rival factions had developed within the National Guard, some demanding tough measures and others urging a reforming military regime. In 1968 Dr Arnulfo Arias was re-elected. His first move was to try to rid himself of his Commander of the National Guard, General Omar Torrijos Herrera. Instead, only 11 days after he had been sworn in for his fourth term, Arias was again expelled (he died peacefully in exile in Madrid in 1988) and Torrijos headed a military junta, which closed the National Assembly and the University, and proscribed all political parties.

It soon became clear, however, that Torrijos himself was one of those who had the determination to carry out far-reaching redistributive reforms and was in addition a leader whose charismatic personality rallied a wide base of support for his policies. He dominated Panamanian politics for the next 13 years, ruling for his first year through his supporters in the military junta, and then, when the hard-liners tried a counter-coup during his absence in Mexico, through a series of civilian presidents. In regaining power, his key supporter was Major (now General) Manuel Noriega, who soon became indispensable. Once back in power there followed a series of measures designed to mobilize popular support and distribute wealth more widely among the regime. The funds came from a new source, the emergence of Panama itself as a centre for 'off-shore' banking under the Banking Act of 1970, for, despite its central position and small population, Panama has never had a surplus on its visible balance of trade. In 1972 a new Constitution was enacted which concentrated power in the hands of Torrijos as head of government with Demetrio Lakas Bahas as titular President. A Labour Code came into force, and community health schemes and an expansion of social services were also prepared. Plans were also made to carry out a degree of agrarian reform through a combination of confiscation for debt, expropriation, donation and purchase; the amount of land affected was small, about 5 per cent of all available arable land, but in the Panamanian context it was a significant step forward. Abroad Torrijos pursued a pragmatic, anti-US foreign policy, established diplomatic relations with Cuba and East European states and in 1975 joined the Non-Aligned Movement, a decisive break with his country's traditional posture of subordination to the United States.

In 1978 Torrijos resigned as head of government but as Commander of the National Guard retained ultimate power in the country until 31 July 1981, when he died in a mysterious air crash in Cocle province. A bitter succession struggle raged for the next three years. When the dust cleared, Colonel Rubén Dario Paredes, who had ousted Colonel Florencio Flores in March 1982, had in turn fallen and General Noriega had emerged as Commander of the National Guard, renamed the National Defence Forces in 1984. The President and Legislative Assembly, directly elected from 1983, remained under the control of General Noriega, who ousted Paredes' choice as President, Ricardo de la Espriella (February 1984) and imposed through rigged elections a trained economist as President. Dr Nicolás Ardito Barletta's devotion to President Reagan and to free market remedies, however, was of no help in dealing with the economy. In due course he too was dismissed, and in 1988 the economy was devastated by a US boycott intended to rid Panama of Noriega, but which only succeeded in bringing widespread hardship on all but the wealthy élite. By then little if anything was left of the extensive programme of reform of the Torrijos years.

The elections of May 1989 were a classic fraud. General Noriega's supporters, it seems, had calculated that they needed just over 100 000 extra votes to ensure victory. So the 20 000 members of the Defence Forces voted five or six times each, in various areas and in the name of those recently dead, while known opposition supporters found themselves struck off the ballot or directed to vote hundreds of miles from their homes. Voting itself was free and exit polls were held, from which it emerged that even some of the soldiers did not vote for the official candidate. When, as the count progressed, it became clear how far the government had miscalculated, and the polls reported the official candidate losing by a margin of three to one, armed plain-clothes police appeared in the polling stations and seized the official returns, replacing them with neatly typed lists of their own. Told of this, however, former President Carter of the United States, who was present as an official observer, called a press conference and within seconds news of the fraud was circling the globe. The government reacted with violence, but failed to suppress the growing anger, and after four days, as armed troops rampaged through the streets striking down opposition demonstrators and smashing their cars, the General declared the election null and void. With breathtaking cheek he blamed the 'unpatriotic actions' and irregularities, not of his own supporters but of the opposition, and remained firmly in charge. Subsequently the Bush Administration stepped up its economic sanctions against Panama, calling for the replacement of the nominal government of interim head of state Manuel Solís Palma and the resignation of General Noriega, and sent a 'brigade-sized force' to the Canal Zone in reassertion of US rights there. Following the failure of an OAS mediation attempt, Francisco Rodríguez was sworn in as President on 1 September, when President Barletta's term should have ended, and the United States government broke off diplomatic relations. But in the end it was the unwise decision of the new National Assembly to name General Noriega Head of Government and to proclaim Panama in a 'state of war' with the United States (15 December), which was followed by attacks by Panamanian troops on US personnel, that led to the decision of President Bush to order armed intervention in Panama early on 20 December. After four days of resistance, General Noriega, who had evaded capture in the initial phase, took refuge in the Papal Nunciature and later surrendered to US troops, while Guillermo Endara, the real winner of the 1989 elections, established a new government. However, despite the fact that democracy had been restored in Panama, the recurrence of US military intervention was deeply resented throughout Latin America.

6 Democratic Consolidation (and Less Cheerful Changes)

Alongside the sad tradition of military dictatorship the belief in democratic government has shown surprising resilience in Latin America. The Second World War gave an important impetus to the consolidation of democratic government in several countries, and although dictatorships persisted, and new ones were created, even in countries like Chile and Uruguay where democracy had seemed secure, the 1980s were to see a striking return to democratic practices. Some of these countries are now experiencing a painful struggle to consolidate democracy against a background of material disadvantage and economic shortage. Nevertheless other nations had achieved democratic consolidation very much earlier than this.

THE DEMOCRATIC REVOLUTION IN COSTA RICA

Although Costa Rica was essentially different from its Central American neighbours, having been settled by non-aristocratic Spaniards who came to the Americas to work their own land and who established a nation of small farms, it, like them, experienced problems of development in the 1930s. Population growth was causing severe social problems in urban areas, especially in and around the capital, San José. Shortage of housing and poor sanitation were exacerbated by unemployment and malnutrition. The 1930s nevertheless saw progressive elements in Costa Rican politics begin to deal with some of these problems by instituting social insurance and minimum wage legislation. The pace of reform was quickened under Dr Rafael Angel Calderón Guardia, who achieved a massive electoral majority in 1940.

The Second World War hit Costa Rican trade and hence government revenues, which derived mainly from import duties and export taxes. However, despite such problems, the Calderón government not only passed important social legislation in the form of a rent freeze and

152

protection for both tenants and workers, but also introduced new welfare schemes including the provision of low cost housing and the establishment of the first full social security system in Central America. Such measures may be seen in the American context as somewhat ahead of their time and it does not come as much of a surprise that Calderón aroused the opposition of the Costa Rican élite. Allegations of governmental corruption were followed by charges of fraud, when Calderón's chosen successor, Teodoro Picado Michalski, won the 1944 elections after a violent campaign, giving the ruling National Republican Party (PNR) a further four years in office.

Meanwhile opposition forces were increasing in number and coalescing around the newly formed National Union Party (PUN), which fielded Otilio Ulate Blanco as its candidate in the 1948 election. The governing PNR nominated Calderón for a second term. After another violent campaign, during which the opposition attacked the PNR for fraud in all recent elections, election day itself was relatively peaceful. However, it was apparent that electoral rolls were inaccurate and opposition supporters had been impeding government supporters in their right to vote. As the opposition victory became clear, the government in turn charged the PUN with fraud and the PNR majority in Congress declared the elections void and rejected the subsequent report of the electoral tribunal. Ulate was arrested briefly and violence escalated.

The Costa Rican tradition of electoral legitimacy and the popular belief that it was really Ulate who had won the elections of 8 February 1948 caused widespread hostility towards Calderón and the National Republicans. Against a backdrop of increasing domestic opposition President Picado tried to stir nationalist feeling by suggesting that the United States was assisting a rebellion led by José María Figueres Ferrer. Figueres was a self-made landowner of Catalan origin, politically a social democrat and by temperament a loner. He had erupted into national life in 1942 with a broadcast speech sharply critical of Calderón and his administration, which had led to his arrest and exile. In exile he publicized his ideas for a 'Second Republic' and in 1945 founded the Social Democratic Party under cover of which he plotted armed insurrection. Two attempts were made to assassinate Calderón; both failed. On 16 December 1947, however, Figueres' agent in Guatemala, together with other exiled leaders, signed the Pact of the Caribbean in which they pledged themselves, together with the Arévalo government, to rid not merely Costa Rica, but the whole Caribbean area, of dictatorship. Hence Figueres was in a position on

10 March 1948 to launch his promised revolution, which he did from his farm.

The revolt, which lasted 40 days, was rapidly supplied with arms and reinforcements (the so-called 'Caribbean Legion') from Guatemala. In face of these the government of a traditionally peaceful country responded hesitantly. Picado called for international help, but the only support came from an unwelcome source, Anastasio Somoza García of Nicaragua. When he agreed to help the government against Figueres and 'communism' and on this pretext sent his troops into northern Costa Rica, leftist elements in the ruling coalition moved into opposition. With some 2000 casualties of the fighting and 500 political prisoners held by the government, Figueres and Picado finally agreed on a compromise candidate for the Presidency and Picado handed over power to him. With this handover, and the departure of Picado and Calderón to Nicaragua, the war ended and the political violence subsided.

After a brief interim Presidency, power was transferred to the 'Junta of the Second Republic' with Figueres in charge. The junta quashed the annulment of the election results and continued to rule by decree until a new Constitution was written and elections held. In this preconstitutional period such radical measures as the nationalization of banking and a tithe on private capital alienated conservatives and moved the centre of political gravity leftwards. The more moderate National Union Party, led by Ulate, did much better than the Social Democrats, led by Figueres, in the December 1948 elections for the Constituent Assembly. Despite this, in the same month Figueres' most famous decree, abolishing the armed forces, met with little surprise and virtually no popular opposition.

The Army, the bloated, potentially insurrectionary institution that had supported Calderón and Picado, had as little real combat value as any other Central American army, and like them had primarily been used by previous governments to reward followers, punish opponents and keep themselves in power. Symbolically Figueres handed over the keys of the principal barracks to the Ministry of Education, so that it could be used as a museum. One week later the forces of Calderón invaded from Nicaragua with the support of Somoza, the main target of the activities of the Caribbean Legion. Costa Ricans of all political persuasions rallied to fight against the invasion. But it was Costa Rica's appeal to the OAS for support under the newly-ratified Rio Pact, that led to Nicaragua being condemned and Somoza's support withdrawn, and so to the collapse of the invasion.

The social welfare reforms achieved under the Junta, moreover, were not reversed by the more conservative Ulate when he came to power at the end of 1949. Ulate survived two revolts, in 1950 and 1951. In 1953 Figueres himself won the Presidency as the leader of the new Party of National Liberation (PLN). His welfare-oriented Presidency was controversial in the domestic context, but it was his continued collaboration with the Caribbean Legion that led to another attempted invasion of the country from Nicaragua in January 1955. OAS assistance was again sought and given. Figueres was thereupon challenged to a duel by his old enemy Somoza, whom Figueres described as being 'crazy as a goat in the summer sun'. He showed a characteristic wit when he accepted the challenge, provided that the duel took place on the deck of a Soviet submarine that Somoza claimed to have captured.

Peaceful transitions of power have regularly been achieved in Costa Rica since that time by a level of compromise and tolerance little in evidence elsewhere in the region. Social reforms achieved by one president have not been reversed by the next and political dissidents have been tolerated to a quite extraordinary extent. Whilst consolidating Figueres' anti-militarist policy, for example, President Mario Echandí Jiménez allowed Calderón, despite his past record, to return and take part in elections. In 1962 he stood for the Presidency itself but was defeated; in 1982 his son was a Presidential candidate. That Costa Rica has been able to remain both democratic and demilitarized is particularly impressive given the complications of its long frontier with Nicaragua. In the time of the younger Somoza relations improved when Echandí ordered the arrest of Sandinista rebels operating out of Costa Rica. But in the late 1970s Costa Rica actively supported the democratic forces fighting against the Nicaraguan dictatorship, necessitating military support from Venezuela and Panama, which also aided the rebels. Costa Rica successfully resisted US pressures to abandon its traditional neutrality since the success of the Nicaraguan Revolution in 1979.

COLOMBIA SINCE THE PACT OF SITGES

As self-appointed President of Colombia, from 1953 to 1957, Rojas Pinilla, whose vanity knew no limits, liked to be known as the Jefe Supremo. He had a wardrobe of more than 300 multicoloured uniforms, ordered busts and pictures of himself displayed throughout the Republic and used to give his friends wristwatches with his portrait on the dial. He was, as is so often the case with military leaders, an incompetent ruler, but he had the support of the armed forces and he proved unexpectedly difficult to dislodge. The major problem was that his Conservative predecessor, Laureano Gómez, doubly bitter at the circumstances of his deposition, refused to make common cause with the Liberals, and it was not until 1956 that his colleagues displaced him and opened talks with their rivals at what was then, incredible as it now seems, the small and almost unknown Spanish fishing village of Benidorm. By then the military government was under increasing criticism and it was at that meeting that the foundations were laid for the Pact of Sitges concluded between the two parties the following year. Before that, the dictatorship had fallen in face of growing popular protest.

Rojas Pinilla hounded his opponents on trivial as well as important issues. Corruption charges were being levelled against him with which he seemed unable to deal and his attempts to create a Third Force with himself at its head were foundering as he had to resort to increasingly obvious methods to pack the Constituent Assembly that was to allow him to stay in power until 1962. His final blunder came when he tried to arrest the Conservative Guillermo Valencia, his leading opponent for the Presidency. Rioting spread throughout the capital and provinces. Valencia was released but the heavy hand of the government aroused fresh anger. On 10 May 1957 the dictator's leading generals gave him an ultimatum to go. He handed over power to a military junta and flew to Hamilton, Bermuda, still unable to realize what had gone wrong.

Thus ended the longest period of military rule in Colombian history. The junta returned power to the civilians and under the Pact of Sitges a 16-year experiment began with *rotativism*, a system whereby the Presidency alternated between Liberals and Conservatives and all Cabinet and other posts were distributed exactly equally between the two parties. The experiment was to last in its unmodified form through the presidencies of Dr Alberto Lleras Camargo (Liberal, 1958–62), Guillermo León Valencia (Conservative, 1962–66), Dr Carlos Lleras Restrepo (Liberal, 1966–72) and Dr Misael Pastrana Borrero (Conservative, 1972-76). By 1960 even Gómez was supporting the pact enthusiastically and the main challenge to it came instead from Rojas Pinilla, who, with the aid and support of his daughter, Senator María Eugenia Rojas de Moreno, tried and failed to return to power as a populist leading a Third Force coalition. But though the turn-out even in the Presidential election dropped to alarmingly low levels, in

1972 only 28 per cent of the registered electorate bothering to record their votes, Rojas' Alianza Nacional Popular (ANAPO) failed to make a breakthrough. Then after 1972 the Liberals, as the party with the majority support, decided to end the Pact and hold on to the Presidency for two terms in succession. Under these centrist administrations all other offices continued to be shared, and the continued effects of steady economic growth brought a new stability and self-confidence which even the endemic guerrilla warfare waged by no less than three different political tendencies was unable to disrupt. Politics remains a national passion, rivalled perhaps only by cycling and football.

Colombia, as an oil-producing country with relatively low domestic demand, actually benefitted from the steep price rises of the 1970s, and the wariness its governments had traditionally displayed towards foreign investment paid off in the 1980s when Colombia emerged as the only nation in Latin America not to have a debt problem. In addition to its oil reserves, Colombia has considerable installed hydroelectric capacity and the opening of the huge coal complex at El Cerrejón in 1984 enables it for the first time to make full use of its reserves, at 3600 million tonnes the largest in Latin America. Colombia, despite the size of its primary sector, has considerable claim to be regarded as a mature economy. Although coffee remains by far the most important export crop, its high quality, which commands a premium price, and the region's freedom from frost, have enabled successive governments to maintain relative price stability, while seeking to diversify in world markets. Colombia has a strongly entrepreneurial culture with a tradition of artisan production and by 1982 manufacturing contributed 20 per cent to GDP.

In the meanwhile, unfortunately, the persistent differential between rich and poor continued to fuel political violence, which, since its revival in the early 1960s, had become endemic. With the collapse of ANAPO's hopes as a legal party, in 1970 many of its members reformed as a guerrilla movement called M-19 under the leadership of Alvaro Fayad. Two other major guerrilla movements already existed, the armed wing of the Colombian Communist Party, the Fuerzas Armadas Revolucionarias de Colombia (FARC) and the Maoist Ejército Popular de Liberación (EPL), not to be confused with the much smaller pro-Cuban Ejército Popular de Liberación Nacional (ELN) founded in 1965. M-19 soon became a serious nuisance, and in 1976 a state of siege was reimposed, while the Liberal governments struggled to contain the situation. By 1982, the Liberals had, however, become divided between the centrists who dominated the party organization and the nominations, and the so-called 'New Liberals', who saw that greater commitment to change was necessary if the guerrillas were to be outflanked. Denied the Liberal nomination, which went to ex-President López Michelsen, the New Liberals ran their own candidate, Dr Luís Carlos Galán Sarmiento, and the unexpectedly dynamic Conservative, Dr Belisario Betancur Cuartas was the surprise winner.

Betancur, taking up the populist call for reform, had promised to negotiate with the guerrillas to bring them within the democratic system and gain peace. By the middle of 1985 he had been successful to a surprising extent and had gained the agreement in principle of the three major guerrilla groups to renounce violence and enter demo-cratic politics. However, at this point the resumption of violence by one of the groups brought the negotiations to a sudden end. Though the FARC persisted in transforming themselves into a legal political party, the ranks of their activists were systematically decimated by assassination squads, and the rise of Colombia as the world's major centre for the illegal trade in cocaine fuelled right-wing retaliation on the attempts of the Left to use this source of funds to their own advantage. In December 1985 11 members of the Supreme Court were killed and the Court building on the Plaza Bolívar, only a block from the Presidential palace, the Palacio de San Carlos, was gutted by fire after guerrillas had siezed the building and the Army had shelled it. The Court subsequently voted that the extradition of major figures accused of cocaine smuggling by the United States was contrary to the Constitution.

Between 1986 and 1990, the Liberal President Alvaro Gómez Hurtado seemed at times hardly to be in control of events, but Colombia despite all its problems remains a democratic country and the armed forces have refused to intervene. In 1989, backed by the United States, the government withstood a declaration of all-out war by the drug syndicates.

THE VENEZUELAN DEMOCRATIC REVOLUTION

The tranformation of Venezuela into a modern, competitive demo-cratic state has been one of the great surprises of the twentieth century. Following the overthrow of Pérez Jiménez, and a brief period of interim rule, elections gave Betancourt 49 per cent of the vote and AD a second term of office; Rear-Admiral Wolfgang Larrazábal, who had acted as interim President, came second for the URD with 35 per cent. Given this background, it is not easy to see how Betancourt, on his second attempt, became the first democratically-elected President in Venezuelan history to complete a full term of office (1959–63), let alone be succeeded by a string of similar presidencies. But such has been the case. Contrary to all expectations, Venezuela has evolved into a complex multi-party system, in which power has passed peacefully, by election, from one major group to the other. One of the factors was undoubtedly the bravery shown by Betancourt himself when he narrowly escaped assassination at the hands of Trujillo's agents in 1960 and his personal commitment to the principle of democracy. His decision to form a coalition government gave him the consistent support of Rafael Caldera and COPEI, which during the period of the dictatorship had moved leftward and become a Christian Democratic party prepared to support continued reform, though in 1960 this cost Betancourt the support of the URD. Nevertheless with the aid of COPEI he was able to withstand the loss of part of the AD's youth wing, who were much attracted by the rising star of Fidel Castro and soon formed a new organization, the Movement of the Revolutionary Left (MIR) with a programme of carrying the armed struggle into the countryside. Yet ironically Castro's personal dislike of Betancourt strengthened him against his own armed forces, to whom he offered a new role as a modern, professional organization, in which for the first time NCOs and men as well as officers would be properly paid and equipped. Above all, Betancourt's government continued the programme of reform already outlined and proceeded to implement the land reform of 1948 in a way which, though cautious, maintained its momentum. By March 1963 Betancourt was able to report to Congress that some 57 000 families had been settled on 1.5 million hectares of land, and it had become clear that the revolutionary Left were failing to make headway in the countryside. Meanwhile in 1960 a state oil company, Petróleos de Venezuela, S. A. (PDVSA), had been established. With no more concessions being granted this organization was intended to take over existing ones as they started to expire in the early 1980s. At the same time Venezuela took the lead in setting up OPEC, of which it has been an active member ever since.

In 1964 Betancourt was succeeded by his old colleague, Raúl Leoni (President, 1964–69), whose relative conservatism did not alienate the campesinos who formed the principal support of the governing party and attracted the URD back into the governing coalition. But divisions over policy weakened its control, and as the oil price fell, the 1968 elections saw COPEI, with historian and political thinker Rafael Caldera as President (1969–74), come to power for the first time. Since neither faction of AD would agree to join it in a coalition, it ruled alone and, despite a shaky start, it came by 1973 to form the basis of a second grouping of parties capable of holding power and in that year AD and COPEI between them obtained three-quarters of the votes cast. However, the steep rise in the price of oil as a result of the first oil shock of the 1970s came too late to prevent the return of power to AD in the 1973 elections.

The new President, Carlos Andrés Pérez, was a dynamic populistic leader with widespread appeal to the urban masses – in 1950 only 31.5 per cent of Venezuelans lived in cities of more than 20 000 inhabitants; by 1971 the proportion was 60.4 per cent. Enjoying the political advantages of a relatively united party and an overall majority in Congress, CAP (as he was known to the public) carried through not only the nationalization of the iron and steel industry, but anticipated the end of the concessions by carrying through the long awaited nationalization of the oil industry in 1976. The 13 existing companies were each given new names and placed under the control of the overall state organization now known as Petróleos Venezolanos, or PDVSA.

Accusations of corruption have been standard practice at Venezuelan elections and CAP succumbed like his predecessors to the Venezuelan electorate's tendency to reject the incumbent government. His COPEI successor, Dr Luis Herrera Campins, was left to deal with the debt crisis, when the high spending and free wheeling days of the oil boom came to an abrupt end in the early 1980s. It was he who took the potentially fateful decision not to renew the agreement with Guyana under which Venezuela's claims to most of its territory had been suspended since 1966. Dr Jaime Lusinchi and the AD, who were successful in defeating ex-President Caldera and the COPEI in 1983, have not only had the initial task of debt rescheduling but have faced increasing problems as oil prices sagged in the mid-1980s. By mid-1988 Venezuela was the only Latin American country apart from Colombia paying both interest and capital on its national debt, but the government, despite a series of austerity programmes, faced a new balance of payments deficit and was unable to get new credit. In these circumstances the choice of Carlos Andrés Pérez as candidate of AD in the Presidential elections was a natural one, and given his bold assertions of how he would stand up to the international financial community his decisive victory over Dr Eduardo Fernández, Secretary

General of the COPEI, was a foregone conclusion. On 1 January 1989 the outgoing government declared a debt moratorium. The declining economic situation was reflected in the violence of demonstrations which tore through Caracas leaving many dead and injured.

CUBA IN ANGOLA AND ETHIOPIA

In Britain and the United States, Cuba is generally regarded as a totalitarian state which is as far removed from democracy as can be imagined. A few, notably Dr Jeane Kirkpatrick, formerly US Ambassador to the United Nations, have gone so far as to argue that the United States should support what she euphemistically termed 'moderately-repressive authoritarian governments', rather than to allow them to become like Cuba. Yet many people in Europe and throughout the world regard Cuba as a democratic country. Ironically, Cuban influence, as in Nicaragua and Grenada, has resulted in the fall of authoritarian regimes, while US policy, as in Chile and Uruguay, has strengthened anti-democratic elements and resulted in the emergence in the region of some of the most appalling governments the world has seen since the death of Hitler.

However, though for a decade after 1964 Cuba continued to be dominated by the personality of its Prime Minister, the formidable and unpredictable Fidel Castro, it was not a dictatorship; nor, since it lacked constitutional forms, was it a democracy. Rather it was what Jorge I. Domínguez has called a 'consultative oligarchy'. During this period, when Cuba was isolated from the rest of the hemisphere and it became clear that the first enthusiastic drive for industrialization had failed, Cuba became increasingly dependent on the Soviet Union. In due course it became evident that a price would have to be paid. To avert this, the desperate course was followed of mobilizing the entire population and maximizing the returns from sugar as the principal basis of the export economy. Hence in 1970 everything was staked on a massive effort to achieve a record harvest of ten million tonnes. In terms of sheer physical effort the figure actually achieved, 8.3 million tonnes, was a triumph. But to achieve it, it had been necessary to divert labour from everything else and even to cut into the coming season, so that production in 1971 was well down. In response the Soviet Union began to insist that if it were to continue to offer support, the economic and political structures of the country would have to be brought into line with the Soviet model, and after experimental elections in the province of Matanzas, in 1976 a Soviet-style Constitution was adopted, under which Castro became President and First Secretary of the Cuban Communist Party, but elections were competitive and policies were debated in the National Assembly and in local assemblies in a way not seen at that time in Eastern Europe. After the Cuban Missile Crisis Cuban attempts to create a revolutionary bloc in the Third World had been largely unsuccessful. The strategy of encouraging revolution in the Western Hemisphere had been largely defensive and soon was abandoned as unproductive. In any case a conspicuous exception was made in the case of Mexico, which after 1964 was the only Latin American country to retain diplomatic relations with Cuba. The failure of the Cuban strategy of rural insurrection was, however, overlooked in the euphoria of the student unrest of 1968 and the spectacle of the United States floundering in Vietnam, as was the fact that Cuba was above all preoccupied with its own economic crisis.

However, Cuba's isolation from its neighbours was even in these years paralleled by very active involvement in other parts of the world which was to bring dividends in international respect and recognition. During these years hardly a week passed in which Cuba did not either welcome the Second Secretary of the Communist Party of Mongolia or send a trade delegation to Zaire. And even within the hemisphere, it was not the Allende Administration in Chile which first broke ranks by re-establishing trade relations with the island state, but the Christian Democrats under Frei. In 1970 Cuba sent a medical team to assist with the Peruvian earthquake disaster, and soon afterwards Castro, who had donated a pint of his own blood, visited not only Peru, but also Allende's Chile and (less probably) Velasco Ibarra's Ecuador.

After 1972 (despite events in Chile) Cuba's diplomatic position was reinforced, above all by relations with the new English-speaking nations of the Caribbean, who had taken no part in the events of the 1960s, and in 1974 secret negotiations were even resumed with the United States. It was the collapse of the Portuguese Empire in Africa that was to offer Castro an opportunity to break out of his constraints. The new Marxist government in Angola was faced with insurrection by anti-Marxist guerrillas backed by the United States. South African forces were actually operating within the country in support of these guerrillas and the survival of the Popular Movement for the Liberation of Angola (MPLA) was at stake. The Soviet Union was able to furnish substantial supplies of arms but trained troops to use them were lacking. Under *Operación Carlota* Cuban troops began to leave for Angola, some by air in civilian clothes, some by sea in hastily-requisitioned fishing vessels, and within months the presence of some 36 000 trained troops had turned the tide in favour of the MPLA government. The Cuban initiative had a dual effect. It gave Cuba a new acceptability in the Third World and enhanced its status in the Non-Aligned Movement, with the result that Havana was selected as the venue for its sixth summit meeting in 1979. Even before the meeting, however, Cuba's ambiguous position as a 'non-aligned' nation closely aligned with the Soviet Union raised misgivings, particularly when in 1978 Cuba sent some 20 000 troops to Ethiopia to serve under a Soviet commander against a rival communist state, Somalia. The Cubans fought well and played a key role in the capture of Dire Dawa and in driving the Somalis out of the disputed Ogaden region. But unlike Angola (from where many of their ancestors had come) they had no special ties with Ethiopia and their subordinate status was clear. Faced with the clear choice between remaining non-aligned and becoming in effect 'the Gurkhas of the Russian Empire', Castro temporized.

At Havana in 1979 the summit rejected Cuba's thesis of a 'natural alliance' between the Third World and the socialist countries, and members were alienated by the way in which Castro took advantage of his position in the chair to check delegates' attempts to condemn the Vietnamese intervention in Cambodia. But they did vote for a resolution affirming that failure to make progress towards a New International Economic Order (NIEO) was the fault of the developed Western nations, and that was the view presented to the United Nations General Assembly, thus recovering some credibility for Cuba. It was only after the Soviet invasion of Afghanistan in December 1979 that Cuba, having to choose between the Non-Aligned Movement and the Soviet Union, voted against the Non-Aligned and forfeited its nomination for a seat on the UN Security Council.

Cuba's position in the Western Hemisphere had been strengthened in 1979 by the revolutions in Grenada and Nicaragua, and its willingness, as previously in Jamaica under Manley, to extend small but useful amounts of fraternal aid. But in 1980 overconfidence brought serious reverses. When in April a busload of Cubans crashed their way into the Peruvian Embassy compound in Havana in search of political asylum, Castro, irritated with Peruvian criticisms of his emigration policy, ordered the guards to be withdrawn and said everyone could leave who wished to do so. Within hours every part of the compound was full of refugees, some 10 000 in all, and the decision to let them go abroad, almost inevitable in the circumstances, was a dramatic confirmation that socialism Cuban-style was not the paradise it had often euphorically been claimed to be. Characteristically Castro turned even this setback to his advantage and won wry smiles. When the refugees arrived in the United States on the *Mariel* it turned out that Cuba had taken the opportunity to empty its prisons and mental hospitals at US expense and a long and unedifying wrangle ensued. The election of Seaga in Jamaica and of Reagan in the United States, was followed by a sharp awareness of Cuban vulnerability. The Nicaraguans, particularly after the US invasion of Grenada in 1983, were warned to make every effort to come to terms with the United States and not to count on Cuban help in the event of open conflict. Help to armed insurgencies in the region, resumed by Cuba after the spontaneous uprisings in Nicaragua in 1978, tapered off in 1981. Unfortunately the Reagan Administration, which continued to denounce it for years afterwards, did not take advantage of its strength to normalize relations with Cuba, and ironically it was to be the changes in the Soviet Union itself, following the election of Mikhail Gorbachev and the policy of *glasnost*, that were to leave Cuba out of step with its former leader and necessary ally.

THE PANAMA CANAL TREATY AND THE SEARCH FOR HUMAN RIGHTS

President Carter identified himself with a strategy of encouraging human rights in Latin America. He was, however, not the originator of the policy, nor was Latin America the arena in which the policy was initially formulated. Human rights as an issue began to take shape as early as 1973 under the Nixon Administration, and, as embodied in the Helsinki Final Act, was seen as a major plank in the Administration's policy towards the Soviet Union. When Congress wrote into the Foreign Assistance Acts of 1973 and 1974 clauses requiring the President to deny aid to countries violating human rights and not to resume aid unless he could certify to Congress that the human rights situation was improving in the countries concerned, it also specifically ended US help in the training of foreign police forces, such as had led to the assassination by the Tupamaros of Dan Mitrione in Uruguay and the association of the United States with the widespread practice of torture in the Southern Cone.

The Carter Administration, with its Southern orientation, had more interest in the Caribbean than any US government since 1965. It saw the trend in the area as being towards, and not away from, ideological pluralism, and believed that in the long run US interests could only be served by coming to terms with this, supporting democratic governments and the extension of human rights. In 1972 the UN Special Committee on Decolonization had voted in favour of independence for Puerto Rico, but the citizens of Puerto Rico had had regular opportunity to vote on their own future and had chosen to remain in their special status as a 'commonwealth' associated with the United States. The third possibility, admission to the Union as the 51st state, had had some minority support; independence virtually none. This meant that the most vulnerable aspect of US policy in the area was the continual unrest caused by its colonial position in the Panama Canal Zone.

In General Omar Torrijos Carter found a pragmatic adversary who was prepared to make concessions in return for the major objective of securing the 'return' of the Canal to Panama ('return' was the term always used, although Panama had only owned the territory, if at all, during the first few illegal days of the nation's existence). No less importantly, Torrijos' political position was strong enough to ensure that the deal went through. Carter's position was less strong; many of his southern Democratic colleagues were unhappy about the retreat it implied and shared the view expressed by the unsuccessful candidate for the Republican nomination in 1976, Ronald Reagan of California. For him it was: 'Our Canal; we built it, we should keep it'.

When in came to the crunch, however, the Treaty did receive significant support from the banking firms with an interest in maintaining stability in Panama. In economic terms this was worth considerably more than the revenues of the Canal, which was looking increasingly outdated. The British liner RMS *Queen Elizabeth II,* which was intended for Caribbean cruising, passes through Gatun Lock with only six inches to spare, and the new supertankers of the early 1970s were too large to use the Canal at all.

From one point of view, therefore, the agreement between Carter and Torrijos, and the successful conclusion of the Panama Canal Treaties of 1977, were triumphs for Panama. Four-fifths of the Canal Zone was to revert to Panama almost at once; the rest, together with the Canal itself, would revert in the year 2000. Panama also received a substantial aid package. In return it agreed to charge only 'reasonable tolls' and to maintain the neutrality of the Canal. Panama further conceded the right of the US to keep a limited number of troops in the Zone, and to continue to do so even after the year 2000. From the

United States' point of view, however, the Treaties were also a triumph. The US stands to rid itself of the Canal at the time when, owing to failing water supplies and the silting up of the waterway, it will have become economically useless; it has gained in return a legal basis for its troops to stay in the region and retains the right to intervene if the neutrality of the Canal is threatened. Seldom has international agreement been such a subtle blend of goodwill and naked self-interest on both sides, and it is the ultimate irony that Carter exhausted virtually all his political credibility trying to get it through a Congress which was too slow to see the point.

THE US AND THE SOCIALIST CARIBBEAN: GUYANA, JAMAICA, GRENADA

In 1972 the US Council on Foreign Relations published Robert Crassweller's *The Caribbean Community*, in which its author urged that the United States should consciously aim to take over the imperial role of the former European colonial powers in the Caribbean.

> Power is intolerant of a vacuum. British influence and activity is now waning in the Caribbean; by some law of the international process, not so much by conscious design as by the nature of power itself, other influences, that of the dollar area and the United States in particular, is coming to replace it, thereby serving existing interests of the United States and creating new ones as well. (Quoted by Jenny Pearce, *Under the Eagle*, London, Latin American Bureau, 1981: 75)

The fact was that as late as 1972 the State Department really did not have a policy towards the new states that were emerging in the Caribbean. Yet by then it was becoming clear that they would play a distinctive role and potentially a very positive one, having the economic problems of Latin America but speaking the language of the United States. Jamaica and Trinidad and Tobago in 1962 were the first of the smaller island states to gain independence, and were in fact the first newly independent states in the region for nearly 60 years. In 1966 they were joined by the island state of Barbados and the mainland territory of British Guiana, which took the name of Guyana. In 1972 these four states took the lead in recognizing Cuba, paving the way for the gradual dissolution of the US boycott of the Castro regime.

Meanwhile, in 1967 the Eastern Caribbean states, which it had earlier been hoped would reach independence as part of a West Indian Federation which had a brief existence between 1958 and 1962, gained autonomous status under a federated structure which was intended to give them at least some chance of competing as independent states. However, the rivalries and jealousies between different islands were still the same, and again the bigger islands sought and obtained independence: Grenada in 1974, Dominica in 1978, St Vincent and the Grenadines and St Lucia both in 1979.

The three biggest island states all continued to attract important numbers of tourists from the United States and developing and maintaining this attraction has continued to be important, not just to them, but to the newer and smaller island states too. It can be a mixed blessing – Dominica actually loses money on its tourist trade, as tourists require expensive food and the like which have to be imported – but no state can afford to forego it. Hence, too, with independence the economic links between the island states and the United States were rapidly increased, the most striking change occurring in Jamaica, whose traditional dependence on exports of sugar to Britain rapidly declined to be replaced instead by dependence on exports of bauxite to the United States and Canada. Guyana, too, emerged as a major bauxite producer. The problem was even greater for the smallest states which had little or no chance of diversifying away from a dangerous dependence on plantation crops, a message abruptly hammered home when in August 1979 Hurricane Allen swept through the Eastern Caribbean and both St Lucia and St Vincent lost almost every mature tree in their extensive banana plantations.

Even before independence, there were signs that these Commonwealth states would inherit a political tradition rather different from anything that the United States had previously been used to. In Guyana elected members had a majority on the Legislative Council after 1945 and at the first elections to be held after universal suffrage was granted, in 1953 the East Indian lawyer Cheddi Jagan and his People's Progressive Party (PPP) gained a substantial majority. Jagan was regarded as a dangerous Marxist agitator by the Eisenhower Administration. In October 1953 on the orders of the Churchill government, Jagan was dismissed and the Constitution suspended. Four years later he was again elected and when re-elected in 1961 looked set to carry Guyana into independence. This time the British government saw no reason to intervene.

However, US concern that Guyana would not on independence

become a centre for communist activity in the region might have diminished but it had not disappeared. Between 1962 and 1964, therefore, with the help of the US trade union organization AIFLD, the CIA took advantage of the racial differences that had led to the formation by another lawyer, Forbes Burnham, of the rival Peoples' National Congress (PNC), to drive a wedge between Jagan's supporters and the Caribbean blacks who formed the majority in the urban areas of the colony. A general strike in 1963 was followed by a sugar workers' strike the following year in which racial violence claimed 170 lives and widespread damage was done to the economy. Hence, at the pre-independence constitutional conference in October 1973 the PNC were able to get the electoral system reorganized on a proportional basis giving fairer representation at the 1964 elections not only to themselves but also to the small third party, the United Force (UF), with whom Burnham was then able to form a coalition.

The new state received an unwelcome birthday present on independence from its neighbour, Venezuela, in the form of a claim to more than two-thirds of its national territory. (Under pressure from the United States, Venezuela agreed to freeze its claim for a number of years but in 1982, during the Falklands War, announced that it would not be renewing the agreement.) But Burnham proved able to make use of even this circumstance to increase his own personal power, when in 1969 he claimed that disaffected and rebellious ranchers in the Rupununi district had received help from Venezuela and he was therefore justified in putting them down by force. Taking an increasingly left-wing stance, he nationalized the Demerara Bauxite Company in 1971 and all the privately-owned sugar estates, notably that owned by the giant Booker McConnell company in 1976. Guyana's third main export, rice, continued to be grown mainly by East Indian small farmers, and in 1983 a ban on wheat imports was introduced to stimulate more domestic consumption. Thus Burnham outflanked Jagan, who after many years of absence returned to the National Assembly in 1976 only to find that he was still ignored. Instead Burnham deferred elections and rewrote the Constitution to create an executive Presidency, under which from 1980 onwards he ruled as a dictator until his death in August 1985, when he was succeeded by his Prime Minister, Desmond Hoyte.

Jamaica, by contrast, has remained a democratic country, though only just, and racial and social tensions have been high. Disturbances in the 1930s led to the formation in 1938 of the democratic socialist People's National Party (PNP) by Norman Manley, an Oxford-educated barrister, and in 1943 of the conservative Jamaica Labour Party (JLP) by Manley's cousin, Alexander Bustamante. When universal suffrage was introduced in 1944, it was Bustamante who gained most. It was he who led the regrettably short-sighted campaign against West Indian Federation and became the first Prime Minister of Jamaica on independence in 1962. Owing to ill-health, he retired from active politics in 1964, but the JLP won a further term of office in 1967.

The years of the JLP governments of Donald Sangster and Hugh Shearer were marred by increasing violence, in part stimulated by the Black Power philosophy then being advocated in the United States. But it was the need for economic reform that helped propel the PNP to power in 1972 under the leadership of Norman Manley's son, Michael. The new government embarked on a comprehensive and far-reaching programme of democratic socialism, and successfully won re-election in 1976 despite accusations that the CIA were trying to destabilize it. Undoubtedly the US government disliked Manley's decision to establish diplomatic relations with Cuba, and to receive Cuban visitors. A Cuban construction brigade working on a workers' housing project was regarded as a nest of spies. Undoubtedly, the US was also concerned with the way in which it consistently failed to get Jamaica's support and vote in the UN, though these equally consistently took a Third World, non-aligned position. But it was the cumulative effect of the first oil shock and the gathering recession that drove Manley first to postpone cuts in public expenditure by seeking a large loan from the IMF and then, when that ran out, in 1979 to seek to 'go it alone' just at the moment when the world recession was about to peak. But if Manley's financial judgement was bad, his commitment to democracy was unshaken, and his party went down to defeat in the elections of October 1980, when the JLP won 51 of the 60 seats in the House of Representatives.

The new Prime Minister, Edward Seaga, was less punctilious. An advocate of the free market, he was rewarded by massive financial aid for being the first foreign leader to visit Ronald Reagan in the White House, and in October 1981 Jamaica again severed diplomatic links with Cuba, being by this time one of the few countries in the world taking such a position. Then in 1983 Seaga held a premature general election. He had broken his word not to do so until a new electoral register had been prepared, but Manley's decision to boycott the elections was a fatal error – the JLP won every seat and the PNP's often violent protests failed this time to rally public opinion against the government.

Despite this fiasco, Jamaica has remained an essentially democratic country, and an older and quieter Manley returned to power in 1989. So far the only Commonwealth Caribbean country to reject the Westminster tradition altogether (if only for a time) has been the 133-square mile island kingdom of Grenada. Grenada emerged into independence under the flamboyant leadership of Sir Eric Gairy, whose knighthood belied his authoritarian nature and his use of the so-called 'Mongoose Gang' against his political opponents. Maurice Bishop, whose father died at their hands, took advantage of Gairy's absence abroad in 1979 (he was in New York to warn the United Nations of a forthcoming invasion of Earth by flying saucers) to seize power in the name of the New Jewel Movement (NJM) with the aid of less than 30 armed civilians. The Provisional Revolutionary Government (PRG) suspended the Constitution and established a socialist regime which owed much more to the British Labour Party than to Moscow and immediately began programmes which resulted in some economic gains for ordinary citizens. On the other hand, Bishop's uncritical public admiration for Cuba aroused concern in Washington without satisfying Marxist elements within the PRG itself. In October 1983 Bishop was overthrown in a military coup led by the Commander of the Army, General Hudson Austin, and supported by his deputy, Bernard Coard. He was subsequently shot by his captors, an event which aroused great horror in the small island community. On 25 October 1983 the United States, responding, it claimed, to the invitation of both the Governor General, Sir Paul Scoon, and the Organization of Eastern Caribbean States (OECS), launched an invasion of the island, and deposed the military government, the members of which were subsequently put on trial. In December 1984 general elections returned a civilian government under Herbert Blaize, who had previously served as Chief Minister in 1960–61 and 1962–67, and whose New National Party gained 14 of the 15 seats in the legislature.

DUTCH AND FRENCH-SPEAKING TERRITORIES IN THE CARIBBEAN

The Dutch Empire in the Caribbean, following the independence of Suriname in 1975, has been confined to the small islands of Curacao, Aruba and Bonaire off the coast of Venezuela. Suriname itself has had a disappointing record since independence, and one which confirms (if confirmation were needed) that the once widely-held view that military coups and dictatorship are peculiar to countries of 'Latin' heritage is quite false. Internal autonomy within the Kingdom of the Netherlands was promised to Suriname in 1942, and by 1954 had been fully achieved, with the political scene being dominated by an alliance between the Creole élite, represented by the Nationale Partij Suriname (NPS) and the substantial East Indian minority, represented by the Verenigde Hindostaanse Partij (VHP). When at elections in 1969 the Creole-based Progressieve Nationale Partij (PNP) displaced the coalition, it was challenged by the new leader of the NPS, Henck Arron, demanding immediate independence and in the 1973 elections his coalition was returned to power and led the country into independence.

The 'Sergeants Coup' of 25 February 1980 involved less than 300 men under the command of Sergeant-Major Desi Bouterse, who protested about pay and conditions for the tiny Suriname Army. The military leaders installed a new government under Dr Hendrik Chin A Sen backed by the left-wing Partij Nationalistische Republiek (PNR) headed by Eddy Bruma. In a second coup in October 1980, Dr Chin A Sen became President as well as Prime Minister. In February 1982 he was dismissed, and Bouterse (now a Lieutenant-Colonel) took an increasingly left-wing position. Over the next two years the situation deteriorated further, under threats from both Left and Right, and in December 1982 the armed forces suppressed all opposition and imposed a state of emergency. After the US invasion of Grenada, Bouterse suspended diplomatic relations with Cuba. Although his ideological position remains indeterminate, he has remained firmly in control of a country whose economy has continued to decline under his authoritarian rule.

The structure of the French Empire in the Caribbean, by contrast, remains substantially intact, and since 1947 Guadeloupe, Martinique and French Guiana (Guyane) have constitutionally been overseas *Départements* of France, electing deputies to the National Assembly. There has been some guerrilla activity in Guadeloupe since 1980, paralleled by political unrest in Martinique, but thus far the benefits of being a small part of a developed modern state have been seen as outweighing any desire for independence. Guyane, once the site of the notorious 'Devil's Island', now a tourist attraction (if that is the right word), has achieved a happier fame as the launching-site for the extremely successful Ariane rocket launch vehicle.

THE NICARAGUAN REVOLUTION

We have already seen the chain of circumstances that left Anastasio Somoza García in control of the National Guard in Nicaragua in 1933. Once the US forces had withdrawn, he lost little time in consolidating his position. In 1934 the hero of resistance to the US occupation, General Sandino, was invited to dine at the Presidential palace, seized on leaving by Somoza's men and murdered. His body was secretly buried under the main runway at Managua airport.

In 1936 Somoza himself assumed power, and ruled in his own name until 1947. Between 1947 and 1950 he ruled through puppet Presidents. He then resumed the Presidency and held it for two decades until he was shot down at a reception in León in 1956. The key to his power, as with Trujillo or Batista, was his loudly-expressed liking of and support for the United States. The story is often told that Franklin Roosevelt asked about Somoza: 'Isn't he a son-of-a-bitch?' and was told by his Secretary of State Cordell Hull: 'Yes, but he's our son-of-a-bitch'. There is no evidence for this story and it sounds unlike Roosevelt; it does, however, sound exactly like Somoza. Somoza in his youth had worked as a bartender and a filling-station attendant in the United States and prided himself on his command of idiomatic American. It was this ability to appear 'one of the boys' that had made him congenial to the US Marines who trained the National Guard, and it was on control of the National Guard that his power rested.

On the death of the senior Somoza power passed to his eldest son, Luis Somoza Debayle (1956–63). His father had been a traditional Latin American dictator who had treated the entire country as his private estate. Luis was more liberal and realized that times were changing; he treated the Presidency as a burden rather than a pleasure, and at the elections in 1963, in which for the first time the secret ballot was employed in Nicaragua, he transferred power to a safe nominee, René Schick. Already a sick man, Luis died soon afterwards and his role as head of the family passed to the Commander of the National Guard, his younger brother, Anastasio Somoza Debayle, known popularly as 'Tachito', who became President in 1967.

Like his father, the third Somoza flaunted his friendship for the United States, implying that it was reciprocated. All too often it was. But the third Somoza lacked both the austerity of his father and the sophistication of his brother and used power so openly in his own self-interest that support ebbed away. Being constitutionally debarred from succeeding himself in 1972, he transferred power to a triumvirate while the Constitution was being rewritten to allow him a new term. As this was still in progress, Managua and the country around was devastated by a major earthquake. Somoza became President of the Emergency Committee, shouldered the junta aside and ran the country despite not holding office. The US government, which had on the advice of its Ambassador done nothing to help 100 000 homeless victims of a hurricane in Honduras, poured millions in relief aid into Nicaragua. But nothing happened. Somoza and his henchmen were too busy buying up all the land on the site on which they proposed to rebuild the city, and it was still in ruins six years later, though by that time its condition was, if anything, worse.

The earthquake showed as clearly as was needed to all concerned that no one in Nicaragua except the Somozas was going to benefit from their rule, and brought about an almost unique political event, a coalition of all opposition elements against the regime: the revolutionary Left organized as the Sandinista National Liberation Front (FSLN), the Church, businessmen and the Conservative Party. The remains of the old two-party system were still retained for cosmetic reasons, but the Chamorros, long the leading family of the opposition Conservative Party, had never accepted the upstart Somozas. The explosion came in January 1978 when the editor of *La Prensa*, Pedro Joaquín Chamorro, whose editorials had been increasingly critical of the regime, was shot down in the street by an unknown gunman.

Attacks were launched simultaneously from the north by the FSLN, and from the south by a democratic opposition front sponsored by Costa Rica and Panama. The National Guard fought viciously to retain its power and privileges (rewards for loyal service included appointment as governor of a Department, a license to collect the local taxes). But the Somozas lacked broad-based support outside the Guard. Owning as they did some 43 per cent of the Nicaraguan economy, they had left too little for others outside their circle, and the tactics of the Guard rapidly alienated what little other support they had. In the last weeks of the conflict, as the Sandinistas fought their way into Managua street by street, Somoza from his fortified bunker ordered his air force to bomb his own capital, regardless of the consequences for noncombatants.

At the State Department this chain of circumstances was viewed with great concern. The Carter Administration had attempted to distance itself from the Somozas, but its instructions had not been followed. By the time they tried to engineer a transfer of power to an acceptable compromise candidate it was too late; the Sandinistas, who had expected such a trick, had already joined the other opposition forces in proclaiming a new Provisional Government from Costa Rican soil, and when Somoza finally fled the country on 17 July 1979, members of the Junta of National Reconstruction and its Provisional Governing Council flew in to take charge of the devastated country (20 July).

The new five-member ruling junta lost no time in confiscating all the property formerly held by Somoza and his family. Unlike the Cubans, however, they did not take savage reprisals against his henchmen, who had for the most part prudently fled. Though a revolutionary regime, in that they ruled by decree and their experience under Somoza had not taught them to have any regard for the formalities of representative democracy, they were not, as alleged by American right-wingers, a 'Marxist-Leninist regime', but a coalition in which the new Christian thought often termed 'Liberation Theology' had a strong representation. There were in fact three priests in the government: Father Miguel d'Escoto Brockmann, as Minister of Foreign Affairs, and the Cardenal brothers as Ministers of Education and Culture. One of the first acts of the new government was to revoke the 1974 Constitution, dissolve the puppet Congress and sweep away the National Guard. The new regime was to rely instead on a popular militia-based force, the Sandinista People's Army. Moreover, on 22 August 1979 a 'Statute on Rights and Guarantees for the Citizens of Nicaragua' decreed freedom of the individual, of speech and of the Press, and the abolition of the death penalty, and despite all the problems of the next few years these guarantees have in general been adhered to and the few reported examples of abuse punished.

The new government was pledged to allow the free expression of popular opinion and maintain a mixed economy. There was in fact no need for nationalization decrees, as the seizure of the Somoza's assets had left the state in charge of the greater part of the economy, including much of the best land. However, the more conservative members of the junta, including the widow of Pedro Joaquín Chamorro, Violeta Barrios de Chamorro, soon became impatient that the formal structures of representative government were not being restored (a Council of State was subsequently established in May 1980) and that the Sandinistas seemed to be gaining power at their expense. They unwisely withdrew from the government, which was subsequently reconstructed in March 1981, still as a coalition, under a junta of three: Rafael Córdova Rivas, Dr Sergio Ramírez Mercado and the chairman and head of state Comandante Daniel Ortega Saavedra.

Assessing the performance of the Sandinista Government is difficult, as after 1981 it was subject to constant attacks by anti-Sandinista forces armed and sponsored by the United States government, and for much of that time has had to operate on a war footing. The effect on the economy has been little short of disastrous. Though the proportion of the economy in private hands has actually increased, to around 60 per cent, the country has been plagued by persistent shortages, rationing of fuel and other essentials, as well as galloping inflation, exacerbated by US financial pressure. However, since 1979 education has been free and is intended to be compulsory, and a major achievement, sponsored by Father Fernando Cardenal, the Minister of Education, has been the national literacy campaign. This campaign, constructed on a model recommended by Colombian (not, as is usually said, Cuban) experts, worked on a pyramid basis to make the maximum use of the few trained teachers available, and succeeded in lowering the adult illiteracy rate in a single season from 52 per cent to 12 per cent. Though this too, has had its critics, who denounced it as an instrument of communist propaganda, the materials used were not at all Marxist and no one who understands how far illiteracy acts as a handicap to full citizenship in the modern world can fail to regard it as a great advance, and one which stands in conspicuous contrast to the neglect of the Somoza years. Alongside this, the achievements in the sphere of national health must also be mentioned. Polio has been totally eliminated and mortality statistics, under Somoza among the worst in the hemisphere, are now much improved.

In November 1984 elections were held under the new Constitution. Opposition parties were allowed to operate freely, but on US instructions, some of them withdrew at the last moment, when it became apparent that anti-Sandinista guerrillas were not able to prevent the elections taking place and hence they were not going to win. Daniel Ortega, the FSLN candidate, was elected President with a respectable but not overwhelming majority, gaining 66.9 per cent of the votes cast; the next best result, (14.0 per cent) went to the candidate of the Christian Democrats (PCD).

CIVIL WAR IN EL SALVADOR

As in Nicaragua, it was the Right that first resorted to violence in El Salvador in 1969 when ORDEN was formed to co-ordinate the activity of 'death squads'. In reaction to this, Salvador Cayetano Carpio, the

Secretary General of the Salvadorean Communist Party (PCS) forsook the path of peaceful co-existence for that of armed struggle. In 1980 a united front was formed in Cuba, through the mediation of Fidel Castro, between Carpio's group and others of like mind. Named after Farabundo Martí, a student martyr, the Farabundo Martí National Liberation Front (FMLN) waged war on the government while its political wing, the Democratic Revolutionary Front (FDR) publicized its aims and objectives. A full-scale civil war followed.

The government of General Humberto Romero had been removed from power by a military coup in 1979, but the armed forces were not able to agree what to put in its place. Though the Christian Democrats were brought into the junta in January 1980 to give a veneer of respectability, the armed forces retained power, while assassinations and kidnappings became routine. Finally, under pressure from the United States, they agreed to accept the radical reforms that were the price of getting José Napoleón Duarte to join the junta (March 1980) and, they hoped, give it real popular support. The reconstructed junta, with military backing, immediately nationalized a quarter of the country's land and promised to carry out the comprehensive land reform that earlier might have averted civil war. But by this stage it was already too late to halt the escalation of violence.

The Archbishop of San Salvador, Monsignor Oscar Romero, had for some time been aware of the depth of feeling against the government in the countryside. Finding that his warnings were not being heeded, he spoke publicly about the threat of violence, and on 17 February wrote directly to President Carter to ask him to cut off the aid being given by the US to the armed forces and to cease its intervention in Salvadorean politics. Finally, saying (in conformity with the traditional teachings of the Church) that the command 'Thou shalt not kill' applied to soldiers as well as to civilians, he addressed an appeal to members of the armed forces themselves to desist from further acts of violence. A few days later, at the end of March 1980, gunmen shot him down as he stood at the altar in the act of celebrating Mass, an open act of sacrilege, committed in a nominally Christian society, which was widely attributed to the emerging leader of the extreme Right, Major Roberto d'Aubuisson. That the intention was once and for all to end the possibility of revolt by any means possible was confirmed when soldiers fired hundreds of rounds into crowds gathering to pay their last respects to the Archbishop at his funeral, and left many dead in the streets. Within days news of the massacre had set the countryside ablaze.

The Church, in this chaos, was unable to continue its work effectively. Archbishop Romero's successor, the Apostolic Administrator of the Archdiocese of San Salvador, Monsignor Arturo Rivera y Damas, lacked the authority of a bishop, and inevitably tended to support the more traditional view of his role, that in the confrontation between government and people it was for the Church to maintain a balance. As with the attempts of the Carter Administration to support the democratic centre in face of the extremes, this policy foundered on the clear intention of the Right to keep the situation polarized. The activities of the death squads continued to be directed towards the soft targets of the centre, killing political leaders, trade unionists and even priests, but they now effectively ended any real possibility of land reform by concentrating their fire, in the most literal sense, on the proposed beneficiaries of the reform.

Administration attempts to build up constitutional government were frustrated even in the US itself, where right-wing Senators and others welcomed d'Aubuisson. By the end of 1980 more than 13 000 had died and some 70 000 were refugees. Though Duarte was appointed President in December, in fact the government had moved to the right, as progressive military influences were eliminated and power increasingly concentrated in the hands of one man, Colonel Gutiérrez. 1981 opened with a 'Final Offensive' by the guerrillas, hoping to sweep to power before Ronald Reagan took office as President of the United States. This desperate course failed, however, as the US aid and training programmes already under way continued to build up, and received increased prominence under the new Administration, whose White Paper, published in February, claimed that 'the insurgency in El Salvador had been progressively transformed into a textbook case of indirect armed aggression by Communist power'. The new Administration, however, also continued to back moves towards a new constitutional government.

At first it looked as if this policy was going to stall on take-off. Elections for the Constituent Assembly in March 1982 were indecisive, leaving the PDC the largest party but the rest of the seats divided between two strong right-wing parties, the old PCN and d'Aubuisson's Alianza Republicana Nacionalista (ARENA). An independent, Dr Alvaro Magaña Borja, became interim President (1982–84), a new Constitution was agreed and in the second elections in April 1984 Duarte won a narrow but clear electoral mandate, obtaining 53.6 per cent of the votes cast to 46.4 per cent for Major d'Aubuisson. It was not until March 1985, however, that the PDC also won a majority share, 33 of the 60 seats, in the Legislative Assembly, and by then, at the cost of some 50 000 lives, the civil war had been fought to a stalemate. Though the guerrillas remained in effective control of much of the countryside, including the entire Department of Chalatenango, and had repeatedly destroyed key bridges (including the bridge on the Pan American Highway over the Río Lempa) on the country's sole major arterial road, the Pan American Highway, as early as 1983 they had been prepared to hold peace talks with the government, which under Duarte became open. In the 1989 elections the FMLN offered to accept a constitutional role. This offer was turned down by the government of President Duarte; the Arena candidate, Alfredo Cristiani, won a substantial victory and a new FMLN offensive was launched when evidence of uniformed 'death squads' seriously compromised the government's credibility.

REAGAN IN POWER: THE NEW AMERICAN PRESENCE IN CENTRAL AMERICA

When the Reagan Administration came to power in the United States in January 1981, it was pledged to 'walk tall', negotiate from strength and 'roll back the frontiers' of communism. Hence, it immediately announced a substantial increase in military aid to the government of El Salvador, where the insurgents were apparently already on the retreat and the risk that the United States might get actively involved was minimal.

In the summer of 1981 the Administration turned its attention to Nicaragua and decided to set up, through the CIA, yet another force of alleged exiles, to operate from Honduras across the border into Nicaragua itself. This decision became effective with President Reagan's signature on National Security Decision Directive (NSDD) 17 of 23 November 1981. In Nicaragua they were described as 'counter-revolutionaries' (contras) and the name stuck, though the anodyne name chosen for them was 'the Nicaraguan Democratic Force' (FDN). Publicly, however, US spokesmen said they had nothing to do with them. The United States wanted only to stop Nicaraguan aid to the insurgents in El Salvador.

The force was built up over the next two years with relatively little attention from the outside world, but at the start of 1984 the contras had still to take control of a single Nicaraguan town. At this point the campaign was stepped up. Co-ordinated from a US warship, naval forces struck on 3 January at the oil facilities at Puerto Sandino.

Similar attacks followed on 25 February on the Atlantic port of El Bluff and the Pacific port of Corinto, and mines were laid which damaged four freighters, one of them of Soviet registration. On 5 April the US vetoed a Security Council resolution condemning the mining of the ports, after the President had told a press conference that he would take no steps to stop it. At a press conference he said that the Nicaraguans were 'exporting revolution'. 'We are going to try and inconvenience the government of Nicaragua until they quit that kind of action', he promised. With commendable restraint the Nicaraguans replied by taking their complaint to the International Court of Justice at The Hague, but in an action of questionable legality the United States refused to recognize its jurisdiction.

Once the growing US involvement had become plain, Congress voted, under the Boland Amendment (26 July), to cut off all funding and to declare it illegal, which it remained until late 1986. Meanwhile, the Sandinista government, who had hitherto been rather sceptical about their value, announced elections for November. The elections were denounced by the White House as 'a sham' before they could even take place. At this point the other states of the region began to become concerned that intervention by the United States could lead to a major upheaval in the region. Representatives of Mexico, Panama, Colombia and Venezuela met at the invitation of the Panamanian government on the Panamanian island of Contadora to discuss a possible initiative and drafted a treaty which was accepted by Nicaragua and three of the other Central American states. Unfortunately, under US pressure, these states afterwards decided that it did not go far enough. At the same time the US encouraged opposition parties to boycott the Nicaraguan elections, refused to send observers and continued to denounce them as false.

The re-election of Reagan in 1984 brought a decision to confront Congress publicly to demand funding for an open US campaign against the government of Nicaragua. The illusion that the contras were Nicaraguan 'freedom fighters' was dropped in favour of a frank admission of US desire to put pressure on the Nicaraguan government. But while Congress failed to vote further funds, behind the scenes in the National Security Council offices strenuous efforts were made to raise funds for the contras from other sources, including channelling the funds from sales of arms to Iran through a Swiss bank account to certain contra leaders. One of these, Alfonso Robelo, later stated in public that he received funds from the NSC staffer Colonel Oliver North.

The disclosure of this transaction caused a furore in the United States. The President, for his part, admitted he was totally unable to recall being briefed on the sale of arms to Iran, even though he repeatedly denounced Carter for the same thing and said he would never do it. But significantly many in the US who criticized him for this did not criticize his support for the contras, even though by this time the International Court of Justice had held that the United States had breached international law in 14 different ways in conniving at the mining of Nicaraguan harbours. In 1989 Colonel North was convicted in Washington of misleading Congress, but acquitted on conspiracy charges after new evidence had been presented suggesting that both President Reagan and Vice-President (now President) Bush had been fully involved in the operation. Ironically, in 1990, in free elections, Ortega and the Sandinistas were defeated by the National Opposition Union (UNO) led by Violeta Barríos de Chamorro, who took office on 25 April with the promise of substantial US aid to help rebuild the shattered country.

THE FALKLANDS WAR

It emerged only subsequently that the Reagan policy for Central America had been originally based on the notion that the military dictatorships of the Southern Cone, in particular Argentina and Chile, would act as proxies for the United States in supplying instructors to El Salvador and the contra forces. Rightly or wrongly this fact seems to have been interpreted in Buenos Aires as meaning that in a conflict with Britain over the Falkland Islands, US support would go to Argentina, and the decision in the British Defence Review of 1981 to withdraw the Antarctic survey vessel HMS *Challenger* from the South Atlantic was taken as a hint that Britain was eager to shed this colonial embarrassment and would make no more than a token protest if Argentina were to take the islands by force.

On 19 March 1982 an Argentine naval vessel delivered a party to Leith on the island of South Georgia. Officially they were there as workmen under contract to dismantle the old whaling station, but in fact they were naval personnel and no sooner had they landed than they raised the Argentine flag. When Britain protested, an Argentine patrol vessel and two corvettes were dispatched to give them 'protection'. Meanwhile preparations were advanced for a landing on the Falklands themselves. On 2 April troops started coming ashore and within hours a large military force had occupied the islands and in Buenos Aires demonstrations against the military government gave way to cheering in the streets.

In London the decision was hastily taken to assemble a naval task force to sail for the islands, while in the Security Council a majority voted for a resolution calling on the Argentines to withdraw and to allow the question to be solved by peaceful negotiation (Resolution 502). The American Secretary of State, General Alexander Haig, offered his good offices, and after a series of journeys across the Atlantic confirmed that there was no question of an Argentine withdrawal. Shortly after the recapture of South Georgia on 25 April, he gave up the attempt. As an ally and the aggrieved party, Britain was therefore able to purchase from the United States the ammunition and equipment needed to minimize casualties and maximize chances of success. It was not possible, as some had hoped, to delay hostilities any longer, as the Argentines had sensibly launched their attack at the beginning of winter and the task force could not be indefinitely held in a state of readiness.

Operating from the British territory of Ascension Island, RAF bombers on 1 May opened the campaign for the recapture of the islands. Their attack on the runway of Port Stanley (renamed Puerto Argentino) was unsuccessful and for the rest of the war aircraft were able to maintain the resupply of the island garrison. The sinking on 3 May of the Argentine cruiser, ARA *General Belgrano*, by a British nuclear-powered submarine, HMS *Conqueror*, with the loss of 368 lives, was followed within hours by the sinking by Argentine naval airmen of the frigate HMS *Sheffield*, and for several days it was feared in London that at any moment the loss of one of the two aircraft carriers would put paid to any hopes the task force might have of recovering the islands. But over the next six weeks, despite serious naval losses, British forces were successfully landed at San Carlos Bay on Falkland Sound, and fought their way across the island of East Falkland. On 14 June, with the surrender of the Argentine garrison in Port Stanley, this bitterly unnecessary conflict came to an end, leaving just over a thousand dead and many more maimed.

The fall of the Galtieri government was the first step in the military withdrawal from power in Argentina, and within a year President Alfonsín had taken office and been greeted (reluctantly) by a telegram of goodwill from Mrs Thatcher, the British Prime Minister. Unfortunately, thereafter on both sides opportunities were missed repeatedly to liquidate the bitterness of the conflict, and when with Brazilian mediation, the two sides officially met at Bern in Switzerland in 1984, the talks broke up within minutes amid recriminations on both sides. In the United States the failure of his mediation attempt, and the bitter hostility of right-wingers within the Administration, had before the end of 1982 led to the fall of General Haig and his replacement by Mr George Shultz. But in Britain the 'Falkland Factor' was widely held to have been important in ensuring Mrs Thatcher's triumphant return to power in 1983. Although research at the University of Essex suggests that in fact the recovery in her party's fortunes was already under way before it happened, the victory seems to have been hailed as an antidote to the depressing effects of the long retreat from empire and remains as an obstacle to a serious resolution of the long-standing dispute over the sovereignty of the islands.

President Alfonsín's greatest achievement was to survive politically until his successor could be elected in fair and peaceful elections in May 1989. However, his failure to deal with the deteriorating economic situation, with inflation rates of 100 per cent per month, ensured that his party's candidate, Eduardo Angeloz, was soundly beaten. Not only did the Justicialist (Peronist) Party candidate, Carlos Saúl Menem, take all the provinces except Córdoba and the Federal capital and win sufficient votes to guarantee his selection as president by the electoral college, but his party also took sufficient seats to gain a majority in both the Senate and the Chamber of Deputies. Menem's election illustrates the continuing Argentine penchant for colourful political figures. With something of a playboy image and an eye for a pretty girl this son of Syrian immigrants reflects the charismatic style that brought Perón himself to power and which helped Alfonsín win in 1983 against a bland Peronist opponent. In his new task, Menem has not been assisted by his striking wife, Zulema, who was immediately likened to the almost mythical Eva Perón. Within months an IMF official was describing the economic condition of the country as 'hopeless'. However, Menem's bold pragmatism has had unexpectedly favourable results in the economic sphere as well as in the restoration of diplomatic relations with the UK.

GRENADA

US support for Britain was certainly deeply resented in Argentina and, indeed, in other South American states. Later in the 1980s anti-Americanism was to be further fanned by the Reagan Administration's campaign against the drug trade. But the episode did not halt the consolidation of US influence in the Caribbean basin – if anything it helped it.

For the fact that Britain was still very much regarded in Washington as an interloper in the US sphere of influence was confirmed by events in Grenada later in 1983. The Reagan Administration had from 1981 onward watched events in Grenada carefully, and appeared to attach a surprising degree of importance to the efforts of the PRG to be taken seriously as an ally of the Soviet Union. At least two major naval exercises – in 1981 and 1982 – were conducted in the region as training for a possible occupation of Grenada. Further, in March 1983, an alleged communist build-up on, of all places, this tiny island was used by Reagan himself in his 'Star Wars' speech to justify his request for a trillion-dollar budget to create nothing less than an anti-missile shield over the United States.

In October, as we saw earlier, events in Grenada took a tragic turn when rivalries within the PRG led to the seizure of power by the Army led by General Hudson Austin and the fall and death of the Grenadan leader, Maurice Bishop. Frustrated by the stalemate in El Salvador, the Administration now had an easy opportunity to demonstrate its resolve, and on the pretext of protecting US lives the island was occupied; significantly without consulting Britain as might have been expected. Released from captivity, the Governor General confirmed that the occupation had taken place at his invitation, the independence Constitution was restored, and a new government was formed with Mr Herbert Blaize as Prime Minister. With this action the Administration confirmed that for the first time since the Second World War it had successfully incorporated the Eastern Caribbean islands into the outer perimeter of its defensive system.

REVOLUTION IN HAITI

With its dominance of the Caribbean thus confirmed, the Administration faced criticism about many aspects of its policy. Nowhere was this more true than in its apparently friendly relations with the unsavoury dictatorship of the Duvalier dynasty in Haiti. The once wealthy territory of Sainte-Domingue, the first country after the United States to gain independence in the Western Hemisphere, had been repeatedly looted and pillaged by gangster regimes, but the Duvaliers, setting new standards in this as in all else, succeeded in making Haiti definitively the poorest country in the Hemisphere.

Their rule began when in September 1957, Dr François Duvalier, known as 'Papa Doc' because of his medical training, won a six-year term as Haitian President. Political opponents claimed that the Army influenced the election results, but the extent of such influence is not clear. Certainly there were soldiers at polling stations, though the Army claimed that this was merely a precaution to ensure a peaceful election. Whatever the level of military involvement in Duvalier's rise to power, once he had achieved it, he lost no time in destroying the independence of the Army, taking advantage of a series of blunders by his political opponents to create in 1959 his own militia, the so-called *Tontons Macoutes* ('Uncle bogeymen'). This paramilitary organization, personally sworn to support the President, comprised the worst scum to be found in Haiti; thugs and criminals who were able to murder Duvalier's political opponents and terrorize the general population. Their arbitrary repression and plunder became so blatant after the assassination of Trujillo that it led to the withdrawal of US aid under Kennedy. The financial drain on the Haitian economy was colossal, official receipts being used as the Duvalier family's private purse. But there was no public criticism; many Haitians believed in the Voodoo cult, and Duvalier carefully encouraged, by his public manner and gestures – black dress, unhealthy pallor, stillness, quiet Creole speech – the belief that he was 'Baron Samedi', a zombie, king of the walking-un-dead. Alternatively he could whip the crowd up into a frenzy of loyalty. When he faced OAS censure in 1963, he roused such a storm of nationalist fervour with a series of obscenities delivered in Creole that the visiting delegation felt unable to challenge his position.

To avoid the fate that had befallen so many of his predecessors, who were overthrown when they sought re-election, Duvalier relied not only on force but on a series of ingenious devices. At municipal elections in April 1961, a year before the Presidential election was due, ballots bore Duvalier's name at the top; when they were counted it was announced that Duvalier had responded to the call of the people for him to serve a further six years. Then in 1964 at the call of the Army the Constitution was amended to allow Duvalier to be elected President-for-life. It was later amended again to allow for hereditary succession. Hence, when in 1971 Duvalier died, and did so contrary to all expectations peacefully and in his bed (the first of Haiti's seven Presidents-for-life to do so), he was succeeded by his son, the tubby and indolent 19-year old Jean-Claude Duvalier, known derisively as 'Bébé Doc'.

Jean-Claude, the world's youngest head of state, ruled initially with the help of his mother, then of his wife. His rule saw some modernization, but corruption and repression were the props of his domination as they had been in the days of his father. Drought and famine struck in 1975 and Haiti, once the jewel of the French crown, became so poor that its major exports were baseballs and blood plasma, drawn from the skinny arms of its starving people for export to private clinics in the United States. Thousands of 'boat people' fled to the United States. Meanwhile, as the president's interest waned, a fierce struggle for power went on around him. Pressure from the Carter Administration brought some symbolic gestures towards liberalization but no real change. As soon as Carter had been defeated (November 1980) political opponents were again arrested and deported and the press curbed. But in 1983, the fateful decision was taken, on the advice of the new Minister of National Defence, Roger Lafontant, again to allow local elections, and in 1984 to hold elections for the National Assembly. The fact that no opposition was legally permitted did not prevent growing unrest at the prevailing poverty and starvation and food riots, as so often before in Haitian history, heralded the fall of the regime and the flight of Jean-Claude in 1985. The Duvalier regime had been one of the walking un-dead all along, and when surprised by daylight, it fell to pieces.

Power passed to the Commander of the Army, General Henri Namphy, while the mob hunted down and killed the hated Tontons Macoutes and looted and smashed everything associated with the Duvaliers. In 1987, under US pressure, elections were held for the Presidency, but the civilian elected, Leslie Manigat, held office for only six months before his efforts to rid himself of General Namphy rebounded and the General deposed him. In September 1988 the second coup of the year replaced Namphy with General Prosper Avril. The coup's mastermind, a Colonel Jean-Claude Paul, soon afterwards collapsed after drinking soup which was subsequently found to be poisoned. But on 11 March 1990 a popular revolt in turn deposed Avril and a new civilian government took office headed by Mme Ertha Pascal-Trouillot, a judge of the Supreme Court. Elections were held again in December 1990. With international observers watching, the people of Haiti voted the way they wanted, and chose as their new President, Fr. Jean-Bertrand Aristide, a priest noted for his work among the poor of Port-au-Prince. Despite, or rather because of, its promising start in the fight against corruption, his government was deposed after only seven months in September 1991 by the armed forces. The new interim government went unrecognised by the OAS and the army remained in charge.

7 A New Start?

As we enter the 1990s, the future of Latin America has never seemed more problematic. The major countries, particularly in the Southern Cone, seem likely to struggle on, always failing to realize their full potential. In a category of its own is Brazil, which, after an introspective phase, could eventually achieve the major power status to which it has for so long aspired. But at the other end of the scale, the smaller countries of both South and Central America seem fated to veer away downward from the path of development of their larger neighbours, into ever more serious problems of poverty.

THE DEBT CRISIS

In the 1980s Latin America has been seen, both by its inhabitants and by many outside observers, as a continent sinking in a sea of debt. The debt issue had been in the making for at least a decade, as investors fell over one another to pour recycled oil revenues from the Middle East into a promising area for development. It became a crisis only when the Mexican government announced it was in difficulty meeting its obligations, and since then the outside world has been obsessed with this one aspect of Latin America's economic difficulties. The voices of those who argue that the so-called debt crisis can only be understood in a wider context, as part of a general crisis of economic development in the Third World, have not always been audible.

In some ways, little has changed since 1983. Brazil remains at the top of the Third World debt league, with a gross external debt of some $115 billion and triple digit inflation. Argentina and Venezuela, too, rank near the top of the league, sharing the limelight with other Third World states such as Indonesia, but even tiny Costa Rica, with a small debt in gross terms, has a massive problem in repaying it. To repay a foreign debt, a country has to trade in such a way as to bring in enough foreign exchange to meet the regular instalments both of principal and interest. If it does not do so, then its own currency will fall in value as it seeks to redress the situation, and its situation will deteriorate very rapidly. The situation for the debtor countries has been much worse than was expected in the 1980s through two circumstances which could not have been foreseen. Interest rates went up steeply at the beginning of the decade and were maintained by the United States at historically very high levels during the Reagan Presidency, so increasing the burden of debt already contracted. At the same time the successful efforts of the Western states to break up the Middle East oil cartel led to a precipitous fall in the price of petroleum, which Latin American states such as Mexico, Venezuela, Ecuador and Peru had hoped to sell at a much higher world price, and other world prices for primary products were forced down in the same way.

TABLE 7.1   *Debt interest as a percentage of export earnings*

Country	Percentage
Argentina	54.5
Bolivia	60.0
Brazil	43.5
Chile	46.5
Colombia	23.0
Costa Rica	28.0
Cuba	—
Dominican Republic	18.5
Ecuador	24.5
El Salvador	14.0
Guatemala	11.5
Haiti	5.0
Honduras	17.0
Mexico	37.0
Nicaragua	17.0
Panama	—
Paraguay	13.0
Peru	34.5
Uruguay	35.5
Venezuela	22.5

SOURCE   SALA 23.

Hence, small though its debt is in world terms, Costa Rica's total debt amounts to 28 per cent of its export earnings, and these are not, in any case, sufficient to meet its import needs – Costa Rica has run a net deficit on its balance of payments since 1956. The main reason for this deficit is that Costa Rica has to import all its oil and this has to be paid for in dollars. Though as a percentage of export earnings Venezuela's debt amounts to 22.5 per cent and Mexico's to 37 per cent, their situation is generally regarded as manageable because all are sub-stantial oil exporters. Argentina, with 54.5 per cent, Brazil with 43.5 per cent, and Chile with 46.5 per cent can only supply their own internal markets in oil, and Brazil has only been able to do so since the early 1980s; hence their situation is less favourable. But these countries have a substantial manufacturing base and the possibility of earning foreign exchange by diversifying their exports. Bolivia's economy, with the collapse in the tin market, is in such a bad way that it has little or no hope of coping with its 60 per cent. Likewise Uruguay's 35.5 per cent is highly problematic, given its limited industrial base and declining economy. A recovery in the price of oil, though repeatedly forecast in the late 1980s, has not materialized. If it does, however, it will benefit the larger economies but the smaller ones will suffer even further, since they lack the flexibility to recover. Costa Rica, the Dominican Republic, El Salvador, Haiti, Honduras and Panama have all run deficits on their balance of payments for years, while Guatemala, Nicaragua and Paraguay have suffered massive oscilla-tions which have been highly disruptive. Some degree of oscillation is, of course, almost inevitable given the very high dependence of most Latin American economies on exports of primary products, the prices of which are set by the consumer countries in a world market which fluctuates violently according to all sorts of external causes. Though all remain critically dependent on the export of primary products, the primary products themselves and the degree of contribution each makes (see Table 7.2), have changed radically in some cases in a relatively short space of time.

A major and quite unexpected change, which could have both good and bad effects for Latin America, is the extraordinary incompetence with which the United States economy has been managed in the past few years. What has been admiringly termed 'Reaganomics' – the belief that a country can at one and the same time spend heavily and keep taxes low – is not new. It is, in fact, precisely the syndrome that has wrecked so many Latin American economies. In the course of one year, 1986, the United States went from being a creditor nation to being a major net debtor – its end of year figure, $286 billion, being nearly three times that of either Brazil or Mexico. Since then the United States has plunged deeper and deeper into debt, as it has had to borrow to fund an ever-worsening trade deficit. In the long term, this absurd situation may benefit Latin American states, freeing them from two generations of subordination to the most powerful economy in the world. But in the short run the prospect of a recession in the world's

TABLE 7.2   *Principal exports as a percentage of total exports*

Country	Exports
Argentina	Corn 9.1, Wheat 13.5
Bolivia	Tin 29.9, Natural gas 59.8
Brazil	Soybeans 9.9, Coffee 9.2
Chile	Copper 46.1
Colombia	Coffee 50.2
Costa Rica	Bananas 22.1, Coffee 32.2
Dominican Republic	Sugar 25.9, Ferronickel 16.4
Ecuador	Crude oil 62.8, Bananas 7.6
El Salvador	Coffee 60.9, Cotton 4.5
Guatemala	Coffee 42.5
Haiti	Coffee 26.0, Bauxite 8.6
Honduras	Coffee 22.7, Bananas 31.1
Mexico	Petroleum 66.6
Nicaragua	Cotton 34.1, Coffee 30.4
Panama	Shrimp 17.8, Bananas 23.3
Paraguay	Cotton 48.9, Soybeans 33.2
Peru	Copper 15.6, Petroleum products 14.1
Uruguay	Wool 19.2, Meat 13.8
Venezuela	Petroleum 84.3

SOURCE   SALA 23.

richest country, resulting in cutbacks in US imports, remains a hazard to Latin American recovery, and, at the same time, reduces any possibility of effective aid from that source.

Unlike Europe, Latin America has never been a major beneficiary of US economic aid. On the contrary, it has been an area from which American companies have drawn huge profits, syphoning off badly needed capital for the benefit of shareholders in the developed countries. It is seldom realized how big these outflows actually are in relation to what goes in, but some individual examples will make the point clear. Between 1966 and 1976 British American Tobacco invested £2.5 million in Brazil, and received in return a capital outflow of £82.3 million. Esso put £1.8 million into Brazil, and drew out £44.5 million, and Firestone gained £50.2 million in exchange for £4.1 million invested. Between 1970 and 1976 the net earnings of British companies trading in Latin America totalled £390.8 million. Over the decade since the debt crisis broke in 1983 new investment in Latin America has been far less than the total of profits repatriated.

What then for the future? Some Western politicians fail to see there is a problem. For them, the Latin Americans ought simply to pay their debts. But if the Argentine economy had not been hit by recession at the beginning of the 1980s the Falklands War might never have happened.

In 1989 the seven major Latin American states banded together to concert their pressure on the developed countries instead of each competing to get in first with a stabilization package. The states concerned did not simply want to put off the evil day, as they had done for five years to no avail. They wanted to be rid of the debt problem. Their remedy, to exchange debt for equity, as Mexico has swapped debt for new investment in tourist hotels and other potentially profitable growth areas, is a slow one, but the evidence is that it should work given time. Again, however, the greatest potential exists for diversification in the larger and more sophisticated economies. As we shall see later, the problem of Latin America is not that it lacks well developed tertiary (service) industries; if anything it has too many of them in relation to the size of its primary producing and especially its secondary manufacturing sectors. What we are witnessing in the advanced industrial countries, as their manufacturing sectors shrink and production is transferred to the Newly Industrializing Countries (NICs) of Asia and the Pacific Rim, is nothing less than the latinamericanization of their economies, with all that that implies for their future social structure. The most striking evidence of change since has come from Mexico. With the aid of the US Treasury Secretary's Brady Plan, it recapitalised its debt, started a massive programme of privatisation, and in August 1992 agreed to enter a North American Free Trade Area (NAFTA) with the United States and Canada.

THE LAND QUESTION

Closely related to the problem of dependence on the exports of primary products is the land question. This has dominated the history of political and social struggles in Latin America since independence and looks set to do so well into the twenty-first century. What makes it qualitatively different is that as populations swell, many countries of the region are running short of food.

The size of the Latin American states is deceptive. Most of them do not have enough good arable land. Only 21 million hectares (12.1 per cent) of Mexico's total land area of 197.3 million hectares is arable, 1.5 million is planted to permanent crops other than forest, and 74 million hectares is pasture. More surprisingly perhaps, less than two-thirds of the arable land is cultivated, and one-third of that cultivated land has to be watered by expensive irrigation systems from a very limited range of water sources. Yet Mexico is a country where, following a major social revolution, successive governments made real attempts to distribute land more equally to all those who wanted it. Between 1916 and 1969 59 413 656 hectares were distributed to 2 525 811 families, much in collective ownership designed to prevent the land again falling into the hands of the few. Despite complaints that these collective farms (*ejidos*) have been inefficient, the evidence is that they have contributed as much to national production as the roughly equal sized private sector. What is in trouble now is the whole of Mexican agriculture. Up to now, difficulties have been masked by the great success of irrigation, the general improvement of productivity, and the success of industrialization, which has led the newly affluent to turn away from the traditional country diet towards wheaten bread and expensive imported foods. Now Mexico, where maize probably originated in its modern form, is actually unable to grow enough of this staple to feed its population, and in recent years has been importing beans, the only significant protein source for the poorer members of the community. Meanwhile, in the border districts intensively cultivated with irrigation waters drawn from the Colorado River or the Rio Grande vegetables and fruit are being grown on a vast scale for export to the United States. Similarly in Bolivia, of the total land area of 109.9 million hectares, only 21.9 million (19.9 per cent) is arable. The land reform which started in 1955 distributed 9.7 million hectares to 208 181 families, and was sufficiently successful to prevent the peasant beneficiaries heeding the siren call of Havana. But in the 1980s, as the economy tottered, governments flitted across the scene and the armed forces disputed among themselves for the pickings, farmers switched into growing coca for the drug syndicates and Bolivia became more and not less dependent on imported foodstuffs.

Left-wing critics of such land reform programmes have long predicted that they are doomed to fail and point to the success of land reform in Cuba. As we have seen, in the early 1960s land was effectively nationalized in Cuba and a system of state farms established. Yet a closer examination suggests that Cuba is in very much the same position as the other Latin American states, and this despite the fact that nature has allotted it a larger share of arable land than most Latin American countries. As early as the 1960s it was having to import black beans, the staple food of the Caribbean area. The drive for industrialization having failed, sugar again became the principal crop and in 1970, the 'Year of the Ten Millions' almost a fifth more land was under cultivation than in 1959–61. But this effort was too great and since then the proportion has fallen back almost to its pre-revolutionary figure. The shortages remain, though the rationing system at least ensures a reasonably equitable distribution.

Some countries, certainly, have been able to postpone the crisis of overpopulation by bringing new land into cultivation. By 1974 Paraguay was cultivating over twice as much land as in 1959–61; Brazil and Ecuador just over and Guatemala just under one-and-a-half times as much. Even now Paraguay has a population density of only 7.5 per sq. km. In the case of Brazil, however, the attempt to open up the Amazon basin has gone seriously wrong, failing to give adequate subsistence to settlers while bringing about the destruction of the rain forest and the potential destruction of the whole ecology of the region. The red laterite soil is thin and lacking in nutrients. The settlers cut a clearing for themselves and set fire to the rest. Most of the nutrients locked up in the vegetation go up in smoke, contributing to the 'greenhouse effect'; the ash for a year or two gives deceptively good crops until the goodness is leached out of the soil, which then bakes dry and rock-hard in the sun. Then the rain tears away the remaining soil and it runs away uselessly to the sea. The ground is useless and the settlers move on to slash and burn more of the rain forest before they give up. Consequently, attempts to divert internal migrants from the northeast away from the great cities of the coast have failed. The would-be settlers have left destruction behind them and headed for the cities anyway and the shanty towns have continued to grow.

In Paraguay, the fact that many of the new settlers are Brazilians has raised ethnic tensions. Ethnic stresses, too, have been exacerbated in Guatemala, where the new lands have not gone to the poor Indian peasants who have to seek seasonal jobs on the lowland plantations, but to Army officers and to their ladino civilian allies. It has a crisis of overpopulation when its population density, 56 per sq. km, is only a fraction of that of Cuba (88), the Dominican Republic (116), Haiti (156) or El Salvador (170). The civil war that has raged in Peru in the early 1980s has also increased tension between the traditionally Hispanic rulers of the country and the large proportion of the population who are peasant farmers of indigenous origin. Like Guatemala and Peru, Bolivia, Ecuador and Mexico also have a large rural population of indigenous origin, while Brazil, Colombia, Panama, Paraguay and Venezuela each have a significant number of indigenous inhabitants still living in tribal areas under traditional conditions.

Natural hazards, in particular earthquakes and hurricanes, add an unpredictable element. Fortunately earthquakes, such as the one that toppled buildings in Mexico City on 19 September 1985, usually affect a relatively limited area, but the Guatemalan earthquake of 4 February 1976, which registered 7.5 on the Richter scale, resulted in 22 778 deaths and untold homelessness over a wide area, wrecked roads and railway lines and embittered already serious social cleavages. In 1987 the eruption of Mt Nevado del Ruiz in Colombia was foreseen, but no precautions were taken, and the destruction by a mudslide of the town of Armero and its inhabitants served as a signal of government incompetence to many of its opponents. Hurricanes kill fewer people, especially if warnings have been given and heeded, but they leave vast numbers of homeless and destroy crops on an immense scale. In 1988 Hurricane Gilbert, the most powerful tropical storm recorded in the Western hemisphere, caused widespread devastation in the Dominican Republic, Jamaica and the Gulf region of Mexico with only a small loss of life; more lost their lives when later Colombia and Nicaragua were struck by Hurricane Joan, but again political considerations contributed to make misery worse when the warm-hearted citizens of the United States, who had generously come to the aid of Somoza's Nicaragua after the Managua earthquake of 23 December 1972, turned their backs on Sandinista Nicaragua.

Not all countries of the hemisphere had increased their cultivation by 1974. Chile (85 per cent) and Uruguay (76 per cent) were cultivating considerably less, and in both cases the countries have since been systematically deindustrialized by incompetent and misguided governments, with the ultimate result that poverty has been increased and thousands have emigrated. Similarly, the underpopulated vast arable plains of temperate Argentina have continued to be farmed extensively. Millions of Argentines have been receiving food supplements from the government in a country which exports food on a vast scale and should be able to sustain its entire population at a level equal to the world's richest countries. A poor 'First World' nation, Argentina seemed to be sinking irrevocably into the Third World, when in 1990 a new Minister of the Economy, Domingo Cavallo, successfully stabilised the currency and set it on the path of recovery.

THE URBAN/RURAL DIVIDE

Latin American countries have long been ruled by small urbanized élites who treat all the problems of their respective countries as if they were those of the capital and its environs. In 1983 40 per cent of Uruguayans lived in Montevideo, 37.3 per cent of Chileans in Santiago, 34.1 per cent of Argentines in Buenos Aires and each of these countries, like Venezuela, was three-quarters urbanized. Also heavily urbanized was Mexico, with 20.1 per cent of Mexicans living in the capital region, which is generally regarded now as the world's largest city. Though Bolivia, Costa Rica, the Dominican Republic, Ecuador, El Salvador, Guatemala, Haiti, Honduras, Nicaragua, Panama and Paraguay retained a rural majority in their population, the same trends were already noticeable in several of these less-developed states. In the twenty-first century the urban population will continue to grow and the problems of overurbanization will increase alongside the continuing spectre of rural poverty.

In 1980 censuses gave Brazil a population of 119 million, Mexico 67 million, Argentina 28 million and Colombia 26 million. For the size of the countries concerned these figures did not yet give rise to alarm – indeed many Latin American politicians still continue to welcome population growth both as a sign of their own virility and as the only natural resource that increases spontaneously. Between 1970 and 1980, however, population increased at least as fast as in the United States in all Latin American countries except Uruguay. Social attitudes, such as the desire for insurance in one's old age, encourage this. So too does the teaching of the dominant Catholic Church. Though artificial contraception is already practised widely among the middle classes, the Church continues to denounce all forms of contraception other than the 'rhythm method', and the technical term for people who rely on that is 'parents'.

Hence, the slowest rates of growth (Uruguay 0.4, Argentina 1.6 and Chile 1.7 per cent per annum) occurred in the wealthier states and the fastest rates were found in the poorer states. Moreover, some were very rapid indeed: Nicaragua growing at 3.7 per cent and Ecuador and Venezuela 3.4 per cent per annum. This means that on all demo-graphic precedents the problem of rapidly growing populations is going to be a problem for Latin America well into the new century. Some 48 per cent of Nicaraguans or Hondurans, and 45 per cent of Mexicans are under the age of 15. Although by the year 2010 this last figure is expected to drop to around 30 per cent, this will only be because the population of older people is expected to increase and not because there is any expectation that those who are in their early 20s then will be limiting the size of their families. In fact in many other countries the figures then will look much the same as they do today. This means that not only, by the standards of the developed countries, will a relatively small number of mature workers continue to have to provide the economic basis for public programmes of housing, education, health care, social services and welfare, but the countries concerned will be hard put even to find work for those. Here too the trends are not encouraging as regards the future of the smaller states. As Table 7.3 shows, the distribution of the labour force in the larger countries already shows a recognizably 'modern' profile, with relatively few people engaged in primary production and a relatively large number in secondary manufacturing industry. Argentina and Uruguay are the most striking examples. But there are warning signs even here. Cuba, despite strenuous efforts to modernize, still has a much larger proportion of its working population engaged in primary production than the countries on which it seeks to model itself. And Chile, while retaining a rather large primary sector, has an extraordinarily large proportion of its population employed in the tertiary services sector. Like Argentina, and, to a slightly lesser extent Uruguay, it resembles in this last respect a modern developed economy such as that of the United States, but without the base of manufacturing industry which would enable it to maintain the level of production and exports that has traditionally been required to support it. The fact that other developed countries such as Britain are going down the same road is not a sign of health in these economies, rather the reverse. The outlook for the twenty-first century, then, is that these larger economies will continue to have difficulty in maintaining their relative position in the world unless some way is found either of expanding production or reducing expectations still further.

As regards the smaller economies, the picture is even more bleak. In Bolivia, the Dominican Republic, El Salvador, Guatemala, Honduras and Paraguay half of the working population, in Haiti three-quarters, are still engaged in primary production. Their future depends on their closeness to subsistence level, the unpredictable chances of flood, storm or earthquake, and on the unpredictable demands of the world market. Manufacturing, too, is closely geared to the needs of the primary sector and shares its problems. The economies are too small to supply a large range of products now universally sought and desired, so these have to be imported, at great cost relative to the money earned by the primary sector. And in both large and small countries the table tells us nothing of the numbers in work. All suffer from high levels of unemployment and underemployment.

Unemployment statistics in Latin America are notoriously inaccurate and little is known outside the major cities. Santiago de Chile, Bogotá, Caracas and Montevideo all have high levels of unemployment. Estimates of the numbers of Mexicans unemployed ranged from 6 to 18 million at the beginning of 1988 and by the year end had risen substantially, probably to over 20 million of the estimated 80 million population. Only those in the state-sponsored union sector enjoyed anything resembling adequate social security. As adults, all Cubans and, more surprisingly, 96.3 per cent of Brazilians are covered by some measure of social security, but in the Dominican Republic, Ecuador, Guatemala and Honduras well under 10 per cent and in Haiti under 1 per cent enjoy any degree of protection. Here too their exposure to the bracing effect of market forces has brought not prosperity, but misery.

Some of the consequences can be foreseen easily enough. The primary sector in all cases is too large and is unable to absorb the

TABLE 7.3   *Individual economic sectors as percentage of total labour force*

Country	Primary	Secondary	Tertiary
Argentina	13	28	59
Bolivia	50	24	26
Brazil	30	24	36
Chile	19	19	62
Colombia	26	21	53
Costa Rica	21	23	48
Cuba	23	31	36
Dominican Republic	49	18	53
Ecuador	52	17	31
El Salvador	50	22	28
Guatemala	55	21	24
Haiti	74	7	19
Honduras	63	20	17
Mexico	36	26	38
Nicaragua	39	14	47
Panama	33	18	49
Paraguay	49	19	32
Peru	40	19	41
Uruguay	11	32	57
Venezuela	18	27	55
UNITED STATES	2	32	66

SOURCE   SALA 24.

growing population of working age. Young men and women will therefore have to seek work elsewhere. Migrants will continue to flock to capitals (and a few major provincial cities) in search of work. They will leave behind in the countryside an aging population who will find it increasingly difficult to provide the necessary food for the burgeoning urban population. They will find when they arrive horrendous problems of housing, food, sanitation and health. Their entrepreneurial skills will be tested to the full as they occupy themselves with all manner of marginal and largely unproductive bits of jobs to try to make a living for themselves and their growing families. They will find great difficulty in making their wants known to those in authority, as the middle classes, striving to keep up their standard of living by doing two or even three jobs at a time, defend their relatively privileged positions. Yet with radio universal and television blanketing all major centres of population in the region the majority of Latin Americans now have the opportunity to compare their conditions directly with those of the developed states, and it would be strange indeed if after a glimpse of life in a Los Angeles penthouse apartment they did not find their own living conditions squalid and inadequate.

QUALITY OF LIFE

Figures for the region as a whole show a marked discrepancy between expectation of life at birth in the larger wealthier states and the smaller poorer ones. Though there are some anomalies, such as the astonishing number of Venezuelans (11.8 per cent) who die in accidents or Guatemalans who are victims of homicide (11.2 per cent), the usual reason for low expectation of life at birth is that far too many babies die before they reach the age of one expressed per thousand live births (infant mortality rate or IMR). The US in 1983 had an IMR of 10.5 and this like rates in Western Europe has continued to fall. Cuba's rate, the lowest reported in Latin America, was 25.6; Bolivia's, the highest, was 124.4. A high IMR is commonly caused by poor nutrition, poor hygiene and inadequate medical services. Though in Bolivia's case high altitude and cold also play a part, among the other countries in the region the three main factors show a striking consistency.

In Argentina, at one end of the scale, the daily calorie intake is 3195, compared with 3647 for the United States, and only some 8 per cent of the population is undernourished, though the National Food Programme is now needed to ensure that food is available. Most houses have piped water and a proper toilet. There are 26.7 physicians

TABLE 7.4   *Life expectancy at birth*

Country	Life expectancy
Argentina	70
Bolivia	51
Brazil	64
Chile	67
Colombia	64
Costa Rica	71
Dominican Republic	63
Ecuador	63
El Salvador	65
Guatemala	61
Haiti	53
Honduras	60
Mexico	66
Nicaragua	58
Panama	71
Paraguay	65
Peru	59
Uruguay	70
Venezuela	68

SOURCE   CEPAL 1982.

for every thousand population. The IMR is low and adult Argentines tend to die of the diseases of an affluent society like the United States or Europe. The commonest causes of death are heart disease (31.9 per cent) and malignant cancers (17.6 per cent).

By almost all standard measures Haiti, the poorest country of the region, stands at the opposite pole. The average daily calorie intake is only 1901 – a figure which is dangerously near the minimum necessary to sustain life – and 90 per cent of the population is undernourished. Few houses have piped water or a proper toilet. There are only 1.2 physicians per thousand population. The IMR is high and, as in Guatemala, El Salvador and even Mexico, adults still die of the diseases of poverty: enteritis, diarrhoea and other infectious and parasitic diseases. The irony is, of course, that virtually all of these can now be cured if adequate medical services are available. Instead, it seems that relying on the free market in health may have brought nemesis on those who deny the right of all to health and trust to the impersonal forces of the market to protect them. The motto of the market is 'Let the buyer beware'. Tragically, Haiti suffers uniquely from the terrible scourge of AIDS, and AIDS, some believe, reached the United States from there as a result of the abhorrent trade in blood products, by which medical corporations have induced poverty-stricken Haitians to sell blood and even parts of their bodies to stay alive while saving the lives of the inhabitants of the world's richest country.

In the twenty-first century medical science will have to be brought on a large scale to the inhabitants of the poorer countries of the region if the inhabitants of the richer ones are to benefit fully from modern developments. Prevention is better than cure and it is all too seldom realized that the demographic explosion in nineteenth-century Europe began with improved hygiene and was well under way before Lister had discovered antiseptics or Pasteur and Koch the bacteria that cause disease. International programmes have eliminated smallpox but yellow fever, once the scourge of the sailors of tropical America and now, though much rarer, still endemic in tropical South and Central America, has yet to follow. Public spending on a vast scale is still needed in many parts of Latin America on the essential but unspectacular necessities of pure water, efficient waste disposal and mass immunization against unnecessary killers such as diptheria, measles and tuberculosis.

All Latin American countries fall short of the United States in terms of quality of life, that indeterminate quality that summarizes the life chances offered by the society to the individual. Those that come nearest are Argentina, Costa Rica, Cuba and Uruguay. In Argentina the middle and upper classes make up 38 per cent of the population; in Uruguay 35 per cent, as against 14 per cent for the El Salvador of the 'fourteen Families' and 12 per cent for Guatemala under military occupation by its own armed forces. Virtually every child of primary school age in Argentina, as in Chile, Costa Rica or Cuba, is enrolled in school and children there have a one-in-three chance of passing through to tertiary education. In Argentina, only 4.5 per cent of those over the age of 15 are unable to read and write; in Cuba 4.6 per cent, and Chile 5.6 per cent. At the other end of the scale, over 40 per cent of Haitians lack even primary education and over 60 per cent are illiterate. Thus the gulf between opportunities for youth in the rich and the poor countries continues to grow.

Since 1960 major literacy campaigns in Cuba, Peru and Nicaragua have achieved striking levels of success, though the second was not followed up and the third has been actively misrepresented by official US sources. Even in the age of the electronic media, literacy is still the essential tool that opens the doors of opportunity. Less spectacular has been a steady advance in general levels of literacy during the same period, and the expansion of secondary and tertiary education. At its best Latin American education is very good indeed. But most, at both primary and secondary level, still depends on badly paid teachers whose frequently inadequate training has often been secured part-time at their own expense and who, through a variety of causes ranging from the chronic shortage of funds for school books and equipment to military purges and closures of schools or colleges, are confined to imparting uncontroversial information learned by rote, in short, training rather than education.

The difference is crucial. For training teaches one to deal with the known and predictable; education is about learning to deal with the unknown and unpredictable, and the lesson of our present century is that we can foresee general trends, but we cannot yet know (if we ever can) what will be the particular incidents or events that turn these trends into political action. Hence, the future of Latin America in the twenty-first century is in a very real sense in the hands of those who plan and provide for the education of its growing masses. Latin America needs a new start, and that can only come from people trained and educated to seek new solutions to old problems.

Postscript: Rio and After

The Rio Conference of 1992 briefly focused world attention on some of these problems, which are, of course, of world-wide significance. As ever, though, Latin America is uniquely well placed to act as a mediator between North and South. When in 1988 the idea that the United Nations should take the lead in problems of environment and development was first suggested, President José Sarney was quick to suggest that the proposed 'World Summit' should be held in Brazil. In the event it was his successor, President Collor, who welcomed more than 120 heads of state and government to Rio and presided over the conference, and ex-President Sarney was not even invited.

The dilemma which faced the 'World Summit', properly the United Nations Conference on Environment and Development (UNCED), was to reconcile the conflicting demands of the South, the less-developed countries, anxious to develop what resources they possessed, and the North, the developed countries, eager to maintain their own standard of living. Not surprisingly, few people were satisfied with the outcome. Only two actual Treaties were agreed. However the United States signed the Framework Convention on Global Warming only because it had been watered down and all binding commitments removed. Malaysia refused to sign the convention on Biodiversity, asserting its right to 'exploit' (i.e. destroy) its remaining tropical rainforest if it chose, precisely as President Sarney had earlier done in Brazil, and no agreement at all was reached which would check the destruction in time to forestall irrevocable loss on a massive scale. Some optimism was generated by agreement on a formidable list of further problems to be investigated, termed 'Agenda 21', and notably on the fact that for the first time in world history, this massive document formally recognised the central role of women in economic development.

The central problem of UNCED was on a global scale the problem of the conflict of interests between Latin America political èlites and the masses of their own countries. The massive security presence mounted to 'protect' the delegates did not disguise the serious economic and political problems of Brazil itself, where on 24 May, on the eve of the conference, President Collor was accused of corruption by his own brother, and within three months was facing impeachment by a Congress dominated by his political opponents. Although no longer official policy, the destruction of the Amazon rainforest at the hands of would-be settlers continued, while the *garimpieros* (gold prospectors) invaded Indian lands, carrying with them disease and other problems.

As so often in the past, President Castro of Cuba stole the show. Though outwardly a hang-over from the past, wearing an extraordinary multicoloured, Central European style military uniform wholly at odds with the new democratic, civilian Latin America of the 1990s, he spoke incisively. In complete contrast with his traditional oratorical style, he used only four of his allotted seven minutes to punch home two simple messages: that it was the imperialist countries that had wrecked the world and that they should pay to put it right. He received applause even by President Bush, whose late decision to attend had brought him into the hall only a few minutes beforehand. Yet his own policies had throughout his career been based on the same strategies of industialisation and monoculture he was now criticising, and he had left behind him in Cuba an economy devastated by the collapse of the Soviet Union, whose only hope for survival, let alone recovery, seemed to lie in the rediscovery, of all things, of dollar tourism.

From the Brazilians, President Carlos Menem of Argentina received a particularly warm welcome. For him, too, the environment remained essentially something to exploit. However the Brazilians had been impressed by the apparent success of Sr Cavallo's economic reforms, which had led in April to the successful refunding of the country's debt on terms which reduced the overall burden by some $10 billion. They were also impressed by the progress made so far on the privatisation of Argentina's large state sector. In addition his visit marked a further step in a new and potentially very exciting development, the creation of a four-country Southern Common Market (Mercosur) of Argentina, Bolivia, Brazil and Uruguay, planned to eliminate trade barriers by 1994.

Among the other Latin American political dignitaries present, President Fujimori of Peru faced the most serious problems. Lacking the political support and experience to mobilise opinion for a severe programme of economic stabilisation, he had in April 1992 carried out an 'internal coup' (*autogolpe*), dissolved Congress and imposed rule by decree, backed by the Army. This action, which represented the first major break in the new democratic solidarity of the continent, was unwelcome in the United States, which was, on the other hand, unwilling to put too much pressure on a friendly government faced by the sole remaining 'Communist threat' in the area, which at the same time was their main hope to control the principal coca-growing region of the continent.

Elsewhere where democratic governments had been elected they remained in power, though sometimes as much by good luck as by good judgment. An attempted military coup in February 1992 in Venezuela against the government of President Carlos Andrés Pérez took the government completely by surprise, but was successfully put down without it achieving the widespread support among the armed forces for which its promoters had hoped. In neighbouring Colombia, the government of President César Gaviria survived the derision that followed when Pablo Escobar, leader of the Medellín drug cartel, 'escaped' from the so-called 'prison' to which he had been consigned after his supposed 'surrender' to the authorities. The 'prison', which he had designed himself, had in fact been a safe command centre from which he had been continuing to control his narcotics empire, and he had only left it when a new Minister of Justice proposed to make it secure. In Ecuador, elections in June gave victory to the conservative leader of the Republican Unity Party (PUR), Sixto Durán Ballén, who took office as President in August.

Even in Central America, the outlook for the restoration of peace had never looked better. In both El Salvador and Guatemala negotiations continued for an end to the guerrilla warfare that had lasted for more than a generation. Progress was slow but in the meanwhile some improvement in economic conditions was evident. At Rio, President Violeta Barrios de Chamorro of Nicaragua had received the constructive tolerance of the Sandinistas for a moderate conservative programme, and was well received by other Latin American delegates. However, President Endara of Panama prudently did not attend, and President Bush's ill-timed decision to stop over in Panama on his way to the conference to meet Endara led to violent rioting which blanketed the headlines on his arrival. The problem, of course, was the continued misery of the Panamanian population, few of whom had benefited from the many promises made at the time of the 1989 intervention.

Only a few of the new island states of the Caribbean shared the fears of their Pacific and Indian Ocean counterparts, that within a generation the rising sea level caused by global warming could threaten their livelihoods. Michael Manley of Jamaica had been succeeded in March by his former deputy, Percival Patterson, thus depriving the Commonwealth Caribbean of their most experienced radical voice, and their contribution to the public debate was muted.

Patterson, who had been forced out of Manley's cabinet for alleged corruption as recently as December 1991, predictably placed the responsibility for global warming on the developed countries, while the Prime Minister of Barbados, Erskine Sandiford, treated the assembled delegates to an Ode in honour of the occasion composed entirely by himself.

For the smaller islands the major issue of 1992 was the so-called 'Eurobanana'. The European Commission proposed in April to support the special preference accorded to Commonwealth bananas under the Lomé Convention, by imposing a Community quota on bananas from the American mainland. This met with stiff resistance from the producer countries, led by Costa Rica, Honduras and Panama, and supported by Germany, the largest importer of 'dollar bananas'. For the smaller states, Eugenia Charles, Prime Minister of Dominica, led the fight for continued preferential terms, claiming that their removal would devastate the economy, not only of her small island state, but of others such as St Kitts and St Vincent, but the issue remained in the balance.

In short, the problem for Latin America and the Caribbean was not so much that the so-called 'free market', that they had embraced so enthusiastically, would not work, but that it would not work in the way that they hoped. Specifically, the beneficiaries were likely to be larger, low-cost producers; the losers, the smaller, weaker economies. Secondly, the action of the market promised to be much too slow to prevent irrevocable damage to the environment – the extinction of species, in particular, could not be averted once their numbers had declined below a critical level, and until that level was reached, there was insufficient motivation, under the unchecked market system, to halt the decline.

Presidents of Latin American States since 1900

ARGENTINA

1898–1904	Gen Julio Argentino Roca (PN)	Elite co-option
1904–06	Manuel A. Quintana (PN)	do.
1906–10	José Figueroa Alcorta (PN)	Vice-President
1910–14	Roque Saenz Peña (PN)	Elite co-option
1914–16	Victorino de la Plaza (PN)	Vice-President
1916–22	Hipólito Yrigoyen (UCR)	Election
1922–28	Marcelo Torcuato de Alvear (UCR)	Radical co-option; election
1928–30	Hipólito Yrigoyen (UCR)	Election
1930–32	José Félix Uriburu	Military coup
1932–38	Agustín P. Justo (Con)	Elite co-option
1938–40	Roberto M. Ortiz (Con)	Elite co-option
1940–43	Ramón F. Castillo (Con)	Vice-President: acting 1940–42; then succeeded on resignation of President
June 5–7 1943	Gen. Arturo P. Rawson	Military coup
1943–44	Gen. Pedro P. Ramírez	Military co-option
1944–46	Gen. Edelmiro J. Farrell	Military co-option
1946–55	Col. Juan D. Perón	Election
1955	Gen. Eduardo Lonardi	Military coup
1955–58	Gen. Pedro Eugenio Aramburu	Military co-option
1958–62	Arturo Frondizi (UCR-I)	Election
1962–63	José María Guido	Military coup; President of Senate
1963–66	Dr Arturo Illia (UCRP)	Election
1966–70	Gen. Juan Carlos Onganía	Military coup
June 8–14 1970	Adm. Pedro Gnavi	Military coup
1970–71	Brig-Gen. Roberto M. Levingston	Military co-option
Mar 22–24 1971	Junta	Military co-option
1971–73	Gen. Alejandro Lanusse	Military co-option
1973	Héctor Cámpora (PJ)	Election
1973–74	Lt-Gen. Juan D. Perón (PJ)	Perónist co-option and election
1974–76	María Estela (Isabel) Martínez de Perón (PJ)	Vice-President; death of President
Mar 24–29 1976	Junta	Military coup
1976–81	Gen. Jorge Videla	Military co-option

206   *Presidents of Latin American States since 1900*

Mar–Nov 1981	Gen. Roberto Viola	do.
Nov–Dec	Maj.-Gen. Horacio Tomás Liendo	do.
Dec 11–22	Vice-Adm. (ret) Carlos Alberto Lacoste	do.
1981–82	Gen. Leopoldo Galtieri	do.
Jun–July 1982	Gen. Alfredo Saint-Jean	do.
1982–83	Gen. Reynaldo Bignone	do.
1983–89	Dr Raúl Alfonsín (UCR)	Election
1989–	Dr Carlos Saúl Menem (PJ)	do.

Con = Concordancia, PJ = Partido Justicialista (Peronists), PN = Partido Nacional, UCR = Unión Cívica Radical

BOLIVIA

1899–1904	José Manuel Pando (L)	Ltd. election
1904–09	Ismael Montes (L)	do.
1909–13	Eliodoro Villazón (L)	Elite co-option; controlled election
1913–17	Ismael Montes (L)	do.
1917–20	Gutiérrez Guerra (L)	do.
1921–26	Bautista Saavedra (Rep)	Republican revolt
1926–30	Hernando Siles (Rep/Nat)	Co-option
1930–31	Carlos Blanco Galindo	Presidential handover
1931–34	Daniel Salamanca (Coalition)	Popular revolt and controlled election
1934–36	José Luis Tejada Sorzano (L)	Vice-President
1936–37	Col. José David Toro	Military coup
1937–39	Col. Germán Busch	Military co-option as provisional President; then election
1939–40	Gen. Carlos Quintanilla	Suicide of President; military co-option
1940–43	Gen. Enrique Peñaranda del Castillo (Coalition)	Military traditional party coalition
1943–46	Maj. Gualberto Villaroel (MNR)	Coup supported by MNR
1946–47	Tomás Monje Guitérrez (Coalition)	Popular revolt; death of President
1947–49	Enrique Herzog (Rep)	Election
1949–51	Mamerto Urralagoita (Rep)	Provisional President, then election
1951–52	Gen. Hugo Ballivián	Presidential resignation and illegal handover
Apr 9–16 1952	Hernán Siles Zuazo (MNR)	Popular revolt
1952–56	Víctor Paz Estenssoro (MNR)	Election; MNR co-option

1956–60	Hernán Siles Zuazo (MNR)	Election
1960–64	Víctor Paz Estenssoro (MNR)	Election
1964–69	Gen. René Barrientos Ortuño	Coup after elections
Apr–Sept 1969	Luis Adolfo Siles Salinas (C)	Vice-President; death of President
1969–70	Gen. Alfredo Ovando Candia	Military co-option
1970–71	Gen. Juan José Torres	Coup
1971–78	Col. Hugo Banzer Suárez	Coup
July–Nov 1978	Gen. Juan Pereda Asbún	Military co-option
1978–79	Gen. David Padilla Arancibia	Military revolt
Aug–Nov 1979	Walter Guevara Arze (PRA)	Compromise candidate; inconclusive elections
1979–80	Lidia Gueiler Tejada (MNR)	Popular opposition to military
1980–81	Gen. Luis García Meza Tejada	Coup: UDP election victory annulled
Aug–Sept1981	Junta	Coup
1981–82	Gen. Celso Torrelio Villa	Military co-option
July–Oct 1982	Gen. Guido Vildoso Calderón	Military co-option
1982–85	Hernán Siles Zuazo (UDP)	Election
1985–89	Víctor Paz Estenssoro (MNR-H)	Election
1989–	Jaime Paz Zamora (AP)	Election

AP = Patriotic Accord, C = Conservative, L = Liberal, MNR = National Revolutionary Movement (MNR–H = Historic faction), Rep = Republican, UDP = People's Democratic Union

BRAZIL

1898–1902	Manoel Ferraz de Campos Salles (Rep)	Elite co-option – limited election
1902–06	Francisco de Paula Rodrigues Alves (Rep)	do.
1906–09	Affonso Augusto Moreira Penna (Rep)	do.
1909–10	Nilo Peçanha (Rep)	Vice-Presidential
1910–14	Marshal Hermes de Fonseca	Elite co-option – limited election
1914–18	Wenceslau Braz Pereira Gomes (Rep)	do.
1918	Francisco de Paula Rodrigues Alves (Rep)	do.
1918–19	Delphim Moreira da Costa Ribeiro (Rep)	Vice-Presidential
1919–22	Epitácio da Silva Pessoa (Rep)	Elite co-option – limited election
1922–26	Arturo da Silva Bernades (Rep)	Limited election
1926–30	Washington Luiz Pereira de Sousa (Rep)	do.
Oct–Nov 1930	Junta	Coup

1930–45	Getúlio Dornelles Vargas (Lib. Alliance)	Military co-option, then election
1945–46	José Linhares	President of Supreme Court
1946–51	Gen. Enrico Gaspar Dutra	Election
1951–54	Getúlio Dornelles Vargas (PTB)	Alliance co-option; election
1954–55	Joao Café Filho (PSP)	Vice-President: Coup/Suicide of President
8–11 Nov 1955	Carlos Luz (PSD)	President, Chamber of Deputies
1955–56	Nereu Ramos	President of Senate
1956–61	Juscelino Kubitschek de Oliveira (PSD/PTB)	Election
Jan–Aug 1961	Jânio da Silva Quadros (Nat. Dem. Union)	Election
Aug–Sept	Raniere Mazzili (PSD)	Resignation of President; unconstitutional succession of President of Chamber of Deputies
1961–64	João Melchior Marques Goulart (PTB)	Vice-Presidential succession to Quadros
1964–67	Gen. Humberto Castello Branco	Coup
1967–69	Gen. Artur da Costa e Silva	Military co-option
1969–74	Gen. Emilio Garrastaszú Médici	Illness of President; military co-option
1974–79	Gen. Ernesto Geisel	Military co-option
1979–85	Gen. João Baptista Figueiredo	do.
1985–90	José Sarney (Dem. All.)	Military co-option; indirect elections and death of President-elect
1990–92	Fernando Collor de Mello (PRN)	Election
1992–	Itamar Franco (PRN)	Resignation of President

PSD = Social Democratic Party, PSP = Popular Socialist Party,
PRN = National Reconstruction Party, PTB = Brazilian Worker's Party

CHILE

Parliamentary Republic

1901–06	Germán Riesco	
1906–10	Pedro Montt	
1910–15	Ramón Barros Luco	
1915–20	Juan Luis Sanfuentes	
1920–24	Arturo Alessandri Palma (R)	Election
1924–25	Gen. Luis Altamirano	Coup
Jan–Mar 1925	Col. Carlos Ibáñez del Campo	Coup
Mar-Oct	Arturo Alessandri Palma	Restored by military
Oct–Dec	Luis Barros Borgoño	

Presidential Republic

1925–27	Emiliano Figueroa Larraín	
1927–31	Gen. Carlos Ibáñez del Campo	Coup
July26–27 1931	Pedro Opazo Letelier	President of Senate
July–Aug	Juan Esteban Montero Rodríguez	Minister of Interior
Aug–Nov	Manuel Trucco Franzani	
1931–32	Juan Esteban Montero Rodríguez	
Jun 4–12 1932	Arturo Puga	Acting
Jun 12–16	Col. Marmaduque Grove	Acting
Jun–Sept	Carlos Dávila Espinoza	
Sept–Oct	Bartolomé Blanche Espejo	Acting
Oct–Dec	Abraham Oyanedel	Acting
1932–38	Arturo Alessandri Palma (R)	Election
1938–41	Pedro Aguirre Cerda (R)	Election
1941–42	Geronimo Méndez Arancibia	Death of President
1942–46	Juan Antonio Ríos Morales	
June–Oct 1946	Alfredo Duhalde Vásquez	
Oct–Nov	Juan A. Irabarren	
1946–52	Gabriel González Videla (R)	Election
1952–58	Gen. Carlos Ibáñez del Campo	Election
1958–64	Jorge Alessandri Rodríguez (R)	Election
1964–70	Eduardo Frei Montalva (PCD)	Election
1970–73	Salvador Allende Gossens (UP)	Election
1990–	Patricio Aylwin Azócar (PCD)	Election

Military dictatorship

1973–90	Gen. Augusto Pinochet Ugarte	Coup

PDC = Christian Democratic, R = Republican Party, UP = Popular Unity

COLOMBIA

1900–04	José Manuel Marroquín (C)	Coup
1904–10	Gen. Rafael Reyes	Election (restricted suffrage)
1910–14	Carlos E. Restrepo (L/Coaln)	do.
1914–18	José Vicente Concha (C)	do.
1918–22	Marco Fidel Suárez (C)	do.
1922–26	Pedro Nel Ospina (C)	do.
1926–30	Miguel Abadía Mendez (C)	do.
1930–34	Enrique Olaya Herrera (L/Coaln)	do.
1934–38	Alfonso López Pumarejo (L)	do.
1938–42	Eduardo Santos (L)	do.
1942–45	Alfonso López Pumarejo (L)	do.

1945–46	Alberto Lleras Camargo (L)	Resignation of President
1946–50	Mariano Ospina Pérez (C)	Election
1950–53	Laureano Gómez (C)	do.
1953–54	Gen. Gustavo Rojas Pinilla	Coup
1954–57	Gen. Gustavo Rojas Pinilla	Election
1957–58	Military junta	Coup
1958–62	Alberto Lleras Camargo (L)	Agreed alternation; predetermined election
1962–66	Guillermo León Valencia (C)	do.
1966–70	Carlos Lleras Restrepo (L)	do.
1970–74	Misael Pastrana Borrero (C)	do.
1974–78	Alfonso López Michelsen (L)	Election.
1978–82	Julio César Turbay Ayala (L)	do.
1982–86	Belisario Betancur (C)	do.
1986–90	Virgilio Barco Vargas (L)	do.
1990–	César Gaviria Trujillo (L)	do.

C = Conservative, L = Liberal

COSTA RICA

1894–1902	Rafael Iglesias	Election
1902–06	Ascensión Esquivel	do.
1906–10	Cleto González Viquez	Election by Congress
1910–14	Ricardo Jiménez Oreamuno	Election
1914–17	Alfredo González Flores	Appointed
1917–19	Federico Tinoco Granados	Coup
Aug 12–Sept 2 1919	Juan Bautista Quirós	
1919–20	Francisco Aguilar Barquero	Resignation of President
1920–24	Julio Acosta Garcia	Election
1924–28	Ricardo Jiménez Oreamuno	do.
1928–32	Cleto González Viquez	do.
1932–36	Ricardo Jiménez Oreamuno (PNR)	do.
1936–40	León Cortés Castro (PNR)	do.
1940–44	Rafael Angel Calderón Guardia (PNR)	do.
1944–48	Teodoro Picado Michalski (PNR)	do.
Apr–May 1948	Santos León Herrera	Revolt and compromise of leading contenders
1948–49	José Figueres Ferrer (PSD) and junta	do.
1949–53	Otilio Ulate Blanco (PUN)	Election
1953–58	José Figueres Ferrer (PLN)	do.
1958–62	Mario Echandí Jiménez (PUN)	do.
1962–66	Francisco José Orlich (PLN)	do.
1966–70	José Joaquín Trejos Fernández (PUN)	do.

1970–74	José Figueres Ferrer (PLN)	do.
1974–78	Daniel Oduber Quirós (PLN)	do.
1978–82	Rodrigo Carazo Odio (PUN)	do.
1982–86	Luis Alberto Monge Alvarez (PLN)	do.
1986–90	Oscar Arias Sánchez (PLN)	do.
1990–	Rafael Angel Calderón Fournier (PUSC)	do.

PLN = Party of National Liberation, PNR =National Republican Party, PSD = Social Democratic Party, PUN = National Union Party, PUSC = Social Christian Unity Party

CUBA

1898–1902	US MILITARY GOVERNMENT	
1902–06	Tomás Estrada Palma	Election
1906–09	US MILITARY GOVERNMENT	
1909–13	José Miguel Gómez	Election
1913–21	Mario García Menocal	do., re-elected
1921–25	Alfredo Zayas	Election
1925–33	Gen. Gerardo Machado y Morales	Coup
Aug–Sept 1933	Carlos Manuel de Céspedes	Revolution
Sept 5–10	Council of Five	
1933–34	Ramón Grau San Martín	
Jan 15–18 1934	Carlos Hevía	
Jan 18	Márquez Sterling	
1934–35	Carlos Mendieta Montefur	
1935–36	José A. Barnet y Vinageras	
May–Dec 1936	Miguel Mariano Gómez Arias	
1936–40	Federico Laredo Bru	
1940–44	Fulgencio Batista y Zaldivar	
1944–48	Ramón Grau San Martin	
1948–52	Carlos Prío Socarrás	
1952–59	Fulgencio Batista y Zaldivar	Coup; election 1955
Jan–July 1959	Manuel Urrutia Lleo	Appointed by leader of Revolution
1959–76	Osvaldo Dorticós Torrado	do.
1976–	Fidel Castro Ruz	Leader of Revolution

DOMINICAN REPUBLIC

1899–1902	Juan Isidro Jiménez	Elections
1902–03	Horacio Vásquez	Coup: Vice-President

Apr–Nov 1903	Gen. Wos y Gil	Coup
1903–06	Gen. Carlos Morales	Coup then election
1906–11	Ramón Cáceres	Forced resignation of President, then election
1911–12	Executive Council	Assassination of President
Jan–Nov 1912	Eladio Victoria	Uncle of strongman in Executive Council
1912–13	Mons. Adolfo Alejandro Nouel	US pressure; resignation of President; election
1913–14	Gen. José Bordas Valdez	Resignation of President
Sept–Nov 1914	Ramón Báez	
1914–16	Juan Isidro Jiménez	
May–Nov 1916	Francisco Henríquez y Carvajal	Congressional election after President impeached
1916–22	US OCCUPATION	
1922–24	Juan Bautista Vicini	Election
1924–30	Gen. Horacio Vásquez	do.
Mar–Apr 1930	Rafael Estrella Ureña	Revolt
Apr–May	Jacinto Paynado	Acting
May–Aug	Rafael Estrella Ureña	Acting
1930–38	Gen. Rafael Leónidas Trujillo Molina (PD)	Election
1938–40	Jacinto Peynado (PD)	Controlled election
1940–42	Manuel de Jesús Troncoso de la Concha (PD)	Death of President
1942–51	Gen. Rafael Leónidas Trujillo Molina (PD)	Controlled election
1951–60	Héctor B. Trujillo Molina (PD)	Acting, then controlled election
1960–62	Joaquín Balaguer (PD)	Controlled election
1962–63	Rafael Bonnelly (PD)	Vice-President; military revolt and resignation of President
Feb–Sept 1963	Juan Bosch (PRD)	Election
1963–65	Triumvirate	Military coup
Apr 25–27 1965	José Rafael Molina Ureña (PRD)	Coup
May–Aug	Col. Francisco Alberto Caamaño Deñó	Flight of President
1965–66	Héctor García Godoy	US intervention
1966–78	Joaquín Balaguer (PR)	Election
1978–82	Silvestre Antonio Guzmán (PRD)	do.
July–Aug 1982	Jacobo Majluta (PRD)	Acting; suicide of Guzmán
1982–86	Salvador Jorge Blanco (PRD)	Election
1986–	Joaquín Balaguer (PR)	do.

PD = Partido Dominicana, PRD = Partido Revolucionario Dominicana, PR = Partido Reformista

ECUADOR

1895–1901	Eloy Alfaro (L)	Civil war
1901–05	Leónidas Plaza Gutiérrez (L)	Election
1905–06	Lizardo Garcia (L)	Election
1906–12	Eloy Alfaro (L)	Election
1912–16	Leónidas Plaza Gutiérrez (L)	Election
1916–20	Alfredo Baquerizo Moreno (L)	Election
1920–24	José Luis Tamayo (L)	Election
1924–25	Gonzalo S. Córdova (L)	Election
1925–26	Junta	Coup
1926-31	Isidro Ayora	Military co-option
1931–32	Col. Luis Larrea	Coup
1932–33	Alberto Guerrero Martinez	Exclusion of elected victor
1933–34	Aberlardo Montalvo	President resigns
1934–35	José María Velasco Ibarra	Election
Aug–Sep 1935	Antonio Pons	Coup
1935–37	Federico Páez	Military co-option
1937–38	Gen. Alberto Enríquez Gallo	Military co-option
1938	Manuel María Barrero (L)	
1938–39	Aurelio Mosquera Narváez (L)	
1939–44	Dr Carlos Alberto Arroyo del Río	Death of President, then fraudulent election
1944–47	José María Velasco Ibarra	Recalled from exile
1947	Carlos Mancheno	Coup
1947–48	Carlos Arosemena Tola	Coup
1948–52	Galo Plaza Lasso (Ind)	Election
1952–56	José María Velasco Ibarra	Election
1956–60	Camilo Ponce	Election
1960–61	José María Velasco Ibarra	Election
1961–63	Carlos Julio Arosemena Tola	Vice President, succeeded on President's resignation
1963–66	Junta	Coup
1966	Clemente Yerovi Indaburu	Military abdication
1966–68	Otto Arosemena Gómez (CID)	Constituent Assembly election
1968–72	José María Velasco Ibarra	Election
1972–76	Gen. Guillermo Rodríguez Lara	Coup
1976–79	Military junta	Coup
1979–80	Jaime Roldós (CFP coaln)	Election
1980–84	Osvaldo Hurtado (PCD)	Death of President, Vice-Presidential succession
1984–88	León Febres Cordero (FRN)	Election
1988–92	Rodrigo Borja Cevallos (ID)	do.
1992–	Sixto Durán Ballén (PUR)	do.

CFP = Concentration of Popular Forces, FRN = National Renovation Front, ID = Democratic Left, L = Radical Liberal Party, PCD = Christian Democrats, PUR = Republican Unity Party

EL SALVADOR

1899–1903	Tomás Regalado	Coup and election

1903–07	Pedro José Escalón	Controlled election
1911–13	Manuel E. Araújo	
1913–14	Carlos Meléndez	Assassination of President
1914–15	Alfonso Quiñones Molina	Resignation of President
1915–19	Carlos Meléndez	Election
1919–23	Jorge Meléndez	Election
1923–27	Alfonso Quiñónez Molina	Controlled election
1927–31	Pío Romero Bosque	
Mar–Dec 1931	Arturo Araújo	Election
1931–34	Gen. Maximilano Hernández Martínez	Coup
1934–35	Andrés Ignacio Méndez	Acting
1935–44	Gen. Maximilano Hernández Martínez	Controlled election
May–Oct 1944	Andrés Ignacio Méndez	Revolt
1944–45	Osmin Aguirre y Salinas	
1945–48	Salvador Castañeda Castro	
1948–49	Manuel J. de Córdova	Coup
Jan–Oct 1949	Oscar Osorio	
1949–50	Oscar Bolaños	
1950–56	Oscar Osorio	Election
1956–60	Lt.-Col. José María Lemus	do.
1960–61	Military junta	Coup
1961–62	Directory (military junta)	Coup
1962–63	Eusebio Rodolfo Cordón	Executive decree
1963–67	Lt.-Col. Julio Adalberto Rivera (PCN)	One candidate election
1967–72	Gen. Fidel Sánchez Hernández (PCN)	Fraudulent election
1972–77	Col. Arturo Armando Molina Bazzara (PCN)	do.
1977–79	Gen. Carlos Humberto Romero Mena (PCN)	do.
1979–80	Junta	Coup
1980	Junta	Resignation of civilian members
1980–82	José Napoleón Duarte (PCD)	Appointed by junta
1982–84	Dr Alvaro Magaña Borja (Ind)	Appointed by Constituent Assembly
1984–90	José Napoleón Duarte (PCD)	Election
1989–	Alfredo Cristiani (Arena)	do.

PCN = Partido de Conciliación Nacional (military), PDC = Christian Democrats, Arena = Alianza Renovadora Nacional

GUATEMALA

1898–1920	Manuel Estrada Cabrera (L)	Assassination of President; First Designate; rigged election

1920–21	Carlos Herrera	Congress declares President unfit to perform duties
1921–26	Gen. José María Orellana	
1926–30	Lázaro Chacón	Death of President; election
Dec 12–17 1930	Baudilio Palma	First Designate; death of President
1930–31	Gen. Manuel Orellana	Military coup
Jan–Feb 1931	José María Reyna Andrade	Resignation of President; interim
1931–44	Gen. Jorge Ubico y Castañeda	Election
July 1–4 1944	Junta	Resignation of President following revolt
Jul–Oct	Col. Federico Ponce Valdés	Chosen by Congress
1944–45	Triumvirate	Revolution
1945–51	Dr Juan José Arévalo Bermejo	Election
1951–54	Col. Jacobo Arbenz Guzmán	Election
Jun 27–28 1954	Col. Carlos Enrique Díaz	Resignation of President following revolt
Jun–Jul	Col. Elfego Monzón	Military coup
Jul 1–8	Col. Monzón and junta	Negotiated settlement
1954–57	Col. Carlos Castillo Armas	Chosen by junta
July–Oct 1957	Luis Arturo González López	Assassination of President
1957–58	Guillermo Flores Avendaño	Chosen by Congress
1958–63	Gen. Miguel Ydígoras Fuentes	Election
1963–66	Gen. Enrique Peralta Azurdia	Military coup
1966–70	Dr Julio César Méndez Montenegro	Election
1970–74	Col. Carlos Arana Osorio	do.
1974–78	Col. Eugenio Kjell Laugerud Garcia	do.
1978–82	Gen. Fernando Romeo Lucas Garcia	do.
Mar–June 1982	Gen. Efraín Rios Montt & junta	Military coup
1982–83	Gen. Efraín Rios Montt	Internal coup
1983–86	Gen. Oscar Mejía Victores	Military coup
1986–89	Mario Vinicio Cerezo (PDCG)	Election
1989–	Alfredo Felix Christiani Burkart (Arena)	do.

HAITI

1902–08	Gen. Nord Alexis	Military revolt
1908–11	Antonio Simón	Military revolt
1911–12	Leconte	Military revolt and German intervention
1912	Tancrède Auguste	Interim
1912–13	Michel Oreste	Death of President
1914	Oreste Zamor	Caco uprising

1914–15	Davilmar Théodore	Caco co-option
1915	Gen. Vilbrun Guillaume Sam	US co-option
1915–34	US MILITARY OCCUPATION	
1915	Dr Rosalvo Bobo	
1915–22	Philippe Sudre Dartiguenave	
1922–30	Louis Borno	Election by legislature
May–Nov 1930	Eugene Roy	
1930–35	Stenio Vincent	Election by legislature
1935–41	Stenio Vincent	Term extended 1935
1941–46	Elie Lescot	do.
Jan–Aug 1946	Frank Lavaud and executive military committee	
1946–50	Dumersais Estimé	Election by National Assembly
1950–56	Col. Paul E. Magloire	Coup, then election
1956–57	Joseph Memours Pierre-Louis	Resignation of President
Feb 1957	Léon Cantave	
Feb–Apr	Franck Sylvain	
Apr–May	Executive Council	
May–Jun	Daniel Fignolé	
Jun–Oct	Antoine T. Kébreau	
1957–71	Dr François Duvalier	Election, possible fraud; re-election, then President-for-life
1971–85	Jean-Claude Duvalier	Hereditary succession
1985–88	Gen. Henri Namphy	Revolution
1988	Dr Leslie Manigat	Election
1988	Gen. Henri Namphy	Military coup
1988–90	Brig.-Gen. Prosper Avril	do.
1990 March	Gen. Hérard Abraham	Revolution
1990–91	Mme. Ertha Pascal-Trouillot	Election by National Assembly
1991	Fr Jean-Bertrand Aristide (FNCD)	Election
Sept 1991	Brig.-Gen. Raoul Cédras	Military coup
Oct 1991	Joseph Nerette	Appointed by National Assembly

FNCD = National Front for Change and Democracy

HONDURAS

1899–1903	Gen. Terencio Sierra	Nominated
1903–07	Manuel Bonilla	Coup
1907–11	Miguel R. Dávila	Coup
1911–13	Manuel Bonilla	Election
1913–20	Dr Francisco Bertrand (L)	Vice-President; death of President, then election
1920–23	Rafael López Gutiérrez (L)	Election
1924–25	Vicente Tosta	Death of President
1925–29	Miguel Paz Barahona (PN)	Election
1929–33	Dr Vicente Mejía Colindres (L)	Election

1933–49	Gen. Tiburcio Carias Andino (PN)	
1949–54	Juan Manuel Gálvez (PN)	Election
1954–56	Julio Lozano Díaz (PN)	Coup: appointed by Congress
1956–57	Military junta	Military coup
1957–63	RamónVilleda Morales (PLH)	Election
1963–71	Col. Oswaldo López Arellano	Coup; election 1965
1971–72	R. Cruz	Election
1972–75	Gen. Oswaldo López Arellano	Coup
1975–78	Col. Juan A. Melgar Castro	Coup
1978–80	Gen. Policarpo Paz Garcia	Coup; then election
1982–86	Roberto Suazo Córdova (PLH)	Election
1986–90	José Simón Azconndel Hoyo (PLH)	do.
1990	Rafael Leonardo Callejas (PN)	do.

L=Liberal, PLH=Partido Liberal de Honduras, PN=Partido Nacional

MEXICO

1884–1911	Gen. Porfirio Díaz	Election
1911	Francisco León de la Barra	Resignation of President
1911–13	Francisco Indalecio Madero (ARP)	Election
Feb 18 1913	Pedro Lascuráin	Secretary of External Relations; resignation of President following coup
1913–14	Victoriano Huerta	Military coup
Jul–Aug 1914	Francisco Carvajal	Flight of President
Aug 13–15	Eduardo Iturbide	Flight of President
Aug–Oct	vacant	
Oct–Nov	Convention	
1914–15	Eulalio Gutiérrez	Appointed by Convention
Jan–Jun 1915	Roque González Garza	do.
Jun–Sept	Francisco Lagos Cházaro	do.
1915–17	Venustiano Carranza	First Chief in charge of the Executive Power
1917–20	Venustiano Carranza (PLC)	Election
1920	Adolfo de la Huerta	Revolution
1920–24	Alvaro Obregón (PLC)	Election
1924–28	Plutarco Elías Calles (PLM)	do.
1928–30	Emilio Portes Gil (PNR)	Assassination of President-Elect
1930–32	Pascual Ortiz Rubio (PNR)	Election
1932–34	Abelardo Rodriguez (PNR)	Resignation of President
1934–40	Lázaro Cárdenas (PNR/PRM)	Election
1940–46	Manuel Avila Camacho (PRM/PRI)	do.
1946–52	Miguel Alemán Valdes (PRI)	do.
1952–58	Aldolfo Ruiz Cortines (PRI)	do.

1958–64	Adolfo López Mateos (PRI)	do.
1964–70	Gustavo Díaz Ordaz (PRI)	do.
1970–76	Luis Echeverría Alvarez (PRI)	do.
1976–82	Gustavo López Portillo (PRI)	do.
1982–88	Miguel de la Madrid (PRI)	do.
1988–	Carlos Salinas de Gortari	do.
	(PRI)	

ARP = Anti Re-electionist Party, PLM = Partido Laborista Mexicana, PLC = Partido Liberal Constitucionalista, PNR = Partido Nacional Revolucionario, PRI = Partido Revolucionario Institucional, PRM = Partido de la Revolución Mexicana

NICARAGUA

1893–1909	José Santos Zelaya (L)	
1909–10	José Madriz (L)	Vice-President; flight of President
1910–11	Juan J. Estrada (C)	Revolution
1912–16	Adolfo Díaz	Election
1916–20	Emiliano Chamorro (C)	Election
1925–26	Carlos Solórzano (C)	Election
1926	Emiliano Chamorro (C)	Coup
1926–28	Adolfo Díaz (C)	Interim
1928–33	José María Moncada (L)	Election
1933–36	Juan Bautista Sacasa	Election
Jun 6–9 1936	Julian Irías	Minister of Interior
1936–37	Carlos Alberto Brenes Jarquín	Interim
1937–47	Anastasio Somoza García (L)	Coup, then election
May 1–26 1947	Leonard Argüello	Election
May–Aug	Benjamín Lacaya Sacasa	Interim
1947–50	Víctor M. Ramos y Reyes	Interim
1950–56	Anastasio Somoza García	Coup; then election
1956–63	Luis Somoza Debayle	Assassination of President; then election 1957
1963–66	René Schick Gutiérrez	Election
1966–67	Lorenzo Guerrevo	Death of President
1967–72	Anastasio Somoza Debayle	Election
1972–74	Triumvirate	Co-option
1974–79	Anastasio Somoza Debayle	Election
1979–85	Junta	Revolution
1985–90	Daniel Ortega Saavedra (FSLN)	Election
1990–	Sra Violeta Barríos de Chamorro (UNO)	do.

C = Conservative, FSLN = Sandinista National Liberation Front, L = Liberal, UNO = National Opposition Union

PANAMA

1904–08	Manuel Amador Guerrero	Election

1908–10	José Domingo de Obaldía	do.
1910	Carlos Antonio Mendoza	Death of President; interim
1910–12	Pablo Arosemena	Election
1912–16	Belisario Porras	do.
1916–19	Ramón S. Valdés	do.
1919–20	Belisario Porras	
1920–24	Ernesto Lefevre	Election
1924–28	Rodolfo Chiari	do.
1928–31	Florencio Harmodio Arosemena (L)	do.
Jan 2–16 1931	Harmodio Arias	Provisional
1931–32	Ricardo J. Alfaro	Coup; interim
1932–36	Harmodio Arias (C)	Election
1936–39	Juan Demóstenes Arosemena	do.
1939–40	Agusto S. Boyd	Death of President
1940–41	Dr Arnulfo Arias (PPA)	Election
Oct 9 1941	Ernesto Jaen Guardia	Interim
1941–45	Ricardo Adolfo de la Guardia	Election
1945–48	Enrique Adolfo Jiménez	do.
1948–49	Domingo Díaz Arosemena	Election
July–Nov 1949	Daniel Chanis	Death of President
Nov 20–25	Rodolfo Chiari	Resignation of Chanis
1949–51	Dr Arnulfo Arias (PPA)	Coup; police co-option
1951–52	Alcíbades Arosemena	Coup; Vice-President
1952–55	Col José Antonio Remón Cantera	Election
Jan 3–15 1955	José Ramón Guizado	Assassination of President; First Vice-President
1955–56	Ricardo Arias Espinosa	Impeachment of President; Second Vice-President
1956–60	Ernesto de la Guardia	Election
1960–64	Roberto Chiari	do.
1964–68	Marco Aurelio Robles	do.
1968	Dr Arnulfo Arias	do.
1968	Gen. Omar Torrijos Herrera & junta	Military coup; Chief of Government
1968–69	Col. José María Pinilla Fábrega	Appointed by junta
1969–78	Demetrio Lakas Bahas (PRD)	Appointed by junta; then election
1978–82	Dr Arístides Royo Sánchez	Chosen by National Assembly
1982–84	Ricardo de la Espriella	Coup; Vice-President
1984	Dr Jorge Illueca	Forced resignation of President
1984–85	Dr Nicolás Ardito Barletta (PRD)	Rigged election
1985–88	Eric Arturo del Valle	Forced resignation of President
1988–89	Manuel Solís Palma	Appointed
1989 Sep–Dec	Francisco Rodríguez	Interim
1989	Gen. Manuel Antonio Noriega Moreno	Coup

220   *Presidents of Latin American States since 1900*

Dec 1989–   Guillermo Endara   Elected; deprived of victory;
             Gallimany (ADOC)   reinstated by US forces

C = Conservative, L = Liberal, PRD = Partido Revolucionario Democrática,
PPA = Partido Panameñista Auténtico, ADOC = Civic Opposition
Democratic Alliance

PARAGUAY

1898–1902	Emilio Aceval	
Jan–Nov 1902	Héctor Carballo	
1902–04	Juan A. Escurra (Col)	
1904–05	Juan Bautista Gaona (L)	Liberal revolution
1905–06	Prof Cecilio Báez (L)	Interim
1906–08	Gen. Benigno Ferreira (L)	Election
1908–10	Emiliano González Navero (L)	Military coup; interim
1910–11	Manuel Gondra (L)	Election
1911	Col. Albino Jara (L)	Military coup
1911–12	Liberato Rojas (L)	
Mar 1–15 1912	Pedro Peña (L)	
1912–16	Eduardo Schaerer (L)	Election
1916–19	Manuel Franco (L)	do.
1919–20	José Montero (L)	Vice-President; death of President
1920–21	Manuel Gondra (L)	Election
1921–23	Eusebio Ayala (L)	Election
1923–24	Eligio Ayala (L)	do.
1924	Luis A. Riart (L)	Interim
1924–28	Eligio Ayala (L)	Election
1928–31	José Patricio Guggiari (L)	Elite co-option; election
1931–32	Emiliano González Navero	Acting
Jan–Aug 1932	José Patricio Guggiari (L)	Election
1932–36	Eusebio Ayala (L)	Election
1936–37	Gen. Rafael Franco (Feb)	Military coup
1937–39	Félix Paiva (L)	Bloodless coup; interim
1939–40	Marshal José Félix Estigarribia (L)	Election
1940–48	Gen. Higinio Morínigo M.	Death of President; Cabinet selection; election 1943
Jun–Aug 1948	Juan Manuel Frutos	Chief Justice; interim; military appointee
1948–49	Juan Natalicio González (Col)	Fixed election
Jan–Feb 1949	Gen. Raimundo Rolón (Col)	Military coup
Feb–Sept	Felipe Molas López (Col)	Overthrew President; then fraudulent election
1949–54	Dr Federico Cháves (Col)	Presidential resignation; then fraudulent election

1954–89   Gen. Alfredo Stroessner (Col) Single candidate election;
plebiscite 1958, re-elected
1963, 1968, 1973, 1978, 1983,
1988
1989–   Gen. Andrés Rodríguez (Col) Coup; then election

Col = Colorado, Feb = "Febrerista", L = Liberal

PERU

1903–04	Manuel Candamo (Dem)	Election
1904–08	José Pardo (Civ)	do.
1908–12	Augusto Leguía (Civ)	do.
1912–14	Guillermo Billinghurst (Civ)	do.
1914–15	Gen. Oscar Raimundo Benavides	Military coup
1915–19	José Pardo (Civ)	Election
1919–30	Augusto Leguía (Civ)	Election and coup
Aug 25–27 1930	Manuel Ponce	
1930–31	Col. Luis M. Sánchez Cerro	Coup
Mar 1–5 1931	Ricardo Leoncio Elías	Provisional
Mar 5–11	Gustavo A. Jiménez	Provisional
Mar–Dec	David Sámanez Ocampo	
1931–33	Col. Luis M. Sánchez Cerro	Election
1933–39	Gen. Oscar Raimundo Benavides	Assassination of President; coup in 1936
1939–45	Manuel Prado y Ugarteche (Civ)	Election
1945–48	José Luis Bustamente y Rivero (PDC)	do.
Oct 29–30 1948	Zénon Noriega	Coup; acting
1948–50	Gen. Manuel A. Odría	Coup
Jun–Jul 1950	Zénon Noriega	Acting
1950–56	Gen. Manuel A. Odría	Election
1956–62	Manuel Prado y Ugarteche	Election
1962–63	Gen. Ricardo Pérez Godoy & junta	Coup
1963–68	Arq Fernando Belaúnde Terry (AP-PDC)	Election
1968–75	Gen. Juan Valasco Alvarado	Coup
1975–80	Gen. Francisco Morales Bermúdez	Internal coup
1980–85	Arq Fernando Belaúnde Terry (AP)	Election
1985–90	Alan García Pérez (APRA)	do.
1990–	Alberto Keinya Fujimori (Cambio '90)	do

AP = Acción Popular, APRA = Alianza Popular Revolucionaria de América,

Cambio '90 = Change 1990, Civ = Civilista, Dem = Democrat, PDC = Partido Demócrata Cristiano

URUGUAY

1897–1903	Juan Lindolfo Cuestas (C)	Assassination of President
1903–07	José Batlle y Ordóñez (C)	Election
1907–11	Dr Claudio Williman (C)	Election
1911–15	José Batlle y Ordóñez (C)	Election
1915–19	Dr Feliciano Viera (C)	Election
1919–23	Dr Baltasar Brum (C)	Election
1923–27	José Benigno Serrato (C)	Election
1927–31	Juan Campisteguy (C)	Election
1931–38	Gabriel Terra (C)	Election; then assumed dictatorial powers
Jun–Aug 1938	Gen. Alfredo Baldomir (C)	
Aug 9–15	César Charlone	Acting
1938–43	Gen. Alfredo Baldomir (C)	Election
1943–47	Juan José Amézaga (C)	Election
Mar-Aug 1947	Tomás Berreta (C)	Interim
1947–48	Luis Batlle Berres (C)	Election
Aug–Sep 1948	César Mayo Gutiérrez	Acting
1948–51	Luis Batlle Berres (C)	Election
1951–52	Andrés Martínez Trueba (C)	Election
1952–67	*Consejo Nacional de Administración*	
Mar–Dec 1967	Gen. Oscar Daniel Gestido (C)	Election
1967–71	Jorge Pacheco Areco (C)	Vice-President; death of President
1971–76	Juan M. Bordaberry Arocena (C)	Electoral technicality; then autogolpe
May–July 1976	Alberto Demichelli	Coup; resignation of President
1976–81	Dr Aparicio Méndez Manfredini	Military co-option; appointment by Council of State
1981–84	Gen. Gregorio Alvarez Armellino	Military co-option
Feb 11–29 1984	Rafael Addiego Bruno	President of the Court of Justice; resignation of President
1984–90	Dr Julio María Sanguinetti Cairolo (C)	Election
1990–	Luis Alberto Lacalle Herrera (PN)	do.

C = Partido Colorado, PN = Nationalist (Blanco) Party

VENEZUELA

1899–1908	Gen. Cipriano Castro	Coup
1908–13	Gen. Juan Vicente Gómez	Coup; in charge of executive power 1908–09; acting President 1909–10; elected for four years 1910
1913–14	José Gil Fortoul	Acting President in absence of President Gómez on campaign
1914–22	Victoriano Márquez Bustillo	Vice-President in charge of the executive power 1914; acting President 1914–22
1922–29	Gen. Juan Vicente Gómez	Elected 1915 but did not serve; re-elected 1922 under new Constitution
1929–31	Juan Bautista Pérez	Election
1931–35	Gen. Juan Vicente Gómez	Coup
1935–41	Gen. Eleazar López Contreras	Death of President; military co-option, then election
1941–45	Gen. Isaías Medina Angarita	Elected by Congress
1945–48	Rómulo Betancourt (AD)	Coup; provisional President with junta
Feb–Nov 1948	Rómulo Gallegos (AD)	Election
1948–50	Gen. Carlos Delgado Chalbaud & military junta	Coup
1950–52	Germán Suárez Flamerich	Assassination of President
1952–58	Gen. Marcos Peréz Jiménez	Military co-option and election
1958–59	Military junta	Popular uprising followed by coup
1959–64	Rómulo Betancourt (AD coaln)	Election
1964–69	Raúl Leoni (AD coaln)	do.
1969–74	Rafael Caldera (COPEI)	do.
1974–79	Carlos Andrés Pérez (AD)	do.
1979–84	Dr Luis Herrera Campins (COPEI)	do.
1984–89	Dr Jaime Lusinchi (AD)	do.
1989–	Carlos Andrés Pérez (AD)	do.

AD = Acción Democrática, COPEI = Social Christian Party

Prime Ministers of Caribbean States

ANTIGUA AND BARBUDA

Independent 1 November 1981
1981–	Vere C. Bird, Sr. (ALP)	Election

THE BAHAMAS

Independent 10 July 1973
1973–	Sir Lynden Pindling (PLP)	Election

BARBADOS

Independent 30 November 1966
1966–71	Errol Barrow (DLP)	Election
1971–85	J. M. G. M. ('Tom') Adams (BLP)	Election
1985–86	Bernard St John (BLP)	Election
1986–87	Errol Barrow (DLP)	Election
1987–	Erskine Sandiford (DLP)	Death of predecessor

BELIZE

Independent 21 September 1981
1981–84	George Price (PUP)	Election
1984–89	Manuel Esquivel (UDP)	Election
1989–	George Price (PUP)	Election

DOMINICA

Independent 2 November 1978
1978–80	Patrick John (DLP)	Election
1980–	Dame (Mary) Eugenia Charles (DFP)	Election

GRENADA

Independent February 1974
1974–79	Sir Eric Gairy (GULP)	Election

1979–83	Maurice Bishop (NJM)	Coup
1983 Oct	Gen. Hudson Austin (NJM)	Coup
1983–84	Nicholas Braithwaite	Caretaker
1984–89	Herbert Blaize (NNP)	Election
1989	Herbert Blaize (NP)	Govt. reconstructed
1989–90	Ben Jones (NP)	Death of PM
1990–	Nicholas Braithwaite (NDC/NP)	Election

GUYANA

Independent 26 May 1966
Executive Presidents

1980–85	Forbes Burnham (PNC)	Election
1985–	Desmond Hoyte (PNC)	Election

Prime Ministers

1966–80	Forbes Burnham (PNC)	Election
1980–85	Desmond Hoyte	Election
1985–	Hamilton Green	Election

JAMAICA

Independent 6 August 1962

1962–64	Dr Alexander Bustamante (JLP)	Election
1964–67	Donald Sangster (JLP)	Election
1967–72	Hugh Shearer (JLP)	Election
1972–80	Michael Manley (PNP)	Election
1980–89	Edward Seaga (JLP)	Election
1989–92	Michael Manley (PNP)	Election
1992–	Percival Patterson (PNP)	Resignation of Manley

ST CHRISTOPHER AND NEVIS

Independent 19 September 1983

1983–	Dr Kennedy Alphonse Simmonds (PAM)	Election

SAINT LUCIA

Independent 22 February 1979

1979	John G. M. Compton (UWP)	Election
1979–81	Allan Louisy (SLP)	Election
1981–82	Winston Cenac (SLP)	Election
1982–	John G. M. Compton (UWP)	Election

226   *Prime Ministers of Caribbean States*

SAINT VINCENT AND THE GRENADINES

Independent 27 October 1979

1979–84	Milton Cato (SVLP)	Election
1984–	James Mitchell (NDP)	Election

SURINAME

Independent 25 November 1975
Presidents

1975–80	Johan Ferrier	Election
1980–82	Hendrik Chin A Sen	Military co-option
1982–87	L. Fred Ramdat Misier	Interim; Vice-President, Supreme Court
1987–90	Ramesewak Shankar	Election
1990–91	Johan Kraag (NPS)	Elected after military coup
1991–	Ronald Venetiaan (NF)	Election

Prime Ministers/Heads of government

1975–80	Henck Arron (NPS)	
1980–82	Hendrik Chin A Sen	Military coup
1982	Henry Neyhorst	Military co-option
1982–83	Lt.-Col. Desi Bouterse	Military government
1983–84	Dr Errol Alibux (PALU/RVP)	Military co-option
1984–87	Wim Udenhout (St)	Military co-option
1987–90	Lt. Col. Desi Bouterse	Military government
1990–91	Jules Wijdenbosch (NDP)	Elected after military coup
1991–	Jules Ajohida (NF)	Elected

TRINIDAD AND TOBAGO

Independent 31 August 1962; Republic 1976

1962–81	Dr Eric Williams (PNM)	Election
1981–86	George Chambers (PNM)	Election
1986–90	Arthur Napolean Raymond Robinson (NAR)	Election
1990–	Patrick Manning (PNM)	Election

ALP = Antigua Labour Party, BLP = Barbados Labour Party, DFP = Dominica Freedom Party, DLP (Barbados) = Democratic Labour Party, DLP (Dominica) = Dominica Labour Party, GULP = Grenada United Labour Party, JLP = Jamaica Labour Party, NAR = National Alliance for Reconstruction, NDC = National Democratic Congress, NDP = New Democratic Party, NF = New Front for Democracy and Development, NNP = New National Party, NJM = New Jewel Movement, NP = The National Party, NPS = National Partij Suriname, PALU/RVP = Progressive Workers and Farm Labourers Union/Revolutionary People's Party, PAM = People's Action Movement, PLP = Progressive Liberal Party, PNM = People's National Movement, PNP = People's National Party, PNC = People's National Congress, PUP = People's United Party, SLP = St Lucia Labour Party, St = Standvaste, SVLP = St Vincent Labour Party, UDP = United Democratic Party, UWP = United Workers' Party

Some Further Reading

The following is a selection of books in English, intended simply to serve as a guide to further reading. It is by no means intended to be exhaustive.

REFERENCE

The South American Handbook, published annually by Trade and Travel Publications Ltd., London.
South America, Central America and the Caribbean, published biennially by Europa Publications Ltd., London.

GENERAL

Anglade, Christian and Fortin, Carlos, *The State and Capital Accumulation in Latin America* (London: Macmillan, 1985).
Archetti, Eduardo P., Cammack, Paul and Roberts, Bryan (eds.), *Sociology of 'Developing Societies': Latin America* (Basingstoke, Hants.: Macmillan, 1987).
Baloyra, Enrique A. (ed.), *Comparing New Democracies: Transition and Consolidation in Mediterranean Europe and the Southern Cone* (Boulder, Colo.: Westview Press, 1987).
Bryce, James, *South America: Observations and Impressions* (New York: Macmillan, 1914)
Bulmer-Thomas, Victor, *The Political Economy of Central America since 1920* (Cambridge: Cambridge University Press).
Cardoso, Fernando Enrique, and Faletto, Enzo, *Dependency and Development in Latin America* (Berkeley: University of California Press, 1979).
Clapham, Christopher, and Philip, George (eds), *The Political Dilemmas of Military Regimes* (London: Croom Helm, 1985).
Gott, Richard, *Guerrilla Movements in Latin America* (London: Nelson, 1970).
Gutiérrez, Gustavo, *A Theology of Liberation* (London: SLM Press, 1988).
Janvry, Alain de, *The Agrarian Question and Reformism in Latin America* (Baltimore, Md.: Johns Hopkins University Press, 1981).
Linz, Juan J., and Stepan, Alfred (eds), *The Breakdown of Democratic Regimes: Latin America* (Baltimore, Md.: Johns Hopkins University Press, 1978).
Malloy, James M. (ed.), *Authoritarianism and Corporatism in Latin America* (Pittsburgh: University of Pittsburgh Press, 1977).
O'Brien, Phil and Cammack, Paul (eds), *Generals in Retreat* (Manchester: Manchester University Press, 1985).
Pearce, Jenny, *Under the Eagle* (London: Latin American Bureau, 1981).
Philip, George, *The Military and South American Politics* (London: Croom Helm, 1985).

228   *Some Further Reading*

Philip, George, *Oil and Politics in Latin America: Nationalist Movements and State Companies* (Cambridge: Cambridge University Press, 1982).
Rouquié, Alain, *The Military and the State in Latin America* (Berkeley, Calif.: University of California Press, 1987).
Thorp, Rosemary, and Whitehead, Laurence (eds), *Latin American Debt and the Adjustment Crisis* (Basingstoke: Macmillan, 1987).
Sheahan, John, *Patterns of Development in Latin America: Poverty, Repression and Economic Strategy* (Princeton, N.J.: Princeton University Press, 1987).
Wesson, Robert (ed.), *The Latin American Military Institution* (New York: Praeger, 1986).
Wynia, Gary W., *The Politics of Latin American Development* (Cambridge: Cambridge University Press, 1978).

INTERNATIONAL RELATIONS

Best, Edward, *US Policy and Regional Security in Central America* (Aldershot: Gower and International Institute for Strategic Studies, 1977).
Duran, Esperanza, *European Interests in Latin America* (London: Royal Institute of International Affairs, 1985).
Feinberg, Richard E.; *The intemperate zone: the Third World challenge to US foreign policy* (New York: W. W. Norton, 1983).
Ferrell, Robert H., *Latin American Diplomacy: The Twentieth Century* (New York: W. W. Norton, 1988).
Martz, John D., and Schoultz, Lars (eds), *Latin America, the United States, and the Inter-American System* (Boulder, Col.: Westview Press, 1980).
Morris, Michael A., and Millán, Victor, *Controlling Latin American Conflicts* (Boulder, Col.: Westview Press, 1983).
Muñoz, Heraldo, and Tulchin, Joseph S. (eds), *Latin American Nations in World Politics* (Boulder, Colo.: Westview Press, 1984)
Munro, Dana G., *Intervention and Dollar Diplomacy in the Caribbean, 1900–1921* (Princeton, N.J.: Princeton University Press, 1964).
Munro, Dana G., *The United States and the Caribbean Republics* (Princeton, N. J.: Princeton University Press, 1974).
Perkins, Dexter, *A History of the Monroe Doctrine* (London: Longmans, 1960).
Wood, Bryce, *The Dismantling of the Good Neighbor Policy* (Austin, Texas: University of Texas Press, 1985).

ARGENTINA

Calvert, Susan and Peter, *Argentina: Political Culture and Instability* (London: Macmillan, 1989)
Corradi, Juan E., *The Fitful Republic: Economy, Society, and Politics in Argentina* (Boulder, Colo.: Westview Press, 1985).
Di Tella, Guido, *Argentina under Perón, 1973–76; The Nation's Experience with a Labour-based Government* (London: Macmillan, 1983).

Rock, David, *Argentina 1516–1982* (Cambridge: Cambridge University Press, 1986).

BELIZE

Bolland, O. Nigel, *Belize: A New Nation in Central America* (Boulder, Col.: Westview Press, 1986).
Bolland, O. Nigel, *The Formation of a Colonial Society* (Baltimore: Johns Hopkins University Press, 1977).
Grant, C. H., *The making of modern Belize* (Cambridge: Cambridge University Press, 1976).

BOLIVIA

Alexander, Robert J., *Bolivia: Past, Present, and Future of its Politics* (New York: Praeger, 1982).
Dunkerley, James, *Rebellion in the Veins: Political Struggle in Bolivia, 1952–82* (London: Verso, 1984).
Klein, Herbert S., *Bolivia: The Evolution of a Multi-Ethnic Society* (New York: Oxford University Press, 1982).

BRAZIL

Bresser Pereira, Luiz, *Development and Crisis in Brazil, 1930–1983* (trans, Marcia Van Dyke) (Boulder, Colo.: Westview Press, 1984).
Fiechter, Georges-André, *Brazil since 1964* (London: Macmillan, 1975).
Flynn, Peter, *Brazil: a political analysis* (London: Ernest Benn, 1978).
Roett, Riordan, *Brazil: Politics in a Patrimonial Society* (New York: Praeger, 1984).
Stepan, Alfred, *Rethinking Military Politics: Brazil and the Southern Cone* (Princeton, N.J.: Princeton University Press, 1988).

THE CARIBBEAN

Barry, Tom, Wood, Beth, and Preusch, Deb, *The Other Side of Paradise: Foreign Control in the Caribbean* (New York: Grove Press, 1984).
Crassweller, Robert, *The Caribbean Community* (Washington, DC: Council on Foreign Relations, 1972).
Manley, Michael, *Jamaica: Struggle in the Periphery* (London: Third World Media Ltd., n.d.).
Palmer, Ransford W., *Caribbean dependence on the United States economy* (New York: Praeger, 1979).
Payne, Anthony, *The International Crisis of the Caribbean* (London: Croom Helm, 1984).
Williams, Dr Eric, *Forged from the Love of Liberty: Selected Speeches of Dr Eric Williams* (Port-of-Spain: Longmans Caribbean, 1982).

230 *Some Further Reading*

CHILE

Monteon, Michael, *Chile in the Nitrate Era: The Evolution of Economic Dependence, 1880–1930* (Madison, Wis.: University of Wisconsin Press, 1982).

Moreno, Francisco José, *Legitimacy and Stability in Latin America: A Study of Chilean Political Culture* (New York: New York University Press, 1969).

North, Liisa, *Civil–Military Relations in Argentina, Chile and Peru* (Berkeley: University of California Press, 1966).

O'Brien, Phil, and Roddick, Jackie, *Chile, the Pinochet Decade* (London: Macmillan, 1983).

Pollack, B. and Rosenkranz, H., *Revolutionary Social Democracy: The Chilean Socialist Party* (London: Frances Pinter, 1986).

Roxborough, Ian, O'Brien, Phil, and Roddick, Jackie, *Chile, the State and Revolution* (London: Macmillan, 1972).

Smith, Brian, *The Church and Politics in Chile, Challenges to Modern Catholicism* (Princeton, N.J.: Princeton University Press, 1982).

COLOMBIA

Fluharty, Vernon Lee, *Dance of the Millions: Military Rule and the Social Revolution in Colombia, 1930–1956* (Pittsburgh: Pittsburgh University Press, 1957).

Hartlyn, Jonathan, *The Politics of Coalition Rule in Colombia* (Cambridge: Cambridge University Press, 1988).

Peeler, John A., *Latin American Democracies: Colombia, Costa Rica, Venezuela* (Chapel Hill, N.C.: University of North Carolina Press, 1985).

COSTA RICA

Ameringer, Charles D., *Don Pepe – a political biography of José Figueres of Costa Rica* (Albuquerque, New Mexico: University of New Mexico Press, 1979).

Bird, Leonard, *Costa Rica: The Unarmed Democracy* (London: Sheppard Press, 1984)

CUBA

Domínguez, Jorge I. (ed.), *Cuba: Internal and International Affairs* (Beverly Hills: Sage Publications, 1982).

Draper, Theodore, *Castroism, Theory and Practice* (New York: Praeger, 1969).

Goldenberg, Boris, *The Cuban Revolution and Latin America* (London: Allen & Unwin, 1965).

Guevara, Ernesto 'Che', *Reminiscences of the Cuban Revolutionary War* (London: Monthly Review Press, 1961).

Huberman, Leo, and Sweezy, Paul M., *Cuba: Anatomy of a Revolution* (New York: Monthly Review Press, 1968).
Mesa-Lago, Carmelo, *The Economy of Socialist Cuba: A Two-Decade Appraisal* (Albuquerque, N.M.: University of New Mexico Press, 1981).

DOMINICAN REPUBLIC

Atkins, G. Pope, *Arms and Politics in the Dominican Republic* (Boulder, Colo.: Westview Press, 1981).
Black, Jan Knippers, *The Dominican Republic: Politics and Development in an Unsovereign State* (Boston, Mass.: Allen & Unwin, 1986).
Gleijeses, Piero, *The Dominican Crisis: the 1965 Constitutional Revolt and American Intervention* (Baltimore, Md.: Johns Hopkins University Press, 1978).
Wiarda, Howard J., and Kryzanek, Michael J., *The Dominican Republic: A Caribbean Crucible* (Boulder, Colo.: Westview Press, 1982).

ECUADOR

Corkill, David, and Cubitt, David, *Ecuador: Fragile Democracy* (London: Latin American Bureau, 1988).
Cueva, Agustín, *The Process of Political Domination in Ecuador* (trans. Danielle Salti) (New Brunswick, N.J.: Transaction Books, 1982).
Wood, Bryce, *Aggression and History: The Case of Ecuador and Peru* (Institute of Latin American Studies, Columbia University Press, 1978).

EL SALVADOR

Armstrong, Robert, and Shenk, Janet, *El Salvador: The Face of Revolution* (London: Pluto Press, 1982).
Dunkerley, James, *The Long War: Dictatorship and Revolution in El Salvador* (London: Verso, 2nd edn, 1985).
Webre, Stephen, *José Napoleón Duarte and the Christian Democratic Party in Salvadoran Politics, 1960–1972* (Baton Rouge: Louisana State University Press, 1979).
White, Alistair, *El Salvador* (London: Benn, 1973).

GRENADA

Thorndike, Tony, *Grenada: Politics, Economy and Society* (London: Frances Pinter, 1985).

GUATEMALA

Black, George, *Garrison Guatemala* (London: Zed Books, 1984).

232 *Some Further Reading*

Calvert, Peter, *Guatemala, a Nation in Turmoil* (Boulder, Colo.: Westview Press, 1985).
Painter, James, *Guatemala: False Hope, False Freedom: the Rich, the Poor and the Christian Democrats* (London: Catholic Institute for International Relations and Latin American Bureau, 1987).
Schlesinger, Stephen C., and Kinzer, Stephen, *Bitter Fruit: The Untold Story of the American Coup in Guatemala* (London: Sinclair Browne, 1982).

GUYANA

Spinner, Thomas J., Jr., *A Political and Social History of Guyana, 1945–1983* (Boulder, Colo.: Westview Press, 1984).

HAITI

Weinstein, Brian, and Segal, Aaron, *Haiti: Political Failures, Cultural Successes* (New York: Praeger, 1984).

HONDURAS

Lapper, Richard, and Painter, James, *Honduras: State for Sale* (London: Latin American Bureau, 1985).
Morris, James A., *Honduras: Caudillo Politics and Military Rulers* (Boulder, Colo.: Westview Press, 1984).

MEXICO

Dulles, John W. F., *Yesterday in Mexico: A Chronicle of the Revolution* (Austin, Texas: University of Texas Press, 1961).
González Casanova, Pablo, *Democracy in Mexico* (New York: Oxford University Press, 1970).
Knight, Alan, *The Mexican Revolution* (Cambridge: Cambridge University Press, 1986) 2 vols.
Reed, John, *Insurgent Mexico* (New York: Clarion, 1969).
Sanderson, Steven E., *The Transformation of Mexican Agriculture: International Structure and the Politics of Rural Change* (Princeton, N.J.: Princeton University Press, 1986).
Stevens, Evelyn P., *Protest and Response in Mexico* (Cambridge, Mass.: The MIT Press, 1974).
Wilkie, James W., and Wilkie, Edna *The Mexican Revolution: Federal expenditure and social change since 1910* (Berkeley, Cal.: University of California Press, 1970).
Womack, John Jr., *Zapata and the Mexican Revolution* (Harmondsworth, Middx.: Penguin, 1969).

NICARAGUA

Crawley, Eduardo, *Dictators Never Die: a portrait of Nicaragua and the Somozas* (London: C. Hurst, 1979).
Pastor, Robert A., *Condemned to Repetition: the United States and Nicaragua* (Princeton, N.J.: Princeton University Press, 1987).
Vilas, Carlos M., *The Sandinista Revolution: National Liberation and Social Transformation in Central America* (trans. Judy Butler) (New York: Monthly Review Press, 1986).
Walker, Thomas W. (ed.), *Reagan versus the Sandinistas: the undeclared war on Nicaragua* (Boulder, Colo.: Westview Press, 1987).

PARAGUAY

Lewis, Paul H., *Paraguay under Stroessner* (Chapel Hill, N.C.: University of North Carolina Press, 1980).
Warren, Harris Gaylord, *Paraguay, An Informal History* (Norman: University of Oklahoma Press, 1949).

PERU

Alexander, R. J. (sel. and ed.), *Aprismo: The Ideas and Doctrines of Victor Raúl Haya de la Torre* (Kent, Ohio: Kent State University Press, 1973).
Bourricaud, François, *Power and Society in Contemporary Peru* (New York: Praeger, 1967).
Fitzgerald, E. V. K., *The State and Economic Development: Peru since 1968* (Cambridge: Cambridge University Press, 1976).
Kuczynski, Pedro-Pablo, *Peruvian Democracy under Economic Stress: An Account of the Belaúnde Administration, 1963–1968* (Princeton, N.J.: Princeton University Press, 1977).
McClintock C., and Lowenthal, A. (eds), *The Peruvian Experiment Reconsidered* (Princeton, N.J.: Princeton University Press, 1983).
Mariátegui, José Carlos, *Seven Interpretive Essays on Peruvian Reality* (Austin, Texas: University of Texas Press, 1988).
Stepan, Alfred, *State and Society: Peru in Comparative Perspective* (Princeton, N.J.: Princeton University Press, 1978).

URUGUAY

Kaufman, Edy, *Uruguay in Transition: From Civilian to Military Rule* (New Brunswick, N.J.: Transaction Books, 1979).
Weinstein, Martin, *Uruguay: the Politics of Failure* (Westport, Conn.: Greenwood Press, 1975).

VENEZUELA

Gil Yepes, José Antonio, *The Challenge of Venezuelan Democracy* (trans, Evelyn Harrison I., Loló Gil de Yanes and Danielle Salti) (New Brunswick, N.J.: Transaction Books, 1981).
Martz, John D., and Myers, David J. (eds), *Venezuela: The Democratic Experience* (New York: Praeger, 1977)
Morón, Guillermo, *A History of Venezuela* (ed. and trans. John Street) (London: Allen & Unwin, 1964).

Index